CALLING MY
DEADNAME HOME

CALLING MY DEADNAME HOME

The Trans Bear Diaries

Avi Ben-Zeev

MUSWELL
PRESS

First published by Muswell Press in 2024

Copyright © Avi Ben-Zeev 2024

Typeset in Bembo by M Rules
Printed by CPI Group (UK) Ltd, Croydon CR0 4YY

A CIP record for this book
is available from the British Library

ISBN: 978-1-73845-281-1
eISBN: 978-1-7384-528-2

publication November 2024

Muswell Press, London N6 5HQ
www.muswell-press.co.uk

To my brother Gil, who showed me that in the end,
love wins.

0

REBIRTH[0]

Hey, Talia barges into my psyche uninvited. Again.

I confess. I tried killing her off, but what was I thinking? I wouldn't be me, Avi — a gay man, psychology professor and immigrant to the United States of America — if it weren't for Talia's survival instincts.

"Go away; you're interrupting my writing flow," I bark when what I could really use is a heart-to-heart with my pre-gender-transition female past.

What are you writing about? She steps closer, brushing her long, multi-coloured hair away from her face.

For a so-called heterosexual woman, Talia's outfit gives drag queens a run for their money — a rockabilly cherries-and-skulls dress that shows off her perky breasts, skinned poodle of a faux-fur jacket, fishnet stockings, leopard-print platform shoes and a bracelet with doll eyes that open and close as she flicks her wrist.

If you saw our photos side by side, you'd say, *No way, this rugged man was once a hyperfeminine woman?* And yes, Talia and I look nothing alike. I'm bald and bearded. My chest is built. But if you'd look closely, you'd see that our eyes have an identical shape and colour: our grandfather's Jewish green with brown-and-golden specks.

You're telling our story, right? Talia cocks her head to one side, refusing to be dismissed.

"I was going to leave you out and focus on my life as Avi," I say out loud; to whom exactly? My empty San Francisco loft? "But I've been rethinking it lately. I can't become who I am without you – the good, bad and ugly."

Ah, Talia mutters, looking young and lost. *Be kind, okay?* Then, poof, she disappears, and I miss her already, and I hate her too, or maybe I hate how hard I've been on her, blaming her for everything bad that's ever happened to us.

*

Talia kept clicking on Ozzie's tribe.net profile. In 2003, this social platform was all the rage in the San Francisco Bay Area. A kind of Facebook before Facebook existed, but edgier.

This fascination with Ozzie was unlike her, or at least that's what Talia told herself. Her usual type was angsty and tattooed, not smiley and buttoned-up. Still, despite Ozzie's suburban, Middle-American clothing, his pics made Talia swoon. His bearishness – beard, broad shoulders and thick belly – was what the feminist scholar Camille Paglia described as more manly than the smooth, hard-bodied gay male ideal, but more Mother Earth than militaristic.

After two days of self-torment, Talia direct-messaged her new crush.   Hey, I like your profile's vibe. What say you to having coffee sometime?

The worst that could have happened would have been what – Ozzie wouldn't have been interested? Or if he had been, he'd have turned out to be a projection? Either way, not the end of the world, right?

He replied right away. I'd love to, but my profile is somewhat misleading. My location says San Francisco, but I live in Massachusetts.

Really? Over 3,000 miles away? Talia was annoyed with Ozzie's deception, but then, he surprised her. I've never been to San Francisco, but I've been itching to visit, maybe even move there. There was something she should know if they were to meet up, though, Ozzie cautioned.

Tell me.

Filling the computer screen were the infamous repeating three dots. Finally, there it was. I'm a trans guy.

Talia didn't know what that meant. To be fair, at the start of the millennium, even in the progressive Bay Area, trans people, especially trans men, were an unknown.

Trans guy? Sorry, I don't understand.

Okay, then sit down for this. When I was born, the doctor yelled, "Congrats, it's a girl!" But I've always known they were wrong. Long story short, in my twenties, I transitioned into the man you see today.

Oh, Talia messaged, the rest of her words getting garbled and stuck before reaching the keyboard.

She sank into the egg-shaped armchair, chewing on her fist. How did Ozzie know that becoming a man was even possible? And if it were ... Wait, was it? And wouldn't that have meant that ...? Never mind, it was too much to absorb at once.

Deal-breaker? Ozzie typed.

No, not at all, Talia replied, heat spreading across her neck and face.

Ozzie's flight wasn't due to arrive at the San Francisco Airport until at least another hour, but there Talia was, pacing about in Arrivals, wearing one of her favourite outfits – a silver-sequin

3

jumpsuit from the Piedmont Boutique in Haight-Ashbury. Would her appearance be too wild for his taste? Or maybe he should be the one concerned about looking so strait-laced? Why care? It was an adventure, right?

Talia hadn't always dressed like a hyperfeminine extravaganza. As a kid, she looked more like a savage pretty boy. She gave buzzcuts to our Barbie dolls and cut her own hair with Mom's rusty kitchen scissors. She was constantly climbing on things, jumping off things, holding her tight fists in front of her unruly, growing chest like a feisty terrier.

People in Talia's small Israeli town taunted her. "What are you, a boy or a girl?"

"I'm a boy," she'd growl. How could they not have seen that?

At first, our parents thought Talia's so-called bravado cute. Their sentiments changed after being summoned by Mrs Hamorah, Talia's elementary school teacher, for an urgent talk. "Your daughter is sitting with her legs too wide apart for a girl," Mrs Hamorah said. She listed other issues – like how Talia had a nasty habit of asking too many questions, and her voice, *oye,* and *vey,* was not at all suited for the school's choir (or any choir for that matter). In the end, our parents agreed that Talia's gendered transgressions needed fixing, and fast.

If the grownups insisted she wear skirts and dresses and talk in female conjugations (fuck Hebrew with its gendered everything), she'd become the femmiest of femmes, queeniest of queens. You'd spot her from miles away, a walking art installation, wearing heels so high they might as well be stilts, her broad shoulders accentuated by a Pepto-Bismol-pink feather boa. *Happy now, Mrs Hamorah?*

Ozzie strode into Arrivals, looking younger and thicker than his photos. He handed Talia an expensive-looking bouquet.

4

"What beautiful flowers," she said, but after one sniff, her eyes watered and she dropped them on a nearby bench. "I'm so sorry, I think I'm allergic to the lilies." Ozzie didn't seem to mind, especially when she leaned in to kiss him. It was a classic rom-com moment – awkward, wacky, the-hell-with-it-all-we're-doing-this smooch.

On their way to the parking lot, Talia felt giddy. Everything looked sharper, more in focus somehow. Greys were greyer and reds were redder. It was all going remarkably well, but wait, the Mazda Miata with its tiny seats! How thoughtless not to have borrowed a friend's car.

Too late. Ozzie groaned as he squeezed into the snug convertible, beads of sweat forming on his brow.

Talia put the top down to buy extra room. "It's more fun that way," she said, wishing that the crisp summer air was a tad warmer for an open air drive. Mark Twain was rumoured to have said, "The coldest winter I ever spent was a summer in San Francisco." Source credibility notwithstanding, that description was spot on.

"What were you like as a kid?" Talia asked, shifting into fifth gear on Highway 101, heading north.

"Everyone called me a tomboy." Ozzie's deep voice reverberated in her belly and chest.

She couldn't imagine him as a girl, much less a woman. And his smell – musky, woodsy – was intoxicating. She steadied her hands on the wheel. "I know what that's like; I was called a tomboy too, and there's no equivalent word in Hebrew, so imagine adding a heavy Israeli accent and raising the corner of your lip in disgust."

"You? No way!" Ozzie gasped. "You're—"

"Feminine and straight?" Talia finished his sentence.

The turn in the road revealed a large stretch of the San Francisco Bay. It wasn't the best view, but the sunny late-afternoon skies added sparkle to the estuary's blue-green waters.

"Wow." Ozzie gulped. "I've been wanting to come here for such a long time."

On a whim, Talia took a detour to the top of Twin Peaks. If Ozzie was losing his San Francisco virginity, it had to be done right.

As luck would have it, the evening was clear, with no infamous fog in sight. Holding hands, they stood on the precipice, overlooking a breathtaking vista — a 360-degree panoramic view of the city, bay and the Pacific Ocean, basked in a red-pink-and-golden sunset. Riding the waves of Ozzie's breath, it was as if it were Talia's first time seeing the rust-coloured Golden Gate Bridge stretching itself over emerald-green waters. Ozzie's heartbeats were hers, and hers were someone else's, the man she'd been waiting to meet her whole life.

"Damn," Ozzie said as they entered Talia's flat.

"Too much colour?" she asked. The tall living room walls were painted clementine orange, tomato red and eggplant purple.

"No, it's perfect, like you." Ozzie's compliment would have normally struck Talia as smarmy, but his tone felt sincere.

"The bedroom's in the mezzanine. Let me show you." Her voice betrayed fear. What if she didn't know how to please him? Ended up offending him?

Determined to keep going no matter what, Talia bee-lined to the bed. Sitting on its edge, she took a deep breath and tapped on the mattress. "Come here, handsome."

Making out was a sweaty affair. Ozzie asked for towel after towel as though Talia's breezy loft had turned into a Turkish bath.

"I'm sorry," he said, catching his breath. "I bet you didn't sign on for having sex with a wet pig."

Ozzie's schoolboy smile turned Talia on, but out of her depth, she reverted to her professor voice. "Lie on your back and spread your legs for me."

"Yes, Ma'am."

"You're my shiny, new boy toy." Heart whooshing in her ears, Talia kneeled by the bed and rested her face between Ozzie's legs, inhaling his testosterone-enhanced aroma. Boldened by his moans, she rubbed her nose, cheeks and mouth against the cotton of his underwear, his wetness spreading against her face.

What had felt like a small, rubbery lump was growing into a firm bulge. Talia sucked on it through the cloth, her down there getting hard and wet. *Now or never.* She yanked Ozzie's trunks to one side. His protrusion sprang out, engorged.

Most people would have mistaken Ozzie's penis for an enormous clitoris, but to Talia, it was a gorgeous, throbbing cock — an award-worthy specimen. She worshiped it until he came in her mouth, screaming.

"Do you want to come?" Ozzie managed to utter.

Talia shook her head no. She ached to say something, but the right words failed to manifest. Ozzie's body was a message that didn't yet make sense.

She rested her buzzing head on his torso. "I love your scars," she whispered, running her fingers on the pinkish-white trails under his pecs.

"Mementos from a different life," Ozzie said.

"Do you still feel connected to that life?"

He gazed at the ceiling. "It's hard to say. I was a butch dyke before I transitioned and part of a close-knit community of butch-femme couples."

"And now?"

"We still hang out, but it's not the same. I've become an outsider, a passing straight dude."

"Must be tough to have to choose between being yourself and people you love." Talia rubbed her belly to soothe whatever was rumbling inside. "Or is the word choice even relevant?"

Ozzie beamed and pulled Talia closer. "We've only known each other for such a short time, so I shouldn't say this, but—"

"Then, don't." She softened her voice. "Feelings can be in-the-moment real but not actually true, right?"

"Can't they be both?" Ozzie sounded disappointed.

"Hold me," she whispered, fed up with words.

In moments and a lifetime, Ozzie's arms disentangled from Talia's body and he started snoring. The noise wasn't harmonious exactly, but it was more like a meditation bell's wakeup call than a chainsaw.

Bolting out of bed, Talia saw herself picking Ozzie's clothes off the floor – white button-down shirt, yellow-and-blue striped tie, khaki pants – and putting them on. The clothes were hanging on her. How could they not have? She was 5' 7" to Ozzie's 5' 11" and weighed about a hundred pounds less.

Fingers trembling, she tucked her hair into Ozzie's tweed newsboy cap, peeked into the full-length mirror and gasped at her reflection. Her curves had all but disappeared, and what emerged was a wide-eyed boy, familiar but nameless, with a square-ish jaw and flat chest.

Do you see me? The boy whispered, locking hazel eyes with hazel eyes.

"I do," Talia mouthed.

What took you so long? he cried, hot tears streaming down his face and neck, staining Ozzie's shirt.

Talia wiped our newborn face with an oversized sleeve. Quivering, we curled into a ball and held our re-birthed self like a father would, rocking back and forth.

"I'm coming home," I heard myself whisper.

"You okay?" Ozzie sounded groggy; then his eyes popped. "Why are you wearing my clothes?"

Teeth knocking against each other, I nestled my body into his Buddha temple, undulating to its soothing waves.

Ozzie wrapped his arms around me. "Wanna talk?"

"Thanks for offering." My voice cracked. "But I'm not sure I'll make much sense."

"Try me."

"Making love to you, I felt like a—"

"Please don't say dyke or lesbian. I won't bear it."

"No, not at all." I swallowed hard. "More, like . . . a man, a gay man."

★

Good ol' sweaty, lustful, romantic Ozzie – I owe him a debt of gratitude for catapulting Talia into the mirror. Life couldn't have been easy for him, exactly, but he liked women, and in this way, he was "normal". At 38 years old, I was rebirthed still attracted to men, a strange creature – a gay trans man in a dick-centric universe of men who love men.

Could I dare dream of finding a gay male lover who'd see me as a real man? Would I lose family, friends and the respect of my colleagues?

One thing I knew for sure – I couldn't unsee the truth. There was only one path forward: to come home to myself, whatever that would end up meaning.

1.

Antithesis

Transition: The First Five Years

(San Francisco, California, 2004–2009)

1

WILD SIDE¾

Nine months into transition and my dick has been growing in powers of ten, throbbing from testosterone. Is that what teenage boys experience in puberty? Hard-ons to anyone and anything that moves, a gentle breeze? Must be hell. I've heard rumours that a famous marine mammal park masturbates its captive dolphins to keep them calm. Poor dolphins! My heart goes out to them, but at least they get some release.

In the middle of meetings, grading, writing, driving, eating, breathing – sexual fantasies invade my brain. Bearded, hairy men with thick bellies, large pecs and broad shoulders kneel at my feet, begging to please. I jack off in bathroom stalls to relieve the pressure. It's annoying, inconvenient, not to mention pathetic. My quest for authenticity has led to this – becoming a horndog caricature.

A shrink might be useful in the early transition process, my GP advised, so I've taken the plunge. I like Jon and even though we're new to each other, I already trust our compatibility as therapist and client. And yes, I have a silly crush on the man. How frickin' predictable. The fact that he's devilishly handsome and wears a motorcycle jacket doesn't help.

"So, what's your main fear around having your first sexual encounter with a non-trans gay man?" Jon asks from his perch on the black-leather armchair.

"A *Crying Game* moment."

"I don't follow."

Right. Jon's not trans, so why should he be familiar with this reference? "It's a movie. A man falls madly in love with a gorgeous trans woman. When she takes her clothes off, he runs to the bathroom and pukes his guts out."

Jon strokes his beard. "I see, so, you're not going on dates because you're worried a gay man will throw up at the sight of your va—"

"Front hole."

"Noted." Jon gives the thumbs up. "But, Avi, do you really think that your fear applies to every gay man in all of the San Francisco Bay Area? The world?"

"Well, maybe not every single guy," I concede. What game is he playing? "Some might be able to suppress their disgust."

"Let me get this straight. All gay men would be revolted by your body?"

"Yes." I can hear how ludicrous I sound.

"Did Ozzie's body disgust you?"

"Not at all. I was very attracted to him."

"And you desire men?"

"Yes, but—"

"No buts for now." Jon smiles. "Is there any evidence non-trans gay men find trans guys attractive?"

"Well, there's Buck Angel."

"Buck, who?" Jon looks puzzled again. He's queer, but

14

I should stop making assumptions about what he knows or doesn't know.

"Buck Angel is this cigar smoking, super muscular trans man porn star who calls himself a man with a pussy." For me, the p-word is anathema. I like using neutral or male terms to describe my plumbing, but I admire Buck's in-your-face *chutzpah*.

"And he's successful?"

"Yes, very. He just signed a contract with Titan Media."

"Ah. So, tell me more about this Buck character."

"He blogs about porn as activism – proof, he says, that gay male sexuality doesn't always revolve around large non-trans dicks." *They came, Your Honour*, I imagine Buck saying in a fictitious court as evidence that non-trans gay men remain gay after orgasming to his bonus hole. *I rest my case.*

"So, how about we put our faith in Buck's wisdom and enough with the catastrophising?"

I laugh. "Sounds good on paper."

"Let's take this a step further." Jon's gaze is intense for a West Coast therapist. "Even if a man gets disgusted by your body, then what? Will you die?"

"On the inside," I say. What kind of therapy is this? We're in a basement office, so at least the setting's right for psychological torture.

"A guy's reaction to your body has very little to do with how desirable you are or what being a man means. So, sure, it'll be unpleasant if he shows signs of repulsion, but I have faith in your resilience."

"I hear you, and I'm terrified."

"From decades of experience, what people dread rarely happens. Fantasy is made of amazing or horrible, but reality has middling shades of grey."

*

Jon's right. It's time I wrote a Craigslist Men for Men ad and click that publish button.

Good ol' Craigslist. It's an online platform that makes this city so preciously weird – a forum for ask, and you shall find. Job? Apartment? Sell some junk? Buy other junk to replace said junk? Cuddle? Fuck? Just describe what you want in as specific details as possible and there's bound to be at least one person who'd see your post and go, *yeah, that's exactly what I'm after.*

And no, I don't feel ready, but I didn't pursue this path to become chicken shit about life, and the worst thing that could happen is in my head.

Or is it?

FTM Top in Search of a Sexually Submissive Bear with a Big ... Heart

Hi gents! I'm a gay man who is also a trans guy (FTM), late 30s, 5'7", slight foreign accent, muscular bearish build and testosterone-enhanced plumbing.

I'm looking for erotic adventures with men who thrive on connected sex and play. Open to vanilla if the chemistry is strong, but my biggest turn-on comes from playing with a man who wants to please me. A hairy beast with a strong personality who craves exploring his submissive desires.

I welcome "emotional baggage" as long as you're introspective and are amused by and curious about your neuroses. I'm Jewish – so I understand.

Outside the bedroom, I'm a nice guy – a social scientist with an artist's soul. I prefer to get to know someone and develop a hot play dynamic over time, but one-offs are great, too, if we hit it off over coffee/tea/a drink.

No previous experience with trans men needed, but let me know what attracts you to write.

Your pic gets mine.

Within half an hour, my ad gets flagged and removed. A large enough number of Craigslist users have agreed that I have violated the terms of use for the Men for Men section. It can't be the X-rated content – my language is tame compared to the other solicitations on this platform. So, ouch.

I sift through the thirty or so responses that have made it through, safe from social policing. Most consist of a single word or phrase, like "Hi," "Hot," and "Still looking?" dick pics attached. The rest are either finger-wagging, "This is a section for men only," fetishistic, "I love eating pussy," or random, "Milk my big, hairy balls, Sir."

As luck would have it, a handful stand out. These men addressed what I wrote, expressed what prompted them to respond and attached face pics along with those of their anatomy.

In the end, it boils down to two candidates, Sammy and Song. Neither are bears, but both are intriguing and handsome. Sammy's kinkier. He's partnered in an open relationship and looking for a connected one-off. Song is more vanilla, but he's a professor writing a book about gender, sexuality and violence. An ally? Someone familiar with trans panic who gets that trans men are ... men? Sold!

Roast ducks are hanging in the window and the menu is in Mandarin. "How adventurous are you?" Song asks. He's the one who suggested meeting up at this family-run restaurant in Chinatown, and except for me, everyone seems East Asian.

"I'll try anything once," I say, hoping I sound more charming than sleazy.

"Really?" Song looks sceptical, but he doesn't realise that as a Middle Easterner, I didn't grow up on bland Jewish-American food.

My dish arrives first – chicken feet with skin and claws. Song gives me an I-dare-you look. Child's play! I nibble on the minuscule bones and suck the sweet-spicy gelatinous layer under the hardened skin.

"So, how did you become interested in studying race and gender?" I ask. Talking shop might ruin any romantic vibe, but I'm curious about Song's research.

"Do you want the academic or personal answer?"

"I'll take personal in a heartbeat."

"But it's easier to hide behind jargon, dammit." There's swelling under his eyes. Too much work and not enough sleep? "Growing up in a predominately white, conservative town, I wasn't just a garden variety gay boy. I was an Asian sissy, a double femininity whammy." Song slurps Jasmine tea with a loud gurgle. "I found refuge in being cerebral, in books and articles about how cultural notions of race and gender enable bullying. Knowledge is power for people like us who are deemed 'other', don't you think?"

"Agreed, but knowledge isn't enough."

"What else, then?"

"Blame my Jewbu-ness, reading too much Pema Chödrön and immersing in Bay Area woo woo speak, but there's also power in compassion."

"You mean having empathy for our abusers? Hell no." Song scowls. "But wait, what's a Jewbu?"

"Jewish Buddhist, but don't worry, I'm not flying on enlightened wings just yet." How do I express edge, nuance and not just the standard spiritual CliffsNotes? "What I

18

meant by compassion is learning how to be kind to our-selves, especially when we become aware of the shit we've internalised. Analysis only goes so far."

Song nods, so I continue, "I hear you that it's hard to have empathy for people who stereotype us. But what happens when things flip and we're the ones who stereotype? I mean, granted, some people experience way more injustices than others, but aren't we all capable of being prejudiced and cruel sometimes?" I've probably said enough, but I can't help adding, "Pema Chödrön makes a compelling point – if we can't find a way to acknowledge shared darkness, how can anything change?"

"I'll give you this; gay men can be prejudiced pricks despite knowing first-hand how toxic discrimination is." Song sips soup from a dumpling and dips its skin into soy sauce. "You know, 'no fats, femmes or Asians'."

"Yeah, that's fucked up." I've seen this disclaimer on too many gay men's hookup and dating profiles. "There's also an unwritten 'no trans guys', except we're not visible enough to be rejected explicitly."

"That's what drew me to include trans populations in my research." Song's getting more attractive by the minute. "But enough about me. What's your research about?"

"I study a phenomenon called 'stereotype threat'. Are you familiar with it?"

"No, tell me."

"It's a fear of confirming negative group stereotypes in high-stakes situations." I pause, trying to become more exacting without launching into a TED talk. "It usually happens when folks pursue careers in which people 'like them'," I gesture the double quotes," are underrepresented or not expected to succeed."

"You mean, like an Asian actor playing a leading male

role in a Hollywood rom-com, instead of the usual genius or villain?"

"This study needs to be done, but I'd imagine that an Asian actor playing Prince Charming might worry that if he doesn't rise to the challenge, it would quote-unquote 'prove' to everyone else that Asian men don't belong in these roles. White male actors feel the pressure to do well, but they don't have to deal with this extra burden."

"Interesting." Song wipes his face with a napkin. "And does your work target specific populations?"

"I've been focusing on the experience of people like me – folks who've been told since childhood that we don't belong in intellectual spaces but pursue them anyway."

"People like you – you mean transgender?"

"No, I was referring to those of us who come from lower social-class backgrounds or anyone who belongs to a group or groups with stigma about their intelligence."

I get why Song immediately thought of my trans identity. Most people guess that gender transition is the most radical change I've gone through. Meanwhile, it was escaping my choiceless working-class existence – transitioning from failing arithmetic in the third grade to becoming an academic. But why should he know that?

"You don't look like a professor," Song says.

"Oh yeah, what do I look like?"

"A hot trucker dude." He winks.

"Thanks for the lift home," I say as Song glides his Volkswagen Beetle into a rarely available parking spot in front of the Clocktower Building. It's my first time inside one of these cars. It has a bud vase with a white daisy – like a toy or a Disney ride.

"Wow, rockstar parking," I add, hoping he'd take the

hint. I'd love for Song to come up for a nightcap and let whatever happens, happen, but he keeps the engine running.

"I had a great time," he says. But if that's true, why is he grimacing? And how come he's grasping the gearshift so tightly his hand is white knuckled?

"You okay?" I ask. It's alarming how Song's demeanour has changed from engaged and playful to this, whatever this is.

"I find you very attractive, but I haven't dated in such a long time. Sure, I've been having sex; that's easy, but intimacy, scary, right?" His smile doesn't reach his eyes.

"I hear you. Going slow would be good for me too."

"Sorry, Avi, I can't do this. It's not you. You're handsome and a great conversationalist. It's me." He puts the car in neutral, then reaches for something in his bag. "Is it hot in here, or what?" he asks, fishing a handkerchief and wiping the sweat off his brow. "I've had HIV for decades, but I'm experiencing unexpected health complications. It's too scary to get close to someone right now."

"If it helps, I'm okay dating men with HIV."

"Stop," Song barks, baring his teeth. "I'm a gay man, okay? I like dicks."

"What hurts, exactly?" Jon asks. It was kind of him to squeeze me in.

"Song was supposed to be an ally. I feel betrayed." The leather couch was comfortable enough last time, but today my lower back screams at its sagging seat.

"Betrayed how exactly?" Jon asks. I don't care how gorgeous he is. This fiasco with Song is all his fault. He shouldn't have encouraged me to jump into the non-trans dating pool before I was ready.

"Song said he couldn't date me because he's a gay man. That he likes dicks," I over-explain.

"And?"

"He doesn't see my trans dick as a dick. Ergo, he doesn't see me as a real man." Why do I have to spell out something so obvious when it's this painful?

"Are you a real man?"

"Jon—"

"Yes or no."

"Yes."

"So why are you so upset?"

"What if I'll never find a guy who sees me the way I see myself?"

"Now we're getting somewhere. You're afraid you might be unlovable. Is that right?"

I nod my head yes.

"Guess what? Being unlovable is what most people who see me are worried about. It's a basic, universal human fear."

"Right," I grunt. So, now I'm a cliché.

"Sammy is next, correct?"

"I guess so, but—"

"No buts. You can do this, brave dating warrior."

"I hate you sometimes."

"That's a sign therapy is working its wonders."

It's 6 p.m. and The Pilsner Inn is just waking up. Two jocks are seated at the bar counter, wearing bright-orange Giants T-shirts and caps. Straight out-of-towners who didn't realise they had stepped into a gay bar?

Early for my date with Sammy – even by my neurotic standards, according to which being on time is late – I order a local bitter brew and listen to Lou Reed crooning on the jukebox. Does walking on the wild side always have to end in tragedy?

Someone here has a penguin fetish. They're everywhere – a penguin mural, penguin cookie jars, penguin figurines and I could go on. Wait, does this have something to do with that gay male penguin couple, Roy and something? Roy and . . . Silo?

It's all coming back now. Circa the late '90s, after courting each other for a while, one of them tried hatching a rock. The zookeepers at Central Park found it so endearing they swapped the rock with a real egg, and the male-on-male penguin couple ended up raising a baby together. Little Tango.

It was our ex-husband, Henry, who broke this story to Talia. He was only twenty-three years old but craved becoming a papa. Poor guy! Talia didn't have the desire to hatch anything, not even a rock.

The orange men turn their heads as Sammy enters the bar. Perhaps I was wrong about their proclivities. My date looks older than his photos, but he's jacked – muscles rippling from a tight-fitting tank top and slim-tapered jeans. He blends in with the Castro neighbourhood's muscle queen scene, but with a notable exception: he's a Black man in an otherwise mostly white crowd. That's San Francisco for you – progressive but with a way to go.

If Sammy's pics are truth in advertisement, hidden in his pants is the longest, thickest penis I'll likely ever see. It's a bit of a stereotype, Sammy joked over email. For the record – I didn't ask for his, or anyone else's, dick pics – and I'm not a size queen, but I'm, let's say, intrigued.

We hug, then take a good, long look at each other. "You're even hotter than your pics," Sammy says.

"Aw, you're a charmer."

"Not really. Truth be told, I'm nervous."

"About what?"

"That you'd find me dull. You teach at university, and I didn't even go to college."

"I grew up working class, so for me, it's all about who the person is. I couldn't give a shit about their title."

Sammy's face lights up. "Agreed," he says and hails the waiter. "A cosmo, please, and another round of whatever he's drinking."

"So, do you have any sexual experiences with trans guys?" My question is abrupt, I know, but after what happened with Song, I want to know how Sammy feels about me being trans, and the sooner the better.

"Just this one. You might know him – Buck Angel," Sammy says.

"*Whoa*, Buck Angel, the porn star?"

"Yes him. We cruised each other at a gym in LA. I had no idea he was trans, until he dropped his towel in the steam room, and let me tell you, I loved making him come."

Hold on. If Buck's the only trans man experience Sammy's ever had, should I even bother taking my clothes off? It's not my trans dick or front hole I'm worried about anymore. All this therapy for dealing with a cisgender guy's trans panic when, ha, what I'm scared shitless about is every gay man's fear: is my body hard enough?

"If you're looking to re-enact the Buck Angel scene, I'll either blindfold you, or we'll have to do it in the dark," I say.

Sammy tilts his head, but then seems to catch on. "I'm not looking for a six-pack. And, yes, I won't lie. I'd love another experience with a trans man. But there's something else that made me answer your ad."

24

"What's that?"

Sammy takes a big gulp of pink cocktail. "I want to please you."

"Say that again, but add Sir."

"I'm begging to please you, Sir."

"Head over to my place?" If we don't do this now, I'll lose my nerve.

Waiting for our taxi, I shove Sammy against the building. A primal force takes over my body as I grind against him, his dick swelling and hardening against my groin.

"Get a room," a group of tipsy pretty boys yells at us.

"We're about to," I shout back.

It's happening, a scene I had never thought possible – a gorgeous man who desires men is naked, kneeling on the cowhide rug, waiting for me to direct whatever happens next.

"Tell me what you want," I say.

"To be yours to do with whatever you please."

"Good answer." I unzip my pants and rub my testosterone-enhanced dick against his lips.

Sammy gasps.

"Blow my cock," I command, and the feel of his mouth and tongue, his ecstatic moans, transport me into wordlessness. I linger there for as long as I can – surrendering to a homing instinct only the body knows. Teetering on the edge of orgasm, I don't want to come, not yet. "Time for your reward." I incline my head in the direction of the bedroom. "Take the stairs to the mezzanine and stand with your back to the bed."

It's organic and easy, throwing this beefy man off balance. One moment Sammy is still; the next, I shove him and he topples into the mattress. "Don't move," I say and strap on a silicone dildo – eight inches with ridges that press against a man's prostate just right. Talia used it on lovers before, so it shouldn't be that different with Sammy.

But against all odds, it is. It so is.

Fucking Sammy, missionary style – his muscular legs in the air, face contorted in pleasure – I'm in my body, no longer an erotic spectator but an actor in the here and now. Energy, dirty and divine, flows from his body to mine, mine to his, until we combust, screaming, then laughing.

Sammy touches the dildo strapped to my pelvis, our over-heated bodies entangled on the sweat- and come-soaked sheets. "It felt like your cock was inside me," he says.

"It was," I say, still flying high. "I felt everything. The base of the dildo rubbed against my dick. I was hard the whole time."

"Fuck, that's hot," he says.

"You're my first."

"Ever?"

"As Avi."

"I'm honoured." Sammy strokes my cheek. "I'm dying to see you again, but—"

"You're partnered, I know, and we agreed to a one-off."

"I wish my boyfriend and I were poly. He's okay with me having sex with other guys, but I need to back off if there's a romantic spark."

"A spark?"

"Didn't you feel it?"

"I did, and I wouldn't change a thing." I'm trying to suppress the wetness in my eyes, but a renegade drop rolls down my cheek.

Sammy smiles. "Hey, Avi'le, I think I know what you looked like as a kid."

"Really?" I'm not sure I want to hear what comes next.

"I sometimes watch Mormon boy choir videos, and there's a tyke that looks like a mini-Avi." He reaches for his BlackBerry and scrolls. "See, doesn't he look like an eight-year-old you?" Sammy's face is glowing, or maybe it's mine reflected in his eyes.

Lingering by the doorway, we hug, then snap back into goodbyes.

"Take care of your precious self," Sammy says, and just like that, he's gone and memory takes over.

Stretching out on the black leather sofa, I listen to Louis Armstrong's "What a Wonderful World". Growing up, Dad used to play this song again and again, singing along to the refrain". "Satchmo! The man was a genius," he'd say.

How did Israel, my father, grow up to be optimistic and kind despite poverty and an abusive father? That vile man, Grandpa Gershon, who tickled Talia's down there, asking, "Does it feel good?"

She didn't have good male role models, my Talia. Even gentlemanly Dad ended up betraying our trust. If maleness spells aggression and cheating, do I even want it? But gender is not a choice, though; it's not a choice.

It's been a month since I lost my gay male virginity to Sammy and no, I haven't been on another date yet, but I'm calmer and more optimistic about whatever sex or love adventures lie ahead.

Anyway, right now, I need to focus on work. It's hard when the sun is shining, the skies are blue and Fort Funston is only a short drive away from the office. A walk on sandy bluffs with a spectacular view of the Pacific Ocean? Yes, please. But that'd mean cancelling my three-hour cognitive psychology class, and as tempting as that sounds, I can't.

Sighing, I head out of the Ethnic Studies and Psychology building towards the student centre for a quick coffee and bite to eat when my phone rings. *Whoa*, just as I never thought I'd hear from Sammy again, his name flashes across the screen.

"Are you somewhere you can talk in private?" Sammy's voice is tense.

"I'm in a busy quad, but you're scaring me. What's up?" The campus is flooded by hundreds of students marching to and from classes, so it's not exactly conducive to privacy, but I'm anxious to hear what he has to say.

"Well, at least find a place to sit down."

"Okay, I'll call you back in a few." It's only a short walk to the empty football field. Sitting on the bleachers, I dial Sammy's number. "So, tell me."

"I did an HIV test, and," Sammy falls silent for a moment, then continues, "I've seroconverted."

"You've tested positive for HIV?" *Duh*, he just told me that.

"I did. A few weeks before we had sex, I went to a play party and barebacked to three different guys in one night."

"Wait, does that mean—"

"Yeah, I'm pretty sure I was in the *acute phase* when we hooked up."

I've read about it. Three to four weeks after contracting HIV, a guy has a tremendously high viral load in his semen, something like a million copies, and is the most effective at spreading it.

"So, to be clear. You're saying that when you and I had the safer sex talk, you knew there was a high probability you had HIV and that your viral load was through the roof, but you chose to conceal it?"

"Yes, but what I did at that party was so out of character, I wanted to forget it ever happened."

"Listen, I'm sorry you seroconverted, but right now, I feel," I swallow a lump of saliva, "shocked. Angry."

"I get that. Believe me, Avi'le, I'm terribly disappointed in myself. I'll die if you test positive."

"I need to end this conversation."

"I'm so, so sorry."

"Goodbye, Sammy."

"Goodbye, Avi; I'll keep you in my prayers."

Somehow, I manage to teach my longer-than-long lecture and the drive home is a blur. I want to cry, but I can't. I want to scream, but I can't. I should have insisted on using condoms, but I topped Sammy with a dildo; surely, that wasn't very risky.

Finally, home, I take a hot shower, make a cup of boiling tea and when my head hits the pillow, I'm more than ready to fall asleep – but no such luck; I'm stuck in consciousness limbo, half awake.

Hi, an apparition whispers, looking dapper and gaunt.

"Lou Sullivan, is that you?" Not every day is one visited by a trans ancestor's ghost.

It's me, brother.

"Getting an HIV diagnosis in 1986 must have been terrifying."

It was, but I found cold comfort in telling the gender clinics that even though they believed that a man like me couldn't exist—

"You'd soon die as the man you truly were – a gay man," I finish his thought.

We're lucky to be us, you know?

"Lucky?" I parrot.

We get to come home to our true selves.

*

29

Jon picks up on the first ring.

"Sorry to call this early," I say and tell him everything that happened.

"Get an HIV test at Magnet. Talk afterwards, okay?"

Magnet is designated as a Men who have Sex with Men (MSM) sexual health clinic in the Castro and is run by the San Francisco AIDS Foundation. It's fairly new, having opened in 2003, but it's already earned a good reputation – getting an HIV test there would be anonymous and quicker than at the GP's.

I'm scared, terrified even, to be honest, but I want to know what my HIV status is, and the sooner, the better.

The building is old, but the clinic's walls smell like fresh paint, and the receptionists look like hip bartenders – a twenty-something twink wearing a T-shirt with an ABBA print and a muscular Daddy type with old-school tattoo sleeves.

"How may I help?" ABBA Shirt asks.

"I'm here for an HIV test."

"Follow me." He leads me into an examination room smelling of ammonia. Gesturing to a chair, he asks, "Is this routine or—?"

"I just found out that a guy I hooked up with seroconverted a few weeks before we had sex." My voice is shrill. "I'm stressed out."

"Did you use protection?"

"No, and I feel stupid about that."

"We've all been there. The important thing is you're here," ABBA Shirt says in a calm voice. "Given the circumstances, we should do an RNA test. It's more definitive because it can uncover the presence of the HIV virus itself." He explains some more about the test, but I find it hard to

30

focus, and my throat is dry. "Fill out these forms." He hands me a stack of papers. "I'll be back."

There are only two options for gender in the demographics section: male or transgender. So, I check the trans box and proceed to the set of questions targeted to guys who fall under that rubric. Do you use your penis for anal intercourse? By penis, do they mean dildo? Or is this a question for trans men who have had bottom surgery? Reading the subsequent questions, my heart drops. Right! How could I not have seen this coming? The transgender box refers to pre-operative or non-operative trans women.

I scribble over my original choice and tick the male box instead. It's 2004, and even here, in this progressive mecca, trans women are considered men, and trans men don't exist. It's the same old formula. Gender equals (assumed) genitals. Should I say something? No, I don't have the bandwidth, and besides, I am male.

When Talia got tested for HIV in 1986 – a year in which the name Human Immunodeficiency Virus had been adopted – waiting two weeks to know her status was a completely different affair. She faced the cold, hard fact that almost everyone who tested positive would soon die a gruesome death. Little did she know that at the same time she was handed a negative HIV result in Milan, Italy, Lou Sullivan, the first openly gay trans man, received a positive diagnosis in San Francisco, California.

While Lou was dying from what the media had dubbed a gay man's disease, his identity as a gay man wasn't recognised – he had, in fact, been denied gender confirmation surgery. The gender clinics at that time believed it necessary for a "real" trans man to be attracted to women. They might as well have stated that heterosexual men are real men and gay men aren't.

ABBA Shirt is back. He takes my stack of papers and nods. "Let's do the test, and we'll see you back in two weeks."

The moment I step out the clinic, I call Jon. "Good job, and whatever happens, I'm here for you," my trusted therapist says. I appreciate his support; I do, but two whole weeks? How the hell will I keep myself distracted?

And just like that it's verdict day. ABBA Shirt, wearing Cher this time, sits me down. He keeps going on and on about safer sex in excruciating detail before delivering my HIV test results. I'm mad at him for prolonging the suspense but hug him on an impulse.

First, I call Jon with the news, then Sammy. "The RNA test came back," I say, hoping Sammy hears me over Castro Street's noisiness.

"And?"

"It was negative."

"Thank goodness." Sammy lets out a big sigh. "Are you still angry with me?"

"Hold on a sec." I walk across the street to the recreation centre. It's a peaceful spot, with a small field and a dog run. "I feel huge relief," I say, putting the phone to my ear.

"I should have disclosed I had high-risk sex. It was unfair to play god with your health."

"Thanks for saying that." Sammy's accountability means a lot, and, of course, I'm culpable too. No matter our safer sex talk, I should have assumed any guy I hooked up with could have been in the acute phase and opted for condoms. I'm a consenting adult, not a victim.

"My partner's furious with me. He's been living with HIV since I met him twenty years ago — you know, back when AIDS used to be a death sentence for most of us — and he's always insisted we use condoms."

32

"I wish you both well," I say, and I mean it. Life must be challenging for Sammy right now, and if he were in front of me, I'd extend my arms for a hug. I'm not at the forgive-and-forget stage yet, but I aspire to get there.

On the drive home, I pass the Buddhist AIDS hospice. Despite the huge medical and social progress since the '80s, too many people are still dying from this virus. How can I be of help?

Back in my loft, at last, I kick my boots off and head to the fridge. A mortality reminder puts things in perspective, and even though I have a shitload of work to do, fuck it; it's time for ice cream and guilty-pleasure TV.

There's someone I need to revisit before devouring a pint of Chubby Hubby and embracing nihilism for the rest of the day, though. Humming a tune about trees of green, I reach for an old and dusty photo album. There she is, little Talia, in a trio of black-and-white photographs – pretending to speak on a toy telephone, holding a doll and sucking on a swirly lolly, a present from Grandpa Gershon.

She had shorn her hair a few days before the photo shoot and was proud of her buzzcut, but Mom had a nasty trick up her sleeve – she covered Talia's head with a large pink ribbon. In the photos, the ribbon looks off-white, like dressing on a wound.

Talia couldn't have known this as a child, but her cries to be seen as a boy would be answered, crossing oceans and time. Being born isn't consensual, and life isn't easy. Still, sometimes its gifts blow the heart wide open.

2

MOTHER SPIDER[2]

"*Shabbat shalom*," my mother answers the phone, over 6,000 miles away.

"*Shabbat shalom*, Mom."

"Israel," she yells, "Talia's on the phone for you."

"Mom, wait—"

"Hi, my darling Avi," Dad says.

"Are we still on for meeting in Istanbul?"

"You bet! We've been looking forward to it."

"We?"

"She'll come around."

Imagine entering Israel holding a passport with a photograph of someone who doesn't look like you, a different gender marker and the wrong name. Even if you don't know much about this troubled, high-security country, you'd probably guess that you'd land in deep trouble at the border.

I've tried and tried, jumped through bureaucratic hoops, but the Israeli government has rejected my request to amend my passport. They didn't care about the notarised copies of my legal name and gender change, approved and stamped by the Superior Court of the great state of California, USA. They scoffed at the official letter from my highly respected American surgeon, a pioneer in his field, attesting to having performed gender-confirmation surgery. They would only accept a letter from a surgeon in Israel, so goodbye and *bon chance*, don't call us and we most definitely won't call you.

Aside from the injustice and irony of it all – a country provides its citizens with passports to guarantee their safe passage – this might be the last nail in the coffin on visiting my ageing parents in the comfort of their home. Mom and Dad are getting frail, and what should happen, god forbid, if one or both become incapacitated? If I tried to enter Israel – and, nope, my birth country doesn't recognise my American passport – I'd be detained, harassed, or even thrown into jail. This thought is too chilling, so for now, I'll focus on getting to Turkey.

It's a thirteen-hour flight from San Francisco to Istanbul and only an hour and a half from Tel Aviv. Still, even a short flight will be harrowing on Mom's body, what with her Parkinson's and incontinence. I appreciate her sacrifice, I do, but I'm dreading her disdain.

"So, what's the family gathering in Istanbul all about?" Jon asks.

"I haven't seen the parents for two years since I started transitioning, and we've all agreed it's high time." I explain the passport situation and how Istanbul will be a relatively short flight from Tel Aviv, even though Mom's illness has progressed.

"So, your mother is making a sacrifice."

Mom's a martyr, I almost say, but the sarcasm dripping from my inner tongue is poison. "Yes, she's making an effort, but she barely speaks to me on the phone and when she does, she calls me Talia and addresses me as a woman."

"Is Hebrew a gendered language like Spanish and Italian?"

"Even more so. If we were speaking Hebrew and I say, 'hey, Jon, I look forward to my next session with you' — *look forward* would be in male form to indicate my gender, and *you* would be in male form too, to indicate yours."

"Pronouns, adjectives, verbs are all gendered?"

"Yup. Crazy, eh?"

"If your mom is resistant to accepting you as Avi, why is she making the trip?"

"Obligation? Wanting to please Dad? It's ironic how my father, who grew up in Peru and Palestine with manly-man ideals, is the one pushing for this reunion."

"And how are you feeling about seeing your parents?"

"It's complicated, but I miss them, so yeah, I want to go to Istanbul."

"When it comes to your mom, what do you wish happens?"

"For her to stop misgendering me, for starters, but beyond that? Having a heart-to-heart."

"Become the child for a moment and give me the full fantasy."

This pain, it scares me. "The dream is a reach, but here goes. I want Mom to tell me she'd love me no matter what, ask how it feels to rebirth, what she could do to understand, be there." I reach for the tissue in Jon's hand. "When I told her I went through chest surgery, she said she was glad I didn't share that information in real-time. 'I'm happy you didn't tell me,' were her exact words." I don't know if I have

36

it in me to go on, but I do it anyway. "I told her that I took a photo of her to the hospital."

"And what did she say?"

"Nothing. She said nothing."

"It won't be easy, but try and keep your heart open on this trip, or else what would be the point?"

He's right. "Thanks; I'll see you on the other side." That's enough processing for now. My flight leaves early tomorrow and I still have a shitload to do.

I land at the Ataturk airport jetlagged and bleary-eyed. It's 2 a.m. local time, and I haven't slept a wink.

The taxi driver averts his eyes and fixates his gaze on the large stag beetle tattoo running from my mid-arm to the top of my hand. If he's a religious Muslim, I pray he knows I mean no disrespect.

I repeat the name and address of the hotel. The man has a poker face, so I try a third time. My Americanised pronunciation must be off-putting, perhaps even more so than my visibly tattooed sin against god. "Okay?" I ask.

He nods and we're off, speeding on a long stretch of highway. I love being in transit – a not-there-yet liminal space that staves off endings. In this dream-like state, we creep up on a city that so generously reveals its majestic, glow-in-the-dark mosques, bridges and palaces. I can't wait to explore every nook and cranny, but I'm desperate for sleep.

Finally, after slaloming in narrow, winding streets, the cab comes to a complete stop. "Hotel here, Sir," the driver says.

I look around, but there's no sign of a hotel, only a vacant parking lot and an entrance to a dim alley. "Sorry, where?" I ask, desperately trying to manifest it.

"There," the man points to the alley's entrance. "The end."

Languageless, I pay and make my way into the darkness, the wheels of my suitcase screeching on cobblestones. The backstreet is in deep slumber, but at the tail end of its shadowy trail is a promising sight – a rundown building with a half-broken neon sign: *H t l.*

"Hallelujah!" a lone figure, wobbling from side to side, shouts from the top of the staircase. "I've been waiting and waiting. I've had images of you dying in a plane crash or being kidnapped. They hate us here, you know."

You. Dying. Kidnapped. In Hebrew, Mom is addressing a woman. I'm standing two feet away from her face. How can she not see me?

"I'm sorry I worried you," I mutter, conjugating *sorry* as a man would.

If only she could speak English well enough, we'd be able to switch from Hebrew to English and avert a cacophony of mismatched gendered exchanges. But we're stuck with Hebrew, with each other, as is.

Poor Mom. She's barely holding herself upright. Has her disease advanced that much? On top of feeling betrayed by her body, my transition must seem like the world's end. So, yeah, as painful as her misgendering is, I vow not to correct her speech.

Keep your heart open, my inner Jon whispers.

I lean in to hug her and she lets me, dangling her arms by her side and arching her back to prevent her breasts from touching my phantom ones.

"I've missed you," I hear myself say.

"Let's go inside," she mutters.

In a sleepless haze, I hand my American passport to the young and cheerful receptionist. Turning to Mom, he asks,

"Madam, didn't you say you were waiting for your daughter? Will she be arriving as well?"

Mom hesitates. "Sorry, my English not so good."

The guy smiles at me with a look that says, *your poor mother must be losing her faculties, I'm afraid.* He doesn't realise that, withering or not, my one-and-only looms larger than Louise Bourgeois' sculpture, *Maman*, a steel spider, over 30 feet tall.

It's a sunny morning and Dad is pacing back and forth in the hotel lobby, smiling from ear to ear like a dolphin.

"My boy. My sweet boy," he cries out and hugs me with the leftovers of his once substantial body.

"*Aba'le*, it's so good to see you." I wrap my arms around his misaligned spine, but I've overreached. The dear man is skin and bones.

"Don't you worry, *chabibi*, this will be a fun vacation and everything will be okay!" He turns to Mom, who is hobbling down the stairs, a pained look on her face, "Right, my Rina?" But Mom doesn't respond.

When Dad is in charge of holiday plans, there's no time to waste. His itinerary is a benevolent dictator's. Once upon a time, Mom and I used to collude in sabotaging Dad's agenda by getting intentionally lost. "No, that's not the way," he'd bristle, but he didn't stand a chance. Getting lost was magical. The moment the blisters on our feet slowed us down, the right café to people watch would materialise, and sure, Dad was defeated, but he was happy too.

This trip is different. When Dad commands, "Today we start at the Grand and Spice Bazaars," Mom and I respond with a "Yes, Sir." When Dad adds, "And then we'll tour the Hagia Sophia and the Sultan Ahmed Mosque!" We salute.

Mom's being stoic, but I can tell that all this doing, doing,

doing is hard on her body. She stoops to the right when she's walking and her pace has slowed to a shuffle.

"How about we rent you a wheelchair?" I ask, unable to take any more of Mom's palpable suffering.

Mom sits down on a park bench. "Tell her she should mind her own business."

Dad sits beside her. "A wheelchair sounds like a good idea, my Rina."

"Don't worry about me. I'm fine," Mom scoffs. "You're doing an excellent job navigating."

"Avi, my child. You okay?" Dad motions for me to join.

I could yell that my heart hurts, but would that make any difference? "I agree with Mom. Grateful to follow your lead, *Aba'le*," I say.

Boldened by being in charge, Dad pushes his luck. Sure enough, Mom and I acquiesce to hopping on a boat to the Princes' Islands and going on a guided horse carriage ride. Mom and I are prone to seasickness and share a hatred for guides, boats and carriages, but having something tangible to attribute nausea to is proving to be a relief.

"Is this your grandson?" our guide asks. She's twenty-something and flirty.

"This guy here is our youngest." It's as though Dad has been calling me son since the day I was born.

Closing my eyes, I meditate to a symphony of sounds — hoofs trotting, carriages rattling, a whistling breeze stroking the tips of the poplar trees — but Mom's silence hisses in my ears. How long can we continue to appease Dad? Pretend to be a family when we'd rather look anywhere but at each other?

When Dad goes out for his afternoon walk, I make my move and knock on the parents' door.

"Who this?" Mom asks in English.

"It's me," I say in Hebrew male speak.

"What do you want?" Here she goes again, addressing a woman.

"Please, may I come in?" I conjugate "may" the way a man does and push the door open.

The room is spacious, with bright-turquoise walls and a queen-size bed, but the window overlooks a busy construction site. How unfair to the parents to have to endure all this banging.

"Why aren't you talking to me?" I hear myself ask.

Mom's hunched on the bed's edge. "What's there to talk about? You've made your choice and what's done is done."

"Do you need help getting up?"

"I'm fine as I am, thank you very much."

"You're angry with me. I get that."

"A mother is never angry with her children. Now, if that's all, may I be dismissed?"

"We have to talk, or else what? Become total strangers?" The uninvited guest, I kneel by Mom's feet on the rough, floral carpet. "My transition must have been hard on you."

"Your father forced me to come on this trip." Mom's chin trembles. "Clearly, it was a mistake."

"Mom, please." I touch her knee, and she wriggles her legs as though my touch sent a shockwave through her system.

I've read somewhere that Louise Bourgeois made *Maman*'s legs disproportionately delicate for such a tall and heavy body. If brought to life, this gigantic mother spider would lose her balance and collapse on herself.

"Look at me," I plead, my heartbeat muting the hammering outside.

"I had a daughter once, but she died." Mom licks her

chapped lips. "I used to talk to my daughter about things I could never discuss with my sons or husband."

"I'm right here." I place my palm on my chest. "You can still talk to me."

"I don't know you."

"What then? Shave my beard? Put on a wig? Get breast implants? Would you recognise me then?" I don't want to lose control, and, goddammit, this is all going so wrong.

Mom's body erupts in spasms, a flood gushing down her cheeks. It's *déjà vu*. I've only witnessed my stoic mother break down like this once. It was in the '80s, right after finding out that her beloved younger brother, Nachman, had been diagnosed with an aggressive brain tumour.

"Go away," Mom bellows. Her spasms attenuate, but she's shaking, mucous dripping from her crimson nose and onto her sky-blue shirt.

Eyes stinging, I grab a fistful of tissues from the bed stand and hand them to her. "How do I comfort you over my death?" I ask, hurt turning to guilt.

And as though the construction's *bang, bang, bang,* isn't enough of a challenge, a sour stench fills the room. What the hell? I look out the window for the asshole who dared take a piss by our open window but, turning back to face Mom the truth stares me in the face – a yellow trail pours down her leg, pooling onto the carpet.

"I feel so humiliated." Mom blows her nose and hangs her head. She didn't ask for American-made incontinence protection pads this time. That would have been a request for a daughter, not a son or whatever I am to my mother. I got a few packs anyway and slipped them into her suitcase, sight unseen, praying they'd help ease her indignity.

In the *bang, bang, bang,* in this urinal mixed with Mom's

42

citrusy perfume, our sorrows blur. "I'm sorry for yelling at you, Mom. I'm sorry for ... your loss." Can she hear my tenderness?

If she does, she doesn't show it.

Taking my cue, I leave Mom be, praying she'd call after me, ask for something, anything.

Nothing. She says nothing.

Dad's being magnanimous today. Instead of suggesting we grab a quick lunch on our way to the next item on his never-ending list, he opts for an extravagant sit-down meal. "This restaurant has great reviews," he says.

While Dad ponders the menu, Mom sits like a statue. Meanwhile, the city is bustling with life. Outside the domed window, heterosexual men sling their arms over each other's shoulders and walk around holding hands.

"Noam's doing well. I was worried he'd never recoup from the war, but his article about Palestinian music in Gaza is getting a lot of attention."

Mom huffs, but Dad ignores her. "Well, your mother and I are very proud of him. His wife isn't loving towards us, but what can you do? It's Gil we're worried about."

Gil. My middle brother who called me a monster, accused me of forcing his sister, Talia, to commit suicide, then cut me off from any contact with my nieces and nephew. His name alone makes me sick to my stomach.

"You know what happened with Gil and his ex-wife, correct?" Dad asks. Mom delivers an elbow stab to his arm. She's right to. This is a sensitive topic.

Poor Dad. Everything he knows about family dynamics comes from his wife. She's always been the one in the thick of things, the fulcrum our family balances on. But even though the dear man isn't skilled at playing a game of telephone, it doesn't stop him from trying to regain ground. "So, the ex-wife accused Gil of—"

"Dad, I know everything." I pre-empt Mom's response this time. "I was there for Gil every step of the way."

"Well, your brother's in a bad way, but I'm still mad at him. He shouldn't be shunning you like this. There's no excuse."

"Thank you for saying that; I'm feeling—"

"Forgive him, *chabibi*. He can't help himself. He's like your mother. You know, two very extreme people." A mutiny! Dad rarely speaks about Mom like this, and never to her face.

Mom manages a sip of water. "I don't blame Gil," she utters, breaking her silence. "He lost his sister."

"I know my transition's hurt you." I fix my gaze on Mom's pale face. "I understand why you're grieving the loss of your daughter, but is there any place in your heart that cares about how I feel too?"

"Israel, make her stop."

"I'm terrified to lose you." My eyes assault the food on my plate with moisture and salt. "Have I?"

Dad asks for the check, and the owner gives him a what-the-fuck-is-wrong-with-you look. Our orphaned plates are overflowing with delectables – grilled eggplant, mint yoghurt, pinto beans in olive oil, stuffed squash flowers, smoked sea bass, artichokes and other Turkish delights. What a shame to let a labour of love go to waste.

While the parents rest in their room, I take off to a nearby *Hammam*. I could use a Turkish massage about now.

The *Hamman* is true to its elegant brochure – domed ceiling, marble columns, white walls and floors adorned with turquoise and gold mosaic tiles. I can't wait for the vigorous pounding to commence, but I'm worried: what if my dick gets dislodged and goes flying into the air? And by dick, I mean the soft pack I've shoved into a pair of tighty-whities, praying it'd stay put. And by soft pack, I'm referring to a realistic-looking flaccid penis that trans guys use in situations where a lack of a bulge in our nether regions might put us in harm's way.

The image of my dick rolling on the *Hammam* floor? Not sexy. Even Stephen King would surely agree that this scenario would be the stuff of nightmares. But enough with the catastrophising! I'm here to relax.

Inhaling deeply on a count of six, then sighing out slowly to the count of eight, my shoulders fall away from my ears. I didn't realise how tightly I've been clenching my jaw. I'm beyond ready to surrender to strong arms, to be taken care of, held.

The attendant demands I take a shower. "But I've showered before coming here," I protest. He must think of me as a dirty and prudish American. Why should he know that some men have bodies they need to keep secret to stay safe? "Alright, follow me," he frowns.

Waiting in the tiny massage room is a hairy bear of a physical therapist, curling and uncurling his fists as though he's preparing to fight. I hop on the massage table, the soft pack lodged in my underwear. Please, please let it stay put.

Thud, thud, thud. Massage Bear's beatings are rhythmic, turning my back and buttocks into percussion instruments. And just as I'm about to reach my edge and beg him to slow down, Massage Bear takes a breather, letting cleansing tears roll down my face, and then recommences with gusto.

Thud, thud, thud.

"But a mother is more like a lioness than a spider," Mom said, looking up at the underbelly of Bourgeois' *Maman.*

"I disagree," Talia said.

45

"Really?" Mom raised an eyebrow.

"A gigantic mother spider is a fierce protector and suffocator."

"Are you trying to tell me something?"

"I'd be lost without your smothering; I mean ... mothering."

Mom giggled, despite herself, then burst into a braying fit of laughter. "No one makes me laugh as hard as you," she said, wiping her eyes with her burgundy coat sleeve.

Thud, thud, thud.

"I love listening to Grandma Rivka's stories," Talia said.

"How comes she doesn't share anything intimate with me?" Mom wrinkled her nose. "All she does is ask for my service."

"You've never respected your mother."

"How dare you?"

"Think about it. You've underestimated Grandma Rivka while idolising Grandpa Simcha."

"The man was a hero."

"Did you know Grandma Rivka talks to Nachman every night before bed?"

"Really?" Mom's tone softened.

"You've lost your favourite brother and she's lost her son."

"I can't imagine. I'd die if one of you kids—"

"Ask Grandma to tell you about their conversations."

"I don't believe in apparitions."

"But Nachman isn't a ghost, Mom. He lives inside her."

"You can be wise sometimes, my girl."

"Thanks, but I'm a mess, and you know that."

"I wish you didn't always choose the hardest path in life."

"Promise you'll ask Grandma about her conversations with Nachman?"

"Thank goodness for having a daughter." Mom's face lit up. "I'd never be able to talk about this kind of thing with Dad or your brothers. Men just don't get it."

Thud, thud, thud.

Mom, your dead child is right here, more alive than ever. I'm begging you, look at me, please, with your heart, not your eyes.

Mom, do you see me?

The parents' flight leaves for Tel Aviv in five hours, but they insist on taking a cab together and walking me to my departure gate. The problem is that it takes us forever to get to the airport, and after clearing passport control, my flight to San Francisco boards in fifteen minutes. I hate the idea of rushing them.

Saved by a courtesy passenger cart, we make it to the gate in the nick of time. Hasty hugs and quick goodbyes, and the next thing I know, I'm handing the attendant my boarding pass.

Turning my head one last time, there's Mom and Dad leaning over the railway, hunched and brittle. Will I see them again? And, how, against all odds, can I hold on to their vividness before their images fade?

"*Bon voyage.* I miss you already, *chabibi*," Dad yells, his voice shrill.

"Goodbye, my son," Mom mouths.

3

ANGEL[3]

Angel's hair smells like Daddy's, the hip barbershop in the Castro – pipe tobacco and cedarwood.

"I don't know how to touch you," he says.

Angel's a trans guy like me, so I'm confused about why he's confused and, frankly, a bit disappointed. I've had steamy erotic adventures lately, but I was hoping to take a break from teaching a guy how to touch my junk. "No pressure. There's a fabulous gelato place around the corner and the flavors are orgasmic," I say. If sex on a first date doesn't feel right, it's better not to force it.

"Avi, I want to do this. It's just that I'm new to transition and I've been a femme-loving butch dyke my whole adult life, you know?"

I don't know what it's like being a lesbian, but Angel's vulnerability is sexy, so I'm willing to learn. "Take off your shirt, handsome," I command.

"Yes, Sir." His chest is flattened by a tight binder. I, too, used to wear one before having top surgery. It did the trick but restricted my breathing – a devil's tradeoff.

"You okay taking the binder off?"

"Will it please you?"

"Yes, as long as you're not crossing a boundary."

"I want you to see me as I am." Angel reveals what could pass for moderate gynecomastia.

"Are your nipples—?"

"Yes, they're sensitive and wired to my clit." Damn, I can't believe he uses the c-word to describe his dick. So many assumptions to shed, but that's always the case, isn't it? Perhaps even more so with the so-called familiar, a person "like me," whatever that means.

"I use 'front hole' for my down there," I say. Neutral or male terms for my gendered parts fit best, and it's good he knows it upfront. "And you?"

"Pussy," Angel says, his face flushed. I try not to cringe, but it's his body, not mine and some non-trans gay men also refer to their anuses as pussies. So, roll with it, right?

I flick my fingers on Angel's nipples, then squeeze them gently, feeling them harden and swell against my touch. He kisses my neck, that soft spot tainted by unwanted childhood touch. But my rebirthed skin is different. It itches to feel his mouth and hands anywhere, everywhere.

We're hard and wet and male *as is*; no justifications for being us. Libidinal and raw, everything belongs.

It's warm and sticky under the silky down comforter. When Mom heard that San Francisco summer nights were cold, she sent it as a special delivery from Israel, as though there were no such goods in the United States.

"You knew exactly what you were doing," I say.

"Oh, yeah, what grade did I get, Professor?" Angel's tone is playful, but the way he says "Professor" reminds me of how Talia used to pronounce that word before academia became a possibility – with defensive disdain.

"I don't have my red pen handy, but I'd say it was a solid B."

"Wow, you're harsh."

"Okay then, A for effort." I rub my beard against his clean-shaven face. "Joking aside, you're an amazing lover."

"Hey, I have a crazy idea." Angel's voice is animated. "The who's who of the gay men's kink scene is throwing a huge play party at the Folsom Street Fair this year. And get this, trans guys aren't allowed."

"That's fucked up."

"Totally, so how about we crash the party?"

"What? You want us to——"

"Yeah, I doubt they'd check my ID at the door, so let's infiltrate and have the hottest, gayest trans–on–trans sex scene ever."

"Careful what you wish for." I reach my fingers and wriggle them under his armpits.

"No, anything but tickling," he yells, giggly and furious. "I'm serious, Avi; it's a hard limit."

Two months of dating and Angel's always at my place. I ask to meet up at his flat and he finally says yes.

West Oakland is a mere fifteen-minute drive over the Bay Bridge and a different landscape. There are no organic groceries here, and the trees lining the boulevard are thin and thirsty.

Inside Angel's apartment, muddy water is drip, drip, dripping from a large hole in the ceiling into a bright orange bucket. "Excuse the nuisance," he says.

"How long have you lived here?" I zip my sweatshirt and pull the hood over my freshly shaved head.

"A few months, and get this, rent-free."

It turns out the place belongs to friends of Angel's who live out of the country for most of the year. "We were part of a shamanic group in the Southwest led by Don Miguel Ruiz." Angel pauses, appearing to expect a response.

"Who?"

"Don't tell me you haven't read *The Four Agreements*?"

"*Four agreements*?" I parrot.

"Sheesh, it's only the most enlightened book on the planet. I'll give you a copy, but only if you promise to read it."

"I might not be up to your spiritual standards, but I hope to exceed your dirty ones. I brought the outfit."

"Shit." His face reddens. "That's hot."

"Wait, what was the shamanic group like?" I should know better than engage with such matters, but I can't help myself sometimes.

"We supported each other in moving from fear to love." Angel's expression changes. "So, the outfit, really? We're doing this?"

"Let me slip into something more comfortable, Sir." My intonation is that of a Southern Belle – Blanche Devereaux's (née Hollingsworth) of *The Golden Girls* fame. Angel doesn't seem to get the reference, but it cracks me up.

Giddy, I grab my bag, walk out the door and into the communal staircase. There's no privacy here. What if a neighbour sees me changing clothes? I'd need to be quick.

Talia's dress doesn't fit. I leave it half-zipped in the back and look at my reflection in the hallway mirror. The garment's tightness and my long, curly blonde wig accentuate my broad shoulders. Talia passed as a woman, and three years into transition, I don't.

Ready as I'd ever be, I knock on Angel's door.

"Who is it?" His voice cracks.

"Drag Queen Massage, darling. Nevah More at your service."

Angel lets me in and tips his fedora. "Nice to meet you, gorgeous. The bedroom's down there."

"Payment first." I stretch out my hand.

"Yeah ... no. Let's see how good your services are."

I'll need to take him down a notch, and wow, I still can't believe we're doing this!

The bedsheets are steeped in Angel's musk. There are also fainter scents. Tobacco? Lavender?

"I'm crazy about you," he says.

I feel that familiar tickle in my nose. *Achoo.* How embarrassing. And another. *Achoo.* "Sorry," I say, disentangling from Angel's embrace and reaching for the Kleenex box on the bed stand.

I blow my nose as soundlessly as I can. "Me or Nevah?"

"I'm sorry to tell you this, but Nevah is, well; how can I put it delicately? Inexperienced at best."

"How dare you?" I swat him on the shoulder. "He's the consummate professional, worth every penny." Then, turning on my side, I thrust my backside against Angel's belly. The bed creaks and digs its claw-like springs into my flesh but Angel's enveloping arms are worth the discomfort. "Role-playing a drag queen body worker was strangely affirming."

"Yeah? In what way?"

Analysis can ruin eroticism, and it's not always clear when it's helpful, but I go for it anyway. "At first, I was like, hell no. Shedding my past's clothing, or anything hyper-feminine, was a huge relief."

"And now?"

"As Nevah ..." I'm trying to reconcile conflicting

52

thoughts, "Talia's clothes fit so badly, it makes me appreciate her aesthetic more."

"I see you," Angel says. It's sweet of him to say, but what does he mean by that, exactly?

"Apropos being seen: how do you feel about being out in public with another man?" I ask. June is Pride month, and Angel is bound to run into people who've known him as a femme-loving butch dyke.

"I worry about being judged by the butch-femme community, but what I really dread is how my diehard lesbian fans will react."

Wait, what? "Fans?"

"I'm a singer-songwriter, didn't you know that?" Angel flips over. "Your turn to spoon me, Daddy," he purrs. At 5'10" and 250 pounds, Angel's taller and larger than me. Still, I wrap myself around him as though he's the cub.

"*Día de los Muertos* is around the corner. I'm sensing the veil thinning between this world and the next," Angel says.

"Who's knocking on the other side?" I might be a Buddhist Jew or Jewbu in Northern California lingo, but when it comes to Bay Area woo, I'm an atheistic anthropologist.

"My father's spirit, for one. You would have liked him, you know."

"I'd love to hear all about your dad." I tighten my arms around him. "And to visit your family in Texas one day."

"That'd be great, but for now, how about a weekend trip to Los Angeles?" Apparently, there's a hoi polloi transgender visibility event in West Hollywood next month, and Angel is the opening act.

"I'll go if you write a song about us."

Angel laughs. "You don't want that. I only write about a relationship when it becomes tormented."

"Count me in for the trip," I say. La La Land — here we come!

"I hope I won't disappoint." Angel shifts from one foot to the other. "I'll be singing from the album I recorded pre-transition." I get why he's nervous. This West Hollywood concert hall is humongous.

"Is your voice up for the challenge?" Renata asks. She's the emcee for tonight's event, a punk rock trans woman, author and activist.

Angel sighs. "I hope so, but it's been cracking a lot since I started testosterone."

"A well-honed instrument is a lot to sacrifice for being who we are," Renata says.

Angel nods. "But if art is truth-telling, this crackling voice is me right now."

The venue is swarming with attractive people, Los Angeles style — a relaxed elegance that makes even the simplest of T-shirts look chic. I kiss Angel's forehead. "Go knock their socks off."

"Thanks, handsome," he says, raising his chin like a cowboy from a '60s Western.

"Ladies, gentlemen and gender benders, it's the moment we've been waiting for." Renata's voice booms from the stage. "We're honoured to feature tonight's shining star, the one-and-only singer-songwriter, Mr Angel Marcos Transgénero."

Angel strides onto the stage, his favourite acoustic guitar strapped over his shoulder, a red feather in his fedora.

"Woohoo," I shout and clap like a diehard groupie.

Angel opens the set with a cover of Gillian Welch's "Everything is Free". It's the perfect song for his changing voice and the crowd loves him. How could they not? He's charismatic as fuck and a total ham.

The second song is an Angel original from his pre-transition album. It goes well at first, but then his voice cracks on the bridge. Angel stops, tries again, falters, then tries again and again, finally stopping dead in his tracks. My stomach's churning gets louder as the audience's chatter dies down.

"Thank you for witnessing my journey," Angel whispers into the mic, placing his hand on his heart. "This is for those who do not have a voice in this world." He somehow manages to bellow out the rest of the song, his voice shrill and uneven, and the beautiful people rise from their seats in a thundering standing ovation.

Minutes after Angel straps his seatbelt on; he falls asleep in the passenger seat. It's a five-and-a-half-hour drive from LA to Oakland and I'm grateful for quiet contemplation. What is it that Mom said with what sounded like witchy foresight? "Be careful, my child; two Scorpios will blow the roof off the house."

Good thing we decided to spend the night at Angel's, or else the rainstorm's damage to the floorboards would have been worse. The orange bucket has overflowed, muddy water seeping into every nook and cranny, and there aren't enough rags so we sacrifice clean towels. That means no shower for either of us, but at least the situation's contained.

Angel's stomach is growling, or maybe it's mine, but the mouldy fridge is empty.

"How about pizza?" I shout from the frozen food aisle at the grocery store, kitty-corner to Angel's flat. Fifteen min-utes from my middle-class San Francisco neighbourhood to

West Oakland, and it's as though trees and organic groceries don't exist.

Angel gives the two thumbs up. "I'll get something healthy," he yells, pointing at a fruit and vegetable stand with onions sprouting green hairdos.

Finally, we're in line to pay. Food in my stomach, then sleep, can't come too soon.

"Angel?" A butch dyke approaches with a swagger, wearing jeans and combat boots. "I almost didn't recognise you."

"George, meet my partner, Avi."

"So, you've transitioned and are dating men now." George's mouth is contorted into an ugly smirk. "Damn, there's so few of us butch dykes left standing."

"So, what exactly are you saying? That I should live a lie?" Angel scowls.

"Whatever, dude," George mutters and takes off.

We walk in silence back to Angel's flat. I'm too exhausted to talk, and besides, I don't know what to say.

"That's the other reason I delayed transitioning." Angel sticks a barely defrosted pizza in the oven. "Being a butch lesbian was a collective identity. We were women who claimed masculinity on our terms. Had each other's backs. Imagine constantly getting kicked out of women's bathrooms, demanding to be addressed as Ma'am." He falls silent for a moment. "I don't know any other way to be, you know?"

I still don't know, but I want to. Does that count?

We stuff our faces and collapse on the lumpy mattress, stinking of sweat, pesto and garlic. I'm falling for him, but it's too scary to think about.

Our romantic date night at the movies is anything but. I've read somewhere that when you're attracted to someone, your pupils dilate. Angel's are the size of moons. All his talk about being into men and now this bullshit.

"Sorry, I didn't mean to ignore you. I'm Camilla," this bombshell of a woman turns to me.

I know who she is – a gender studies professor and a professional dominatrix, the Martha Stewart of the BDSM world. She's attractive by conventional standards, a lipstick femme with a narrow waist and big breasts. Every hair on her coiffed head is in place. Her every utterance has the correct diction. So perfect I could scream.

"Nice to meet you too; I'm—"

"Oh, good, here's my date, Bex," Camilla says. We're joined by an Angel look-alike, sans testosterone, holding an extra-large bucket of popcorn reeking of fake butter.

"Avi and I are going to the new Tarantino flick," Angel says.

"It's Disney for us." Camilla laughs as though she said something witty.

"Nice meeting you both," I grumble, grabbing Angel's hand and giving it a small but firm yank.

"Call me." Camilla gives Angel a forties starlet look.

"Yes, Ma'am," Angel tilts his cap.

During the previews, I lean into Angel's body. "Are you in love with Camilla, or is it just lust?"

"No, and no." He rolls his eyes.

"To be clear, I'm open to polyamory; it's the lying that bugs me."

"Stop being so fucking insecure."

It's a good thing the movie starts. I don't want to say stuff I'll regret.

"You still coming over?" I ask when the end credits appear on the screen.

"You still want me to?"

"Sure," I mutter.

Walking in resounding silence, we pass South of Market's growing homeless encampments. "I might have flirted with Camilla as a butch reflex." Angel kicks a crack pipe into the gutter.

"Aha."

"Please understand, a butch dyke is how I've expressed my masculinity for most of my life." Six months together and I sort of get it, but our gendered histories and desires are worlds apart.

"Do you even want to be with a man?" We're at my front door, but I don't take my keys out.

"I've always been attracted to men, but I used to be too masculine for straight guys and the wrong gender for gay men."

"So, if we weren't together—"

"I'm finally starting to pass, so I'd be dating and having sex with cis men."

"Exploring your desire makes sense, and the last thing I'd want is for you to feel trapped."

Angel's about to say something when his phone rings. "Sorry, sweets, but I need to take this." Ten minutes later, he barges through my front door. "You realise how much I could use a stable job?"

"Of course."

"Camilla just offered me one."

"In adult entertainment?"

"Yes."

"Doing stuff by yourself or with her?"

"Both, but it's all very professional."

"Can't you see she's trying to seduce you? Gosh! You have this blind spot when it comes to this woman."

"Don't say that."

"It's true."

"I meant, don't say blind spot." Angel slows down his speech, articulating every word like a schoolteacher talking to a particularly obtuse student. "Think about it. It's offensive, ableist language that puts down people with disabilities."

"Fuck you," I snap. I get what he's saying, but I hate how he's saying it.

"This negative energy," he gestures a make-believe bundle between his palms and outstretches his hands towards me, "is yours, not mine. So here, I'm giving it back to you."

Is there a halo over his head, or is smoke blowing out of his ass? "What's your part in what's happening?" I yell.

"I should leave," he snarls.

"The fourth agreement?"

"What?"

"I read Don Miguel Ruiz's book. Not that you've asked." God, I'm fuming. "Is this what you call doing your shamanic best?"

Angel runs at me with closed fists. "How dare you mock my spirituality?" he yells.

I shut my eyes, letting my arms hang by my side. I don't trust him; no, I don't trust either one of us to not get physical. Two pacificists. How the hell has it come to this?

"You make me insane," Angel cries, grabbing my arms with both hands. His body is shaking, or maybe it's mine. I can't tell anymore where the rage resides or who the hurt underneath it belongs to.

"Call it quits?" My question should be rhetorical. It's madness, I know, but my heart wants us to work.

"We need help," Angel says.

He's right. Of course, he's right.

*

"What brings you here?" The couple's counsellor asks. The man came highly recommended. Apparently he's queer, a trans ally, and doesn't beat around the bush.

"It's only been six months, but our relationship has cancer," Angel says, sitting as far away from me as the sofa allows.

The counsellor turns to look at me. "Do you agree?"

"That's a morbid way of putting things, but yes."

Angel complains about my jealousy, my drifting off to faraway places in punitive silences. I elaborate on Angel's holier-than-though complex in the finest of details.

"I have a strong hunch what the main problem in your dynamic is. Ready?" the counsellor asks.

We nod our heads, eager for a diagnosis. After all, this guy is an expert.

"Your connection suffers from a lack of authenticity."

Angel and I look at each other. Really? That's the best he can do? We might have a problematic relationship, but one thing's for sure, we're both as real as it gets.

"Hear me out. Neither of you is turning to the other to disclose, much less to ask for, what you want."

"You're wrong." My anger wells up. "Angel's a pro at declaring what he needs. He told me point-blank that he wants to work in Camilla's dungeon no matter how I feel about it."

"What if what Angel wants is something deeper?" The counsellor motions for Angel to say something.

"Like what?" Angel sneers.

"I'd venture a guess that you'd like Avi to learn how to trust you," the counsellor says.

"How can I trust Angel when he's dishonest with himself about his feelings for Camilla?" Yeah, yeah, it wasn't my turn to speak, but fuck it.

"Would the two of you be willing to brainstorm how to get to a place of trust?"

Angel's eyes narrow. "If Avi knows me better than I know myself, what's the point?"

"I'm sorry," I say as we exit the clinic and step into Market Street's bustling madness.

"About what?"

"About being such a bad communicator."

"I need to go. Talk later?" Angel looks somewhere to my right.

"Sounds good," I mutter, half-disappointed, half-relieved.

We don't talk. Instead, our breakup happens over email. Angel writes a well-manicured goodbye with gratitude and well-wishes. My thank you and *buh-bye* are just as respectful. The counsellor was onto something about our lack of authenticity, but I'd diagnose us as not being able to stay vulnerable with each other when it counts most.

So that's that, another dream brought to its knees.

And freedom.

There's that too.

Perhaps in some distant future, Angel and I will shift into friendship mode and go cruising together in gay bars. We never did crash the gay men's Folsom Street party, but we could get into other types of good trouble.

Come to think of it, I'd love a queer trans guy co-conspirator. Almost all the trans men I know are partnered with women. Some have sex with men on the side, but few are in primary relationships with men. So, maybe it's the end of romance but the start of something new for Angel and me. We'll see what happens down the line; right now, my heart's too raw.

*

It's been, what, about a year since Angel and I broke up? And *boom*, I get a text from Camilla, "Sorry to catch you off guard, but would you be open to meeting up? I'd like to ask you something." . Okay, I admit that I've been following Angel's singer-songwriter career on social media, but I've had zero contact with him or his inner circle. So, what's Camilla's invite all about?

"Sure. I'll be grading papers at Café Flore this evening and into the wee hours, so feel free to drop by," I write back. Truth is, I'm dying to know what's up her sleeve. It'll be hard not to ruminate, but thankfully, this massive stack of student essays should help.

"You look busy," Camilla interrupts my grading frenzy. Goddamn, the woman hasn't changed an iota.

"Perfect timing; I could use a break." I set my red pen to the side. "Please, join me."

She sits with her back straight, clutching her purse in her lap. "Thanks for making the time."

"This is all very mysterious."

"I'll jump right into it then. I'm editing a book about transgender identities and wanted to ask if you'd contribute a chapter."

"Can I get you a drink before we get into the nitty gritty?" I ask.

"A glass of red wine would be lovely." She smiles as though the elephant isn't crowding our space.

I order at the counter. Pinot noir for Camilla, Cuba libre for me. So, what's her true agenda? I'm not a gender scholar and she knows it.

"Why a trans identities book?" I hand her the wine glass.

"Well, I'm a cis dyke, but—"

"A dyke? Really?" A sip of the cocktail tickles my throat. "Not bi? Pansexual? Queer?"

"Yes, a dyke," Camilla says, the elephant looming so large now it's sucking the air out of the room.

"I've heard the rumours and if they're true, you're getting married to a man." I take a big gulp this time and spit out my words, "For the record, even if I were attracted to women, I'd never date someone who calls herself a dyke. How invalidating."

"For the record, you're not my type either."

I smile despite my efforts at a poker face. "Fair enough."

"We'd love it if you were part of our wedding party." Camilla's diction is flawless, as if she'd rehearsed this invite. "Angel wants you as his groomsman, but he's too proud to ask."

She must really love him if she's doing this, and, anyway, who am I to judge how she identifies or how Angel should react to being seen as what? Butcher-than-butch but not quite a man?

Wait, am I being an ass? Perhaps Angel's gender isn't binary like mine. Or maybe I'm taking things too personally when it's not about me.

Still, it pains me that Angel would marry someone who identifies as a woman who loves women. And why commit to Camilla at all? Why not explore his queerness, a new way of being in the world?

"You look lost in thought," Camilla says.

"Yes."

"Yes?"

"Yes, to being a groomsman but tell Angel he should get over himself and shoot me a text."

I will dance at Angel's wedding. I miss the guy and wish him happiness, even if I don't understand his choices. In the end, not all trans men are alike. It's the difference that highlights our humanity, right? And, who knows, maybe one day Angel will dance at my commitment ceremony to a bearish prince or two. Three is a lucky number in Judaism, and a man can dream.

4

WHO HOLDS JESUS?[4]

Waltzing into Dad's big 80th birthday bash in my provincial Middle Eastern hometown would be the sensationalist stuff of a tabloid exposé. Avi's "after" to Talia's "before". *Read all about it! This bearded beast* (Avi's face superimposed on the Loch Ness Monster) *was once upon a time a beautiful woman.*

Legally, there's no excuse not to go. After a long battle, the Israeli government finally changed my passport. First name: Avi. Gender: Male. My current photo – that of a lumberjack of a man – has replaced Talia's drag queen mug shot.

My heart's leaning towards going. I want to celebrate the dear man's life, but what if my presence ruins his special day? My parents excepted, no one else in my family had seen me as Avi. They haven't witnessed the gradual changes over the past four years – hyper-femininity to androgyny to rugged masculinity. The whispering and gawking are bound to distract from the man of the hour.

There's another issue. Gil. Imagining his face close up

sends shivers down my spine. (Does the Loch Ness Monster have a spine?)

"You'll need more than talk therapy to cope with your physical manifestation of stress," Jon says and refers me for short-term somatic work.

So here I am at my new therapist's office. It's less leather and more Boho – macramé wall hangings, Moroccan rugs and vintage rattan.

"So, what brings you here?" Ronald has a reputation for being a touchy-feely therapist, a Mexican American ex-ballerina gay mother hen.

"I'm trying to decide if I should go to a family event back in Israel and the stress makes me choke," I say.

"Metaphorically?"

"No, literally. I've been gagging on liquids, like coffee or water and sometimes even on my spit." I'm not sure why it's embarrassing to admit this, but it is. "Gasping for air isn't an attractive look."

"Have you ruled out medical causes?"

"My GP's convinced it's a laryngospasm." Ronald tilts his head to the side, so I explain, "A vocal cord spasm that's triggered by stress."

"Ah," he says in universal therapist speak. "And what's at the core?"

It's daunting to explain who I am from scratch, but I try. "After I transitioned, my brother, Gil, accused me of forcing his sister to commit suicide."

"His sister, you mean . . .?"

"Talia." Ronald still looks confused, so I add, "That's what my pre-transition name was."

"I see."

"Gil told me I disgusted him, that I was a monster." It

fucking hurts to speak about this, and, besides, is it helpful or retraumatising? Still, I soldier on. "Gil's cut me off from his and my nieces and nephew's lives. It's been four years since I've seen any of them."

"That must be very challenging. Were you close?"

"Big time. It'll kill me if they think I've abandoned them or if . . ."

"They, too, see you as a monster?"

"Yes, exactly."

"Let's use EMDR." This acronym stands for "Eye Movement Desensitisation and Reprocessing" and is effective for trauma-based stress. Instead of the traditional finger-movement approach, whatever that means, Ronald would be alternating between tapping my right and left knees and asking me to share whatever comes up. Cryptic, but I'm game.

Tap, tap, tap. "What are you thinking about?" Ronald asks.

"Unfiltered or with some interpretation?" It's weird to puke my thoughts out.

"Whatever comes up, exactly as is." He gives me a reassuring nod. "Let's try again." *Tap, tap, tap.* "What are you thinking about?"

"Jesus."

"C'mon, Avi, it's not that hard."

"No, I mean, Jesus, as in, I saw an image of Jesus."

Ronald's hand flies to his chest. "Why do you think *he* visited with you?"

I'm flooded with thoughts. None, which I care to share. A visitation? Whoa, not so fast there, bud. It wasn't Jesus, okay? It was an image of Jesus. Big difference.

"Avi, are you being resistant?" My silence seems to have unnerved the guy.

"Thoughts come and go. There doesn't always have to be a reason, right?"

"Jesus doesn't just come and go," Ronald says. On the bookshelves by a statue of a green Buddha is a framed picture of the Sacred Heart. How have I not noticed that before?

"Who holds Jesus?" I hear myself ask.

"Interesting, say more."

"Jesus holds the suffering of the world, right?"

"Correct."

"People pray to Jesus to ask him for things."

"All the time."

"Is there a prayer to help Jesus hold this vast human grief, or is he supposed to do that alone?"

"I don't know of any such prayer." Ronald closes his eyes in what looks like deep contemplation. "Wait, let's bring this back to you. What makes you ask?"

I have no clue why an image of Yeshua Ha-Nozri appeared in my mind's eye. But a Jewish atheist (with Buddhist leanings) or not, I feel moved to join in communal prayer to help carry his burden. That's all I have.

As self-hating as it sounds, I can't stand most Israelis – the loudness, nosiness, lack of personal space – yet here I am, flying El Al, the Israeli Airlines, stuck in a shrimp-sized chair and sandwiched between a mother and daughter who keep yelling over me.

The mother tries to get my attention. "What brings you to Israel?" she asks in English with a heavy Israeli accent.

"Vacation."

"You Jewish?"

None of your fucking business dangles from my tongue, but I nod and put on my headphones. What better time to practise mindfulness?

Inhale, exhale, inhale, exhale ... Gil.

My brother emailed this morning that he'd be the one picking me up at the airport. He's decided to try and forgive me for the shame I've brought on the family. How fucking magnanimous.

I want to rise to the occasion, be there for Dad, for "the greater good," as I told Jon, sounding holier than I had intended. But will I be able to, or will I lose it and ruin Dad's party before it even begins?

May I be safe, protected and free from inner and outer harm, I chant sotto voce to my favourite loving-kindness track. It usually works, but this time, I'm punching Gil in the face, again and again, his blood spilling at the altar of my righteous indignation. *I hate you, I hate you, I hate you.*

There's Jesus again with the same white robes, his hair long and flowing. Why Jesus? Why not Moses? He, too, had suffered, gone through hell and high water to voyage to the holy land, only to be barred from entering by a vengeful god.

No offence, but I'd take Moses over Jesus. Then, maybe I, too, will be forbidden entry into this troubled land. Something wrong with my new passport that denies me entry, perhaps? "Hey, I tried," I'd tell my family.

Jesus' image is hovering without consent. What is "he" trying to say?

Tap, tap, tap. I bang my thighs, attempting self-induced EMDR.

I'm not alone. Right at this very moment, trans people all over the world are journeying to family reunions, terrified of rejection and pain. What is it that makes us so repulsive to people who've proclaimed to have loved us before we became the best versions of ourselves?

*

69

Ben Gurion airport looks more modern, cleaner, but its hustle and bustle are just as claustrophobic. People don't keep physical distance in this part of the world. Spitting Hebrew with guttural "ch," they rub against me, elbowing in lines for passport control.

Finally, at the booth, I hand my documents to the dour-faced border police officer.

"A new passport? I'll need to scan it." He takes his time before looking at me again. Is his upper lip curled, or am I imagining it? "What elementary school did you go to?" he asks.

"What kind of question is this?"

"Are you refusing to answer?"

"HaNadiv in Herzliya, the city. It has the best cemetery views in town."

"I'm also from Herzliya, the city," the man says, his face softening. "Your mother's maiden name . . . are you related to Benjamin Urieli?"

"He's my uncle."

"I voted for him for town mayor. Great man."

Great man. Right. A man who is a proud, card-carrying member of the most right-wing party Israel has ever had. A man who threatened Talia with hiring a guy to rape her so she would finally have children.

"You haven't been back in over four years. So, why now?" my enemy asks.

None of your business, you fucking fascist, I almost say, but I know better. I've paid a heavy price for refusing to serve in the Israel Defense Forces, and I'd do it all again, but this visit isn't about me. "It's my dad's 80th birthday," I hear myself say.

"Mazal tov." The officer stamps my virginal passport. "But next time, don't wait so long. Your parents aren't getting any younger."

*

Red suitcase in tow, I amble through the green customs lane into arrivals. The barriers meant to separate the visitors from the travellers are useless. People barge through them, shrieking loved ones' names and leaping into each other's arms. *Ahalan! Ahalan!*

My motherland's cultural warmth is as real as its aggression. I need to remind myself of that more often or I'll get stuck in . . . Wait, is that . . .?

"Avi?" Gil asks, his green-brown eyes the colour of bloodline.

And no, I don't want to punch him, and no, I don't want to hug him. And, no, I don't know what to do with my body.

"Let me help you with this." Gil's hands are shaking as they reach for my suitcase. "I looked at your Facebook pics, so I was sort of prepared, but wow, you're so masculine." Gil's addressing me in Hebrew male speak, gendering me correctly.

"Forgive me if I don't talk much. I'm exhausted." I'm aware of my distanced delivery, but I can't pretend that everything's okay and I don't have the bandwidth to process. Not now. Maybe never.

"Sure, no worries." My brother sounds cheerful, as though nothing's wrong. What a mindfuck!

In the car, Gil cranks the radio on. It's the news; what else? "Rising violence in the West Bank after Palestinian Terrorists opened fire, injuring Israeli civilians."

This country is high on victimhood and rationalised anti-Palestinian violence. And here I am – a traitor to my people, family, gender, to mother nature herself. If it weren't for Mom and Dad, I'd never set foot in this place again.

Beyond exhausted, I try to nap, but my brain is buzzing, trying and failing to shut itself off.

I glance at my brother. His left hand is on the wheel, the right on the gearshift. He's still handsome by social standards but weathered – drier skin, thinning hair, a small hump growing under his chin.

If there's hope for Mom and me, is there hope for Gil and me?

The parents have moved into a modern penthouse in an apartment complex built over the foundations of our old family home. The balcony is its selling point – twice the size of the living area with a view of what's left of the town's rustic greenery – orchards of citrus trees.

"My two children, together." Mom's face is glowing. I'm happy she's happy, but really? After everything we've been through, how can she and Gil pretend everything's okay? Can someone scream, please?

Mom shows me to the guest bedroom, which she's nicknamed "the grandkids' room". A five-foot tattered teddy bear is taking up half the bed, holding a plush heart-shaped pillow embroidered with "I LOVE YOU" in all caps – a tenth anniversary present from Gil to his ex-wife, Sigal.

"I'll leave you be," Mom says and hobbles out the door. Stoic or not, I can tell she's in pain, even though her balance has improved somewhat with new meds and physical therapy.

Alone, at last, I toss teddy on top of the wardrobe and plop myself on the bed, utterly exhausted. Gil and Sigal's divorce was bitter, so why is the damn stuffed animal even here? I used to resent Sigal for what she had put Gil through. Now, I'm questioning everything my brother's ever shared about his marriage.

The mattress is stone hard. I wriggle, desperate to make it cosy somehow, but it doesn't give. Dying to get some rest, I place the duvet on the polyfoam and use the sheet as a blanket. Some more squirming, and finally, I settle on a semi-comfortable sideways pose and shove a milk chocolate bar into my mouth. The first bite tastes like a childhood prayer. May the sugary sweetness stave off the monsters under the bed. Amen.

And just like that, it's party time.

Standing on the parents' balcony, I spot them – Anna, Tamar and Daniel – my beloved nieces and nephew, getting out of Gil's car, all dressed up for Dad's big day. Wow, they're so grown up!

Do they know what to expect? Will they be horrified at the stranger who's missed them more than he can say?

Breathe, just breathe.

Daniel and Anna are the first to sprint through the front door and jump into my arms. "Avi, our Avi," they cry, "We've missed you so, so much." I can't believe it; how in the world is it possible they're not freaking out?

Fears evaporating, head whirling, I want to yell, *I didn't abandon you*, but all I can do is squeeze these precious beings, again and again, until we're one big mess of tears, snot and laughter.

Tamar, the youngest, has been hiding behind Gil's back. "I don't remember him," she says, pointing at me. Makes sense; she was only five when my brother disowned me.

"It's your uncle," Gil says. This is the best-case scenario, right? Mom must think so, rounding the corner, beaming. So why does Gil's easy-breezy demeanour make me see red? Why can't I be more generous towards my brother, open my heart?

Refocusing on Tamar, I extend my hand. "Wanna see the balloons?" She grabs it with the same winning grin she had as a chubby baby. Tamar can't remember, but I do. The way she fitted so perfectly in my arms is imprinted on my skin.

"Uncle, look," Tamar says. The catering company has transformed the balcony into a proper party venue – tables covered with fine linens, centrepieces with white roses, calla lilies and baby's breath flowers. Attached to the chairs are blue and white helium balloons swaying in the warm Mediterranean breeze.

Guests swarm in, bringing gifts in shiny, colourful packages. "Mazal tov," they yell, hugging and kissing with Middle Eastern warmheartedness.

"Grandma," Tamar lets go of my hand and rushes towards Mom, "presents!"

Someone taps me on the shoulder. Turning around, I see a familiar face – my cousin, Tirtza. "Remember me?" she asks. Tirtza hasn't changed much since I've seen her last, so why wouldn't I? But this question rears and re-rears its head.

"Remember me?" Yet another cousin asks.

"How about me?" It's Mom's best friend, tilting her head.

"And me?" A neighbour I'd recognise anywhere has joined the collective *Who am I?* game.

Do they think my brain has somehow gotten re-wired, my memories erased? Does re-birthing on Mars cause that?

Dad raises his glass and the guests fall into a hush. "Thank you, dear family and friends, for coming tonight." He chokes back tears. "Thank you, my Rina, for organising this event and being by my side for over five decades."

Mom leans against the table, wearing all white, like a bride. She motions for the microphone with a shaking hand, but Dad isn't done. "And a big thank you to my son, Avi, my youngest, for coming all the way from America."

"So, you're a man now?" Uncle Benjamin whispers. So far, I've managed to avoid him, but he's made sure to stride towards me, and like it or not, here he is. "You probably think I wouldn't be okay with it, but I get it." His hushed voice is a normal person's shout. "Who wouldn't want to be a man?"

His question is rhetorical, so I don't say anything. Besides, Mom is speaking now and I want to hear what she says.

Uncle Benjamin takes a swig of red wine, then leans into my ear. "Now here's what I really want to know . . ."

Please, please, may he not ask about surgery or genitals.

"Do you have a girlfriend?"

No, Sir, I'm a flaming homosexual, the consequences-be-damned me wants to say. Instead, I swallow hard, and my saliva goes down the wrong pipe. No, no, no, this can't be happening, but it does – my vocal cord spasms, closing my airway.

Mouth gaping, I pray for air, but I can't breathe. Panicked, I tilt my head back as far as it goes and press the notches behind my earlobes, right above the jaw. It's a trick I've learned from a Laryngospasm support group and thank goodness, it works. My vocal cord relaxes its death grip, but a high-pitched whistling sound screeches out of my throat, complete with drool.

Uncle Benjamin slaps me hard on the back. "Stop, please," I plead, but my voice hasn't fully come back yet, so he whacks me again and again.

"Better?" he asks.

"Enough," I yell.

Mom stops mid-speech and all eyes are on me. No more surreptitious peeks but a free-for-all staring contest. Are they looking at my hips and chest for any signs of *her*? Do they see a man? A bearded lady? And why the hell should I care what they think? I don't want to, but I do.

"Grandpa and Grandma, how about thanking me for being super fabulous?" Anna shouts.

Dad reclaims the microphone. "Indeed, you are, *chabibti*," he says, and the crowd bursts into laughter, refocusing on the leading man. "Mazal tov to Israel, till 120!" Mom's cousin, Chana, yells. "Mazal tov," people scream in a cacophony of pitches and intonations.

Choking fit over; I take a seat. The grandkids have prepared a multi-act performance – taking turns singing, dancing and wishing their beloved *Saba* many more happy and healthy years to come. Holding onto the coattails of Dad's smile, I too wish him well, *ad mea ve esrim*, or for however long he has left.

The truth is, it's not Dad who should have thanked me; it's me who should have thanked him. Anna shared that Dad was the one who broke my ex-communication spell. Without asking his wife or sons for permission, Dad gathered the grandkids and told them that Talia was Avi now, that they had a brand-new uncle.

"We were in seventh heaven you were alive. Why didn't they tell us earlier?"

I'm afraid to ask, but I do anyway, "Wasn't it weird for you to hear about my gender change?"

"It was at first, but then it wasn't," she said.

It's funny how the whisperings of unconscious fear make us, so-called adults, underestimate youngsters' resilience and wisdom.

My childhood friend, Adva, arrives during dessert. "Mazal tov," she bellows, bestowing a surprisingly strong round of bearish hugs for someone with such a delicate frame. I'm first in line, Dad's second, and to her horror, Mom's third.

"Thank you," Mom says through gritted teeth. She's never liked Adva, even though Adva has been part of our family landscape since forever, having grown up across the street.

Adva looks me up and down. "Wow, wow, what a hunk."

"Stop it," I say, blushing like a schoolboy.

"How about a walk in the old neighbourhood?"

"Let's." Stretching my legs would be perfect right now, and I can't wait to catch up with her one-on-one.

Our street has gentrified somewhat, but many houses are still dilapidated and the pavements are cracked. Herzliya the city, is the so-called wrong side of town. It's the proletariat, ugly stepsister of Herzliya by the Sea, one of the richest neighbourhoods in Israel. Still, the fragrance of oranges mixed with honey-smelling alyssum brings back memories of little Adva and little me running wild and free.

"But seriously, when you wrote you were a man, I wasn't all that surprised," Adva says, leaping over a pothole as if she were playing hopscotch.

"Really?"

"There were signs." Before I can even ask what she means by that, Adva sprints into a tiny park with a swing set. "Wanna?" she shouts.

I squeeze my bottom into the child-sized flat-board seat. "How's Penina?" I ask, grabbing onto the chains.

"Mom died," Adva yells, her brown hair swooshing around her face as she swings upwards. "Fat and lonely."

"Oh no, I'm so sorry." I step back as far as I can, then reclining, I extend my legs, surrendering into the forward momentum.

77

Adva's going strong. "The skinny guy." She's up. "From Chevre Kadisha." Down she goes. "Couldn't haul Mom." Legs extended. "Out the door." Legs in.

I need to get off this damn thing. It's pinching my ass, and besides, I forgot that swinging makes me nauseous. Untucking my legs, I dig my feet into the dirt.

"So, we dragged her body," Adva yells, heading upwards. "And the song on the radio?" She's on her way down. "We're going on a journey, hopa, hey, yay, yay." One moment she's up, up, up on top of the world, crooning and laughing with gusto, the next, she dives down like a bird of prey.

I'm trying to contain the wild braying within, but resistance is futile. Roaring, I clutch my belly. "You're horrible," I manage to utter.

"No, you are." Adva snorts.

"Get off the swing. I beg of you."

"Ready?" Adva jumps off mid-air, skims the ground and hops into my arms.

"Crazy woman," I say, toppling backwards.

"I knew you'd catch me." She giggles. "You always have."

Most of the guests have already gone and the servers are putting leftovers away. Did my family even notice I had stepped out?

"Where's Dad?" I ask Mom, who is busy orchestrating the clean-up from a kitchen chair.

"He's gone to lie down for a bit."

"Go see your dad. I'll help your mother in the meantime," Adva says.

I find Dad awake, stretched out on the bed in his fancy birthday outfit and shoes.

78

"Hi, my youngest."

"Did you have a good time?"

"It was the best night of my life. I've been trying to re-member every detail, but I forget things, *chabibi*. The doctor told me I have Alzheimer's."

"Oh no—"

"I don't know how much time I have to be me." He takes out a creased and stained note from his shirt pocket. *I love you, Aba'le*, it says in Hebrew in Talia's handwriting. "Love" conjugated in female form. "I take it wherever I go," he says.

"Thank you for being the sweetest dad ever," I kiss my father on his wrinkled forehead.

This bittersweet "Full Catastrophe Living", as the medi-tation teacher Jon Kabat-Zinn calls it – how can our hearts hold it all?

"That beast's about to pounce." Adva points at romantic, creepy teddy. Wait, has he moved since I last tossed him on the dresser?

The bed is narrow, but our bodies fit just right. Adva's warm lap is a nest for my heavy head, an invitation to dis-appear into a dream. I fight the urge. If I fall asleep now, it'll screw up my night. Besides, I'm enjoying her company way too much.

I tell her about EMDR and Jesus, curious what her take is. Adva is what people in Israel call "*roochnit*", a de-rogatory term for spiritual, which is in itself a disparaging term here.

"That was a real visitation," she exclaims.

"Why would Jesus seek out my company? Doesn't he have more important things to do?" I counter.

"He can visit multiple people at once."

"How do you know?"

"I've talked to Abraham."

"Really?" I get a second wind. "Abraham, Abraham? The biblical daddy of all Jews?"

"Not exactly Abraham himself. It's a name for a group of entities."

"Ah," I say, more confused than ever. As fascinating as the Abraham multiple-personality business is, I can't keep up the pretence of taking it seriously. "I've been dying to hear about the play you're in."

Her face brightens. "It's an anti-government piece, of course. But it's also so much more than that. There's love, sex and death. All the good stuff."

"Does Abraham make a cameo?"

"You're an asshole." Adva hits my face with a pillow. "Listen to this, a wounded soldier was wheeled in to see us perform last night. His mother told me she wants him to experience the world, despite his horrific condition."

"What's happened to him?"

"Most of his head had been blown off," Adva says, somewhat unscientifically. "Something to do with being locked-in, if that makes sense."

"Locked-in Syndrome! Yeah, I've read about it. Being fully conscious and aware but trapped in a completely paralysed body. What a nightmare."

"He communicates by moving his eyes."

"Remind me to shut the fuck up the next time I whine about a long plane ride or a relative playing *Who am I?*"

"Anyway, at the end of the show, I strip half-naked and sit on someone's lap—"

"No, you didn't."

"I did! The breathing tube and huge hole in the guy's head were freaky, but I got over myself. I put his hand on my cheek and let his arm slide down with gravity. It was like he was stroking me."

Adva is such an amazing human. So, why does Mom dislike her so much?

"Advoni, tell me a bedtime story about when we were kids, 'kay?"

"I'll tell you my favourite Talia story," she says.

"You were four and I was five. We played in my room for a while, having a great time, but then your mom came to pick you up. I tried blocking the door, but she said she needed you to come home.

"After dinner, I yelled at the top of my lungs that I wanted to see my bestie again. 'Now', I shrieked, 'right now'. In the end, my parents got so sick of my screaming they made my older brother — the jerk, remember him? — take me across the street.

"Your daddy was bathing you. I leaned over to say hi, and you yanked me in, with all my clothes on and my shoes too!

"I walked home drenched in soap and water. 'You're in such deep shit, missy', my brother said, but I didn't care! I got what I wanted . . . more time with you!"

The sticky cobwebs of sleep are taking hold of my brain.

"I love you, Avi, my brother, my best girlfriend turned homo," Adva says.

"I'm sorry for your loss," I hear myself mumble, letting go into a blessed fog.

What time is it? Someone must have pulled down the blackout shades. Adva, was it?

I feel my way into pitch darkness and click the light switch. There's a note on the dresser. I grab it, blinking.

Didn't want to wake you to say bye, it says in Adva's handwriting. She's added a wave – that's what her name means in our mother tongue –

and a heart.

It's 6 a.m. local time, meaning 8 p.m. in San Francisco. No wonder I'm ravenous. It'll be good to have a bite and a few moments to myself before the parents wake up.

Entering the kitchen, a shadowy figure makes me jump. "G'morning. How about coffee and toast?" it asks.

"What are you doing here so early?"

"I wanted to check on you before I went to work," Gil says.

I still don't get it. How did my brother go from cutting me off to this, whatever this is? Pretence or a true change of heart? Even if he's being genuine, it's too little, too late, doesn't he think? *If you want us to connect, as in really connect, own up to your shit*, I'm tempted to yell, but it's not worth it.

"Did Dad tell you about his diagnosis?" Gil asks, pouring water and finely ground Turkish coffee into a metal pot.

"Yes, he did."

"I can't bear the thought of Dad losing his mind." Gil stirs the coffee, filling the kitchen with an earthy, nutty aroma. It's been years since someone made me a brew and this pouring ritual – foam first, coffee second – is comforting for a moment. But then I remember. Coffee makes me choke.

I tap my thigh three times, calling on my inner Ronald.

"You look deep in thought. Care to share?" my brother asks.

"It's too early in the morning to think or speak clearly," I say. If this were an EMDR session, I'd have spilled it un-filtered. *If you can talk to me so easily right now, why the fuck did you make me into a demon, an untouchable, someone you needed to keep away from your kids? Do you realise how much you've hurt me?*

But this isn't therapy and I don't trust Gil's reaction. In two minutes, we could both get out of control. He and I are similar that way, especially when we feel wronged. And I've managed so far to contain the drama, so no, I'm not risking a fight.

A sip of Turkish coffee and something miraculous happens – I don't choke. I don't even fear choking.

"Hey, kiddos," Dad says, shuffling into the kitchen. "Your mother's still asleep, but I'm ready to rock and roll." He's wearing his signature silk pajamas. Growing up in a working-class family, we'd taunt him about being a dandy. The dear man didn't deserve our mockery, but we took him for granted back then.

Gil embraces Dad's shrunken body. "Good morning, Daddy-O."

"Thank you, *chabibi*."

"My turn." I give Dad a gentle squeeze and a peck on each cheek.

"Thank you, thank you, *chabibi*."

I pray that his sons' hugs and kisses tattoo on Dad's psyche and give him solace, even when his brain no longer knows who he is. And, yes, I could write him a new note to put in his pocket – to replace Talia's, *I love you*,

conjugated in female form,

אני אוהבת אותך

with Avi's in male form,

אני אוהב אותך

But if Dad forgets her, or me, or thinks of me as her, I vow to love him just the same.

Tap, tap, tap.

83

Three times Dorothy clicked her ruby-red slippers because *there is no place like home*. Three, in Judaism, is symbolic of luck. Three is also a trinity, holy – a mythical figure, made of multitudes, wishing all beings to be safe, free and at ease.

I'm no expert in theology; I don't even believe in a god, but I trust that the grief I carry isn't mine alone. That maybe, just maybe, in my better moments, I could hold it with others, for others, for myself, who is not as separate from others as I'd sometimes like to believe – not even from the brother who betrayed me when I needed him most.

5

CANDY FROM A STRANGER[5]

What was I thinking? A week-long LGBTQ+ silent meditation retreat sounded like a great idea when I booked it three months ago. Now, not so much.

I could have vacationed in Hawaii and gone swimming with giant sea turtles in clear, turquoise waters. Instead, I'll be sitting on back-breaking cushions, 6 a.m. to 9 p.m., surrounded by people who gurgle and breathe too loud. That's what I get for being a JewBu.

Gosh, I'm whiny. It's probably my stomach speaking, empty and growly after the long drive from San Francisco to hippy-dippy Saratoga Springs. First things first, though – I need to claim a bedroom. A glance at the visitors' map shows my assigned cabin at the periphery of the grounds, a twenty-minute hike from the restaurant and main lodge. Making it to dinner on time might be pushing it, but I want a room with a reasonably comfortable bed and, who knows, maybe even a view.

"Hello," I shout as I enter the dimly lit hallway. "Anyone here?"

The cabin seems empty. Still, I knock on the door of the one bedroom with windows overlooking the lush wildflower garden. When no one answers, I slam it wide open and step into a pleasant, no-frills chamber, basked in the tail end of a golden California sunset. It has sparkling-clean, dark hardwood flooring, bay windows and a painting of a fat Buddha hanging above the bed, his enigmatic smile illuminated by the soft, pink-and-yellow light.

Bracing for a bed of nails, I flop myself on the mattress, but, surprise, surprise, it's comfortable. Damn, this simple room is far better than, dare I say it, a *fancy schmancy* Hawaiian resort. After all, I'm here for spiritual growth or at least to cultivate some inner peace.

Right? Right!

I should get going, but my body sinks into the mattress, getting heavier and heavier, my muscles relaxing their hold. Get up! I slap myself on the cheek. This isn't the time to dawdle. Hangry-ness and patience aren't good bedmates, and I'll need loads of patience to keep still for hours on end.

On the count of three, I fish my childhood teddy bear from my knapsack. "*Veni, Vidi, Vici,*" I whisper, propping my retreat companion's matted body against the pillow. Not quite a Buddhist sentiment, I concede, but I declare this room mine, goddammit and teddy my watchman.

I'll need the loo, then I'm out of here.

Foraying into the hallway, I count three more empty bedrooms and freeze. The bathroom is missing a door. There's a stall for the toilet, but the communal shower is exposed, with no curtain, not even a curtain rod.

An invitation for voyeurism might be part of this cabin's granola charm, but it's far from ideal for a trans guy who'll most likely be sharing this place with non-trans men. On the bright side, being on a silent retreat means that even if some of my housemates experience a "tranny surprise" moment as they glimpse my naked body in the shower, they'd need to shut up about it. I wouldn't have to explain or educate. *Namaste.*

Light-headed, I grab a windbreaker and torch and hurry down the narrow path towards the dining hall. I forgot how cold it gets up north after dark. I pull the hood over my head and quicken my pace, dried leaves and brambles shattering under my boots.

Whoa, who is that? A shadowy figure careens towards me, its carry-on bouncing unevenly on a surface meant for hiking boots and backpacks. I raise the torch and make out the person's face. Drew! My least favourite person in my queer meditation group. As if the exposed shower situation weren't challenging enough.

"Hey, Drew," I yell, pointing the light under my chin.

"Hiya, Avi," Drew shouts back.

The path is barely wide enough for one person, let alone two men and a carry-on. I turn sideways to let him pass, but he comes to a complete stop, a metre from my face, reeking of soured cologne. When did he become so stinky?

"*Ugh*, I don't think I can do a week of silence," he whines.

"Really? I can't wait for the silence to begin."

"If you change your mind, let's cut class and hang at the heated pool."

Hell, no. I'm here to deepen my mindfulness practice. Besides, my recent farce of a date with Drew, or whatever that was, still stings. But, instead of speaking my mind, I mumble something incoherent and continue my trek, praying he'll choose the room furthest away from mine. Better yet, how about he hops into his Mercedes Benz convertible and zooms back to San Francisco?

The dining hall is bright and warm. About sixty people or so are milling around, returning their trays and helping clean up. Except for a few folks from my meditation group and a smattering of familiar faces: Bay Area Buddhist circles? Craigslist? I don't know these people.

One of the strangers, this dude, well, he's bugging the hell out of me – rocking his head side to side and thumping his thighs. It'd be weird behaviour regardless, but it's especially grotesque when everyone around him is quiet.

The more I think about it, the more righteous I get. How dare this dude, Rocky, I'll call him, take up so much space with his loud gestures? I hate, hate, hate him.

Wait, what? I try to stifle a laugh, but it escapes my mouth without consent. Hate, really? My mind is so frickin' judgmental. What if Rocky is anxious? How about a modicum of compassion? And, anyway, how can I hate someone I don't know – projection, much?

Famished, I inhale what's left of a quinoa salad, stuff my mouth with sticky cornbread and down it with sips of boiling tea. Belly full, I'm ready to become more equanimous. Or am I?

"Five minutes to the bell," a retreat coordinator announces on a megaphone. "After the third ring, follow me to the Heart Lodge, and no more talking." Talking? Who's been talking besides the loud voices in my head?

The lodge is larger than I had expected, about 2,000 square feet, with pine floors, a stage and a stone fireplace that doubles as an altar. On its mantel are purple-and-white orchids and a bronze Buddha. Below the stage is a medley of meditation cushions in primary colours. Just looking at them hurts my back. But further out are wooden folding chairs arranged in a semi-circle. "Aha," I hear myself utter, rushing to put dibs on a middle seat. It's not the epitome of comfort, but it'll do.

My fellow meditators have been trickling in. Before long, they divide themselves into two groups: the cushion people and the chair people. Rocky is a cushion person. He seems calmer but humps his pad before settling into a meditation pose.

Jerked by the sound of the bell, we stare at the stage. Our meditation teacher, Larry Yang, has arrived, looking like a spiritual daddy in white slacks and a blue button-down shirt with a white shawl draped over his shoulders.

"Welcome, beloved community." Larry observes his flock with an infectious glow. "Our goal on this retreat is to go inwards, supported by each other's open-hearted presence. In this spirit, I ask that you respect others' silence and personal space, however antsy or bored you might become. And for the love of the Buddha, refrain from cruising. We're all sex-positive here, but this is neither the time nor place. Now, let's meditate."

I settle into a semi-comfortable pose, back straight and close my eyes. Inhale, exhale, inhale, exhale . . . Drew.

*

Drew leans towards me, his angular face half-lit by tea candles. Is he trying to seduce me? His suggestion to grab a drink after our group meeting had a friend vibe, but Martunis is famous for its strong martinis, and now I can't tell.

The tiny backroom in this iconic gay piano bar is where the karaoke magic happens. Uneven-sized mirrors compete for wall space, while a ceiling mirror reflects the room's highlight – a grand piano. Singing is for the brave or the foolish: whoever ventures on stage receives a piano accompaniment only, without the usual machine controls and adjustments. And Martuni's typical audience? It's a vicious crowd, hungry for a healthy heckle or the rare applause.

"Let's sing a duet," Drew says.

"I got kicked out of choir in the third grade." Can he hear the terror in my tone?

"So that's a no, I take it."

"Correct. It's a favour to you and everyone here."

"In that case, mister, I'll serenade you." He decides on Leonard Cohen's "Hallelujah", which happens to be my favourite heartbreak song and marches to the limelight.

Maybe it's the second Apple Sour Martini or the way Drew's claimed the stage – a David to the audience's Goliath – or how he looked at me, and only me, just now; I'll say yes to whatever happens next.

"Hallelujah, Hallelujah ..." the audience joins in the fourth and last verse.

"Hallelujah," I mouth along.

"Ha-lle-lu-jah," Drew draws out the coda, milking each syllable.

People rise from their seats and burst into a round of applause. I join the clapping. "Bravo," I yell, "Bravo." Drew's all smiles, stopping for pats on the back and some high-fives before returning to our table.

"Fantastic singing, Sir." The waiter has appeared out of nowhere, with two fresh martinis on the house.

"Yes, what an amazing performance," I say.

"How about we down these real quick and go to my place? I have a hot tub in the backyard."

"Tempting, but—"

"What?"

"You need to know something first."

"You're hot, and I'm horny and versatile, so anything goes."

"I'm trans."

"Trans?" Drew cocks his head.

"Yes, transgender."

"You're becoming a woman?"

"No, I've transitioned from female to male."

Drew chokes, mid gulp, spraying pink, sugary liquid over his shirt. "Sorry, it's all very confusing," he says, dabbing his collar with a napkin.

I try to catch Drew's gaze, but he looks away. "Damn," he mutters, "it's impossible to tell by looking at you."

I assume he means well, so I don't say anything. There's no good response to this so-called compliment, anyway. Trans men are men who look like men. What else *should* they look like?

"You've led me on." Drew downs the rest of his drink with a single gulp.

"How did I do that exactly?"

"Great, now you're offended. Call it a night?"

★

I hate, hate, hate being late! How did I miss the 6 a.m. wake-up bells for the first meditation sit of the day? I leap out of bed, throw on a pair of jeans, slip into my boots and dart out the door.

The fresh outdoor air is an adrenaline shot. I break into a sprint, praying to make it on time. My bladder's about to burst and my nightshirt clings to my body, tacky from sweat, but fuck it; peeing and showering will have to wait.

The meditation hall is filled to the gills and steeped in a deep hush. Tiptoeing towards an empty seat on the far side of the room, I swallow my *sorry, sorry, sorry* when I can't help but brush against people's knees. Silent retreats call for silent apologies.

And just as I've almost got away with being late, Larry opens his eyes from his perch on the stage and stares at me. Yikes, is this how my poor students feel when I glare at them for being even one minute behind schedule?

Still, I'm here, and that's what matters, right? Lowering myself into the chair, I cringe at its roaring creakiness, and Rocky, of all people, looks at me with reproach. Really, dude?

Determined to stay present, I close my eyes and focus on the cool air entering my nostrils. How have I not noticed the tight band wrapped around my head? What have these poor muscles been trying to protect me from?

Hawaiian turtles are awesome, but this meditation retreat is what I needed – holding and being held in communal silence, an intentional non-doing. I'm committed to the now, to whatever good, bad, or ugly invades my brain with a tyranny I can't control.

Inhale, exhale, inhale, exhale ... Fuck you, Drew.

Inhale, exhale, inhale, exhale ... No, thank you, Drew. Thank you for reminding me that who I am has nothing to do with how men like you choose to see me.

When the meditation bells finally ring, I sprint back to the cabin. It's high time to take care of my bodily needs, shower and reset, even if it means missing a meal.

The cabin looks more lived-in – my roommates haven't left a mess exactly, but hanging on the clothes rack is a baseball cap with a silver fox print, and next to the welcome mat are a pair of slippers and a vaguely familiar carry-on.

Drew's room must be the one across from mine – walking past the open door, I can smell his cologne. Whatever. I can easily ignore him.

What's important is that the bathroom's in decent shape. Admittedly, there are toiletries all over the sink, but it's otherwise clean. I disrobe, glancing over my shoulder. The no door, no shower curtain situation isn't relaxing exactly. But fuck it, a man's gotta get clean. Besides, everyone's at lunch.

Turning the shower dial to just below scalding, I place my hand under the stream. Yup, lobster hot is just right. Positioning myself under the nozzle, at last, I surrender to the water's heat and pressure, my shoulders relaxing away from my neck.

"May I be safe, protected and free from inner and outer harm," I hear myself chant. Before getting kicked out of my third-grade choir, I used to bellow my little heart out, but hardly ever since. It's another silence born of indignity.

Propping my hands against the tiled wall, I stick my bottom out, letting the strong stream massage my lower back and glutes. What bliss, swaying my hips back and forth, serenaded by the splashing water. Hey, what if I dared sing to an admittedly self-critical audience of one? Isn't that why I'm here – to be bold and vulnerable?

Okay, okay, I'll do it, but what should I sing? I know; how about "Dancing Queen?" That's it. I make a fist, pretending to hold an imaginary microphone in front of my mouth. Gosh, I'm ridiculous, but who cares?

"You are the—" I start bellowing, then freeze, sensing the intruder, even though my back is to the doorframe. It's like the world has gone into slow motion, and my body has a mind of its own. It pivots to face the hallway and my worst fear comes true. A man is standing there, staring at me.

No, this can't be happening! What the fuck is *he* doing here? I'm looking through a narrow tunnel, and at its end is Drew's face, looking me up and down.

"Boy, was I wrong about the trans thing," Drew smirks. "I'm hard for you."

Get out slowly, my inner Larry says. *Don't look at him, and whatever you do, don't let him break your vow of silence.*

I see my hands doing their hands' thing. They turn off the water, grab a towel and wrap it around my dripping wet torso. If only I could shrink to two dimensions, but, no, my body rubs against Drew's as I dash out the doorway and into the hallway.

"Wait," he yells.

Is he following me? I can't tell, but I hasten my walk, then dart inside my room, slamming the door shut with a loud thud. How dare he have ogled me like that? Pressing against the door with all my weight, the towel slips from my waist.

Fuck you, I scream inside my head, naked and panting.

What would Larry say about now? I don't know anymore. What would he say? He'd want me to find him, right? That's it. Find Larry. I throw on some clothes, toss the damp towel on the window shutter and hug teddy against my chest, sniffing its tattered head. I can do this.

Wait, am I imagining it, or is someone knocking? Yes, the thumping's getting louder. It must be Drew, right? Who else could it be? And if I open the door and it's him, I might scream my lungs out and then what? He'll have destroyed what I've come here to do: my commitment to silence. No way am I letting that happen, but Drew, or whoever it is, is not giving up.

I can't anymore. That's it. Whatever happens, I'm done playing hide and seek. I fling the door open and it's Drew.

Of course it is. He's blocking the exit, holding a bag of chocolate truffles. "Want one?" he asks.

Fuck off, asshole. I think it, but don't say it. Instead, I duck under his arm, noticing, in horror, that my hand reaches to grab one of the truffles – a chocolate ball wrapped in a red, shiny wrapper that crinkles inside my fist.

"Hey, sexy," Drew yells after me. "Join me at the pool."

My legs takes me in the opposite direction of the pool and into an open meadow. Leaning against the rough trunk of a walnut tree, I try taking a loving-kindness inhale, but my lungs reject it.

What devil possessed me to take the chocolate? What the hell is wrong with me?

You could have screamed, *Stop!* Instead, you egged him on. "Yes, it tickles, Grandpa Gershon," you said. You wanted his candy.

The sugar made your teeth hurt, but you craved more, more, more. It felt good, right? Sure, you were only eight years old, but you knew it was wrong. You could've said no.

You made him do it. You made all of them do it.

Remember how shitty you felt on your thirteenth birthday? Your boobs were an insult, the bra an injury. So why the hell did you choose a bra that made your titties stick out from your shirt, perky and inviting? Molest me, they said.

Once a slut, always a slut.

What were you thinking, looking at yourself in the hallway mirror? You should have stayed in your room.

"My girl's all grown up," he said, standing behind you and staring at your budding breasts as though ogling your body in the mirror didn't count. He brushed your hair to the side and kissed your neck, nuzzling lips and nose against your smooth whorish skin, sending shivers down your spine. You told yourself you didn't like it, but if that was true then why were your nipples tingling, your down there wet?

He sniffed the dirty on you. They all did.

Normal people scream when they're accosted in the dark, the air too thick to breathe. Not you. You wanted Gil's friend's candy. That's why the older boy snuck into your teen bedroom late at night, right, bitch? So, he didn't stop when you begged him to please, please, not orgasm inside your filthy hole. He knew you didn't mean it. You'd been asking to be bred.

Mommy, Mommy, wake up; I've been – What? Did you really think she'd believe the R-word? Why would she when all she needed to do was take one look at you, and . . . What a disgrace!

The silent ride to the ER. Parents in the front, their hussy of a child in the back, blood and semen dripping from the soiled flesh between its legs. Humiliating!

At the hospital. Blinding lights. Gloved fingers. A speculum pinching raw flesh. The bitter morning-after pill that made you puke your guts out.

That's what happens when you cry out for abuse, for more candy.

Look at me now, a so-called mature man who's learned so much from therapy and Buddhism – yeah, right – I still took the truffle.

Shove the candy down your throat and choke on it, you worthless piece of shit. You know you want to.

Hey, a child-like voice emerges from somewhere, the woods, my soul?

"Hey," I murmur, my body cold as a corpse.

None of this was fair, she whispers.

"It's ruined me," I say, the truffle's flesh erupting inside my clenched fist.

You took the candy to survive, she says, *but I'm here, and I love you.*

"How can you love me when I hate you?"

You don't hate me. You hate what's happened to me.

I open my hand and shake it. The candy's carcass collapses onto the earth, its glossy red wrapper garish against moss green and charred clay. By some grace, my tainted palm finds its way to a place of rest, that tender spot on my chest.

It's not just me that's here, she says. *So is Grandma Rivka. Trustworthy people loved you too, you know, and dogs count too.*

"Thank you," I whisper.

Call on me if you need me, she says, disappearing into the blue skies above or infinity within.

"You asked to see me?" Larry is seated behind a desk in a cosy office adjacent to the Heart Lodge.

"I need your guidance," I say, then tell him everything that happened with Drew and my unravelling at the meadow. It took a few hours for me to recoup, and I almost got in my car and drove home, but I'm glad I stayed.

"Thanks for sharing." Larry's expression is soft. "I will have a stern conversation with Drew, but more importantly, how's your heart?"

"Right now, I'm okay." I take a deep breath, and this time, my lungs don't resist. "It dawns on me that if I hadn't committed to the silence, if I would've engaged with Drew or called a friend, then . . ."

"You would have avoided the damning self-talk?"

"Yes, and that would have been a shame." I'm surprised

at what just came out of my mouth, but Larry nods in what looks like agreement.

"How about you get in touch with little Talia more often?" he asks.

2.

Thesis

Talia's Story

(Israel, Italy, USA, 1973–2001)

6

SACRIFICE IS SEXY[5]

Since coming back from the meditation retreat at Saratoga Springs less than a month ago, Talia has been haunting my thoughts and dreams, asking to be reconsidered, integrated.

Please, take another look at who you think I am. If I surprise you, maybe you'll learn to appreciate me more; at the very least, forgive me. I'm not as bad as you've made me out to be, you know?

To inhabit the man I aspire to become means reckoning with my past's identities, including and beyond gender. Talia crawled from under Israeli working-class, right-wing rocks – and I get that it was an admirable feat – but her survivalist coping skills came at what cost to herself and others?

"You win," I hear myself say. "I'll write your origin story."

Finally! Where will you begin?

"In third grade."

Of course. She sighs. *Third grade.*

★

"The whole world hates us," Talia's third-grade teacher, Mrs Hamorah, repeated her favourite mantra. The woman's face was moist and red, forty kids huddling around her like buzzing bees.

Thirty-five degrees Celsius and humid made pontificating hard. The classroom had no air conditioning. There was barely any reprieve from June's thick, burning heat, save for the occasional warm breeze from the one window overlooking the small-town Israeli cemetery.

In different universes, Jewish kids our age read books like *Peter Pan* and *Charlie and the Chocolate Factory*. A boy that never grows up? Weird. Roald Dahl? Twisted. But Mrs Hamorah proclaimed that these were tales for "sissies".

"Gather around, kids, and I'll tell you the story of the battle of Tel Hai," the woman shouted, the overgrown, black, curly hairs sprouting from her armpits dripping sweat, forging yellowish trails on her flowery dress. Mrs Hamorah must have been in her early forties, but to Talia, she looked as ancient as the witch in *Hansel and Gretel*.

"Picture this. The year? 1920. The place? Tel Hai, a small and peaceful Jewish farming village in the Galilee." Mrs Hamorah closed her eyes and became still like a monument.

Sitting at her feet, we looked at each other, wide-eyed. Was our teacher okay?

"The attack came from nowhere," Mrs Hamorah barked. "Swarms of vicious Arabs from Jabal Amil in Southern Lebanon converged on the gates of Tel Hai, yelling *Death to the Jews!*"

Our eight-year-old semi-circle erupted into a tephra of gasps.

"Don't you worry, boys and girls," Mrs Hamorah said, with a tone that could have been mistaken for empathy. "What happened next was the stuff of true heroism.

102

Galloping to the farmers' rescue came Yosef Trumpeldor and his ten brave men. They fought with cunning and determination, like David warring against Goliath, and scared our enemies away."

Relieved, we were ready to move on to a different, perhaps more cheerful topic.

"But!" screamed Mrs Hamorah, her eyes moist. Her exclamation didn't sound too promising. "Trumpeldor's hand was blown off, its stump gushing blood. He had also suffered gunshot wounds to his stomach." About to climax, our teacher's voice pierced our eardrums, "As Trumpeldor lay dying, he uttered, *Never mind, it's good to die for our country*!"

Talia had a hard time falling asleep that night. When she finally drifted into a deep slumber, she dreamt of red fountains made of human flesh.

While Talia was made to listen to Mrs Hamorah's gruelling stories about the atrocities levelled against the Jewish people – and chastised for her terrible singing voice, failing arithmetic and sitting with her legs too wide apart for a girl – our older brother, Noam, was drafted into military service. At a mere nineteen years of age, he was placed in a tank battalion on the Suez Canal.

On a scorching Yom Kippur, 6 October, 1973, many of Noam's fellow soldiers were away from their posts and tanks, fasting in honour of the *Day of Atonement*, relieved of their gear. But Noam's platoon sergeant was notorious for being a hard-ass. "In your tank for an exercise," he ordered. While Noam and his fellow soldiers obeyed this sadistic command – despite the high holiday and their need for a break from the punishing heat – Egyptian and Syrian forces began a synchronised attack against Israel.

The war came as a total surprise to Israeli intelligence, the whole country, and, of course, our older brother. Noam's tank got hit, the sounds of battle shattered his eardrums and the smell of burnt flesh knocked him unconscious.

On that same sweltering Yom Kippur day, Talia was doing her nightmare of a chore – hanging laundry outdoors on the large, creaky carousel.

"No rest for me," she chanted as she picked her favourite wooden clothes pins to hang her garments while relegating the half-broken plastic ones for Mom and Dad's underwear.

Mom's colossal bras were handmade by the elderly Russian lady who lived next door and smelled like mothballs. Talia worried that her maternal lineage's booby curse would infect her too and her small but developing chesticles would soon erupt and overripen. Wasn't it bad enough she couldn't pee standing up, and now this?

The air-raid siren of war interrupted Talia's mind wandering. She was used to the single continuous pitch of the "this is only a test" variety, but the sound kept ascending and descending this time. Was Talia misremembering, or had Mrs Hamorah said that this oscillation meant war? Like, for real?

Talia froze, telling herself that she must be wrong. But the sound kept pulsating up and down, up and down, up and down. As Egyptian troops swooped into the Sinai Peninsula and Syrian soldiers into the Golan Heights, blood rushed back into Talia's limbs and she ran inside the house screaming.

In uniform, Noam looked like the mural soldier adorning the entrance to our dreaded elementary school – chiselled and handsome. "He gave his life for you!" This message was

104

written in large block letters underneath the hero's image. Sacrifice was sexy.

The mural solider was a prodigal Jewish son, rock hard, made from the toughest elements of the mother earth he stood protecting. Too strong to wither away into a skeletal creature in a Nazi concentration camp. Too cunning to choke on Zyklon B, to allow his fat to be turned into soap, his skin into lampshades and other Jewish-made objects. No fucking way!

Passing this image six days a week – and, yes, to add extra torture to our young existence, we only had the Sabbath off from school – well, it scarred us forever. If this young man died so we could live, we needed to give back, right? And even though how to do that exactly was muddy, one thing was clear – at eighteen, we'd be drafted into the Israeli Defense Forces, men for three years, women for two. Until that fateful day, we needed to be good little boys and girls and listen to what we were told.

After Noam returned from war, wounded, different, but alive, Mom decided to bake her famous chocolate cake.

Mom hated the kitchen. She was a terrible cook and a worse baker, but, by a twist of fate, that modest cake made of white flour, margarine, sugar, eggs and low-grade cacao was always pure magic. Crispy on top. Moist on the inside. Just right.

Talia volunteered to help and was given the task of stirring the batter. While Mom looked away, Talia licked the raw paste off the spatula, sugar crystals tingling her tongue. Since Noam's return, she'd been getting away with being sneaky.

A sudden, ear-piercing noise made Talia jump. The windows and walls shook as if they were coming undone. "It's the sound of freedom. The fighter jets are here to keep us safe," Mom said.

"Noooooooo," Noam screamed from the living room. He must have been having another one of his fits. Talia hesitated. She wanted to run to our older brother and put her arms around him, but we didn't show this kind of "weakness" in our family. What if Talia wouldn't know what to say? What if she'd embarrass him?

"I'll be there in a second, Noam," Mom shouted. She opened the stove to stick a toothpick into the cake. It came out with a sticky brown residue. "Not ready yet," Mom muttered as she slammed the oven door shut and walked out of the kitchen with Talia at her heels.

Noam was curled up on the living room floor sobbing, the small of his back pressed against the velvety gold sofa. The rays of the harsh Middle Eastern sun forced their way through the blinds, imbuing him with a messiah-like halo.

"What's the matter, honey?" Mom asked.

"Not a hero, not a hero, not a hero," Noam chanted, rocking back and forth.

"Yes, you are. I'm so proud of you—"

"Stop it!" Noam barked.

"I know it hurts right now, but your pain will go away one day."

"I've seen my friends blown into a million bloody pieces. And for what? Some twisted Zionist ideology?"

"You were protecting your country." Mom's face flushed. "I'm proud of you."

"How can you call yourself a mother," Noam raised his eyes to meet hers, "if you're willing to sacrifice your child for your country?"

"How dare you?" Mom's eyes turned steel blue.

A hint of burning wafted from the kitchen – had the cake been in the oven too long? Talia inched forwards. "Mom, what about the cake?"

"Quiet." Mom rubbed her temples. "Why do you always have to poke your nose where it doesn't belong?"

"That smell. Make it stop," Noam screamed.

Talia sprinted into the smoky kitchen. She opened the oven door and gasped. The cake was charred, ruined.

"Am I a good mother, little one?" Mom asked from the doorway.

Talia gasped, mustering the strength to answer the way Mom would have wanted her to. "Yes, you're a very good mother."

"You love my chocolate cake, right?"

"It's the best cake in the world." Talia wiped her eyes with her sleeve. This was true. There wasn't any other cake like it.

"I let the cake burn. I kept thinking about turning the oven off, but I'm that kind of mother, you know, the one who'll drop everything to listen to my child."

But *cake, shmake*, the apex of childhood trauma was yet to come.

"You sound like the radio," Grandma Rivka said, chopping tomatoes, cucumbers and onions into minuscule pieces with a butcher's knife. Years later, after Grandpa Simcha died and before the stroke that robbed her soul, she'd hide the same knife under her pillow to fight off intruders.

"The radio? What do you mean, Grandma?" Talia had been absent-mindedly perusing the latest copy of *For the Woman* – a magazine that offered beauty and other tips, like how to get the guy – and was unaware of humming "Ani ve Ata", a song about changing the world. It was Noam's favourite. At least it had been before he returned from war, same and different from the brother she'd known.

"You have a beautiful voice, and don't let anyone tell you otherwise."

"Thank you, Grandma." Talia's unceremonious dismissal from the school choir the month before still stung, and she hadn't opened her mouth to sing since. Well, at least until now, in the safety of Grandma Rivka's kitchen.

"Your mother tells me you're having nightmares. What's going on?"

"Mrs Hamorah terrifies me; Noam shakes a lot, and there's this older girl . . ." Talia's voice trailed.

"What girl?" Grandma blotted her eyes with a rag. The onions made her cry, but Grandpa liked his salad just so.

"It's not a big deal." Talia regretted having opened her big mouth. She didn't want to burden Grandma with the bullying; besides, she couldn't risk our family's interference. Talia, the tattletale? Now, that would have made her the ultimate pariah.

"Grandma, tell me about your life in Russia as a girl."

"You're too young to hear such horrors."

"You always say that, but I want to know what little Grandma was like."

"I know you do, Talusinka, my sweet. One day, I promise." Done with the salad, Grandma turned to peeling potatoes for her one-and-only casserole. She didn't have much of a cooking repertoire – Grandpa Simcha demanded the same breakfasts, lunches and dinners, day after day, year after year, decade after decade. Still, she made these same bloody dishes with love, pouring generous amounts of olive oil on that one salad and choosing the freshest eggs for that one casserole.

"It's time for your lesson," Talia said.

"Already?" Grandma wiped her hands on her apron. "Give me two minutes; I'm just about done."

Talia donned a pair of Mom's old glasses to appear more tutor-like. Luckily, they had no lenses, or her vision would have blurred. "Ready?" she asked, wielding a red pen.

"Yes." Grandma took out a large notepad and handed it to her granddaughter.

Talia scribbled furiously. RIKVA. Damn, the letters switched on her again. She got it right the second time. RIVKA. "There, now read it out loud, please, Grandma."

"Ree . . .vvvv . . .kha," Grandma uttered. "Rivka! That's my name!"

"I'm so proud of you, Grandma," Talia said, and like a spell, this humble scullery with its brown cabinets and yellow laminate countertops transformed into a castle. Grandma? into its beaming queen.

Meanwhile, at school, Mrs Hamorah's stories of a glorious death kept coming at us like a record-setting artillery strike.

"Gather around, kids, and I'll tell you the most riveting story of Chanukah," said Mrs Hamorah.

At this point, we were a little uneasy and who would blame us? Still, we had no choice but to sit and listen.

"At the time of the Maccabees, the Greek king Antiochus demanded all Jews abandon their faith and worship him as if he were a god. Why, might you ask? Antiochus wanted to humiliate the Jews and defeat our spirits. That's true of all our enemies, past, present and future."

"Who are the Maccabees?" Talia asked.

"You'll learn soon enough. Now listen," Mrs Hamorah pressed her index finger to her lips and carried on, "One day, a Jewish woman called Chana along with her seven sons were summoned to appear before Antiochus. The king demanded the boys bow to an idol, a sculpture of a false god carved in his image. Chana's eldest refused and was dismembered. His mother and brothers were made to watch his remains cooked in a cauldron."

Talia tried covering her ears, but resistance was futile. Mrs Hamorah smacked her lips and continued, "One after the other, the boys refused the king's command to bow to the false god, and into the cauldron they went. The only son left was Chana's youngest, a sweet-natured boy with honey-coloured locks and green eyes."

We couldn't take it anymore and cried out for Mrs Hamorah to reassure us Chana's youngest wouldn't get cooked. We knew we had to be brave, but this story was becoming too upsetting.

"Silence," Mrs. Hamorah yelled. "Antiochus tried to bribe the boy with gifts. *If you bow down to this idol, I'll let you live*, the king said. When the child refused, Antiochus pleaded with Chana to convince her son to change his mind. The boy was a fledgling, your same age boys and girls."

"Did she save him, Mrs Hamorah?" It was Yossi, the class bully who had never participated willingly before.

"What do you think, Yossi? Have you not been paying attention to what I've been teaching you lot? To Trumpeldor's legacy? Now, no more interruptions."

Mrs Hamorah's eyes glimmered as if they had caught on fire. "Chana kissed her youngest on his forehead and said, 'I'm proud of you, my son, for refusing to worship the false god!' So, King Antiochus killed the boy and cooked his remains in the same cauldron as his brothers. Grief-stricken, Chana jumped into the scalding pot and was boiled to a crisp."

The woman scoured our terrified faces and banged her fist on the table. "Boys and girls, there wouldn't be any

Jewish people left without great sacrifice. Chana and her seven sons died, so you could be born!"

Our teacher's gruelling tales changed everything. Chanukahs of years past had been simpler, more joyous affairs, untainted by the image of a mother throwing herself into an aromatic stew that had once been her family. Grandpa Simcha used to light the candles on the *Menorah*, us grandkids huddling around him, singing off-key, and gorging on Grandma Rivka's *sufganiyot* – mouth-watering, deep-fried jelly doughnuts.

But, now, we were no longer innocent fools. The red jelly dripping from our mouths was Chana's blood that was Trumpeldor's blood that was Noam's fallen friends' blood – the life force of heroism and nationalism and thicker than water. Talia had never eaten the body of Christ, but she had consumed the bodies of Chana and her seven sons.

Midway through third grade, Mrs Hamorah summoned Mom for an urgent talk. Her daughter was becoming a serious troublemaker. "She doesn't have much aptitude for school and she's behaving, how can I put it, unladylike," Mrs Hamorah groaned. "But I'm confident we can teach her how to become a productive member of society."

Mom looked distracted. "Yes, yes," she muttered and turned towards Talia, who had been forced to tag along. "What's that bite on your ankle?"

"Nothing." Talia shrugged.

"It looks infected, missy. I told you to stop petting stray dogs."

"Perhaps Talia should see the school nurse?" Mrs Hamorah offered.

"Good idea," Mom said and dragged Talia down the hallway. They knocked on an office with a red Star of

David painted on its door, and as luck would have it, there was no wait.

"It's a human bite," the nurse exclaimed.

"I got into a fight." Talia gazed at the floor. The cracks in the green linoleum were Petri dishes for colonies of black and grey mould. "This girl called me a 'lezzie', so I pushed her, and she bit me."

"Savages," Mom muttered.

"This might hurt." The nurse donned gloves and examined the bite. "Well, the good news is the wound is less than three centimetres, and no teeth are lodged in it." The woman attempted a smile neither mother nor daughter reciprocated, so she continued, "the bad news is there are indeed signs of infection."

"How bad?" Mom asked.

"We need a culture, so I'll take a swab."

"Ouch," Talia yelped, but Mom gave her a shushing look, so she didn't utter another peep until after the nurse finished cleaning and dressing the wound. "What's a 'lezzie'?" Talia asked.

Mom turned to the nurse. "While we're here, can you please examine my daughter's abdomen? The girl's been complaining about bellyaches."

"I can't feel anything unusual," the nurse said, poking Talia in the gut, then taking off her medical gloves and throwing them into a bin. "I'll give her antibiotics for the infection, but I suspect the stomach pain is psychosomatic."

"Psycho what?" Talia was confused, and her ankle was throbbing.

"Where did I go wrong with you?" Mom shook her head.

Talia missed her best friend. Adva was a year older and had grown up across the street. She always knew how to make everything brighter with her rolling laughter and mischievous plotting. Like that time Adva convinced Talia to create a pool inside Mom and Dad's enclosed shower. It seemed like a good idea at first, but the water level refused to go up, and, instead, they ended up flooding the house.

Or that time they found *Playboy* magazines under Gil's mattress. "Will our breasts get this big?" Talia pointed at the bleach-blonde centrefold's silicon chest. Talia's face must have leaked the horror she felt because Adva said not to worry – she, Adva, knew a spell they could use that would guarantee just the right boob size.

"What spell?" Talia demanded to know.

"*Abracadabra*," Adva said, and they both laughed so hard they peed their pants.

It sucked that Adva's dad moved his family to Greece in the middle of the school year. The two friends had been exchanging snail mail since, and, no, it wasn't the same, but still, it was something.

Dear Adva,

What is a lezzie? Mom will not tell me. A big girl bit my ~~ankel~~ ankle. Her teeth were ~~shapr~~ sharp like a ~~sahrk~~ shark. How is Greece? Do you like ~~gonig~~ going to the beach there? Do you have new ~~freinds~~ friends? I miss you.

Your best ~~freind~~ friend ~~foerevr~~ ~~foerevr~~ forever,
Talia

"I don't want to go to school," Talia screamed, clutching her belly. "I want to stay home with Noam."

"You know he can't take care of you and, anyway, what nonsense," Mom muttered.

"But my tummy hurts."

It was Passover. Still, Mom burst into her favourite Purim song, "If you feel pain, you—"

Talia scowled, refusing to play along.

"C'mon, sing with me, child." Mom chuckled and crooned again, "If you feel pain, you—"

"Stomp on it with your feet?"

"That's right. So, get dressed, and off you go."

At school, Talia found our teacher overcome by unabashed glee. "Yay, Passover! Let's play Jewish Jeopardy. Who can tell me why the Egyptians killed our first-born sons?"

Finally, a fever! Talia had been praying for such a gift. A fever meant the adults in her life believed her when she said she wasn't feeling well. It also meant missing school and spending time with Grandma Rivka. Win-win.

Our grandmother planted her favourite granddaughter in a sunny armchair on the covered porch, overlooking a sweet-smelling rose bush, and doted on her with tea and oranges.

"Mom doesn't like me," Talia said.

"Your mother loves you." Grandma Rivka fluffed Talia's pillow.

"She loves me, but she doesn't like me."

Grandma Rivka laughed. "You're too smart for your own good."

"Tell me your story, Grandma. I'm ready, I promise." How much worse could it have been than what happened to Chana? Or to our older brother, for that matter, who hid under tables when he heard a loud noise?

"The girl should know her history," Grandpa Simcha said, appearing from nowhere and startling them.

"You're home early," Grandma said.

"The guys complained it was too hot for construction work." He took a swig of water from a canteen strapped to his waist. "The youth of today, I tell you. If only they knew what working in hard conditions meant."

"Your lunch is ready." Grandma inclined her head towards the kitchen.

"You're not doing the girl any favours by shielding her from the truth. She needs to grow a thicker skin, that one."

Grandma tsked. "Let children be children. Just because we were robbed of our innocence, why should our grandkids?"

In his late sixties, Grandpa Simcha was still a formidable force – as the unofficial arbiter of our town, people came to him to settle disputes rather than go to court. His word was law. A strong and strapping man, he constructed our house with his bare hands and fixed his own false teeth. And Hebrew? He learned to speak it from a dictionary after arriving in Palestine in the 1920s, disillusioned by the revolution and scarred by systemic and visceral antisemitism.

"Listen here, girl," he said, sitting beside Talia on a creaky wooden chair. "When your grandmother was your age, she came home from school to find—"

"Enough," Grandma said.

"Either you tell her, or I will."

"Then she'll hear it from me."

"Very good, it's settled then. I bid you ladies goodbye for now."

Talia waited until Grandpa Simcha was out of earshot. "Please, please, Grandma, tell me. I'm a big girl."

"First, let's check if your fever's come down." Grandma Rivka shook a mercury thermometer up and down. "Open your mouth, please," she said and placed it gently under Talia's tongue.

The thermometer was cold and slippery. What if it broke and the loosened mercury killed her? Gil had told her this kind of accident happened all the time. He had also warned that gypsies kidnap girls her age and put them in barrels. "The girls can't grow upwards, so they grow sideways and become barrel shaped." This way, Gil explained, people took pity on them and threw more coins into their begging plates.

"Oh good, your temperature is down to 37 degrees Celsius," Grandma exclaimed. She gazed at her grand-daughter fondly. "And where have you drifted off to, my sweet?"

"Nowhere." Talia was moved by how attentive the older woman was – the only adult who asked Talia how she was doing and waited for the answer.

"So what I'm about to share, well, it's not an easy story to tell or hear." Grandma Rivka's expression clouded and she moaned as she lowered her aching body into the chair. "And if you need me to stop, that's okay. We can always continue another time."

Talia gestured she understood.

"So, like Grandpa said, I was eight years old. Your age. My mother, your great-grandmother, died when I was four. And as the oldest child, my father, your great grandfather, looked to me to become a parental figure to my younger siblings."

"That's why you're so good at being a grandma."

"Thank you, my love." The kind woman patted Talia's head. "On a day like any other, I picked up my young-est brother, Shemaiah, from school. We were almost home when we heard people shout and a man screaming. Terrified, we hid behind a tree and peeked at the crowd. A group of villagers surrounded your great grandfather, and then . . ." Grandma's face paled, and she stopped speaking.

"Then what, Grandma?"

"The men attacked your great-grandfather. He tried fighting them off, but there were many of them and only one of him." Grandma's breaths were fast and audible. "And then," she shut her eyes, "they hung him from a tree to die."

"Why?" Talia gasped.

"Because he was Jewish," Grandma said.

That's how Talia learned about a Jewish lynching or pogrom. She couldn't wrap her head around it. (I still can't.) And when four years later, Talia heard Billie Holiday croon "Strange Fruit" on a vinyl record in Herzliya, Israel, the lyrics – trees with blood on their leaves and in their roots – felt personal.

Re-imagining my beloved grandmother's face, reliving her unimaginable trauma, and having to pass it on to her kids and grandkids – to me, who she wanted to protect more than anything; I can still feel it in my body. And I so wish I could go back in time, to Grandma's kitchen, and tell her how much I appreciated her bravery and trust, how much I adored and admired her, how much I loved her.

If I could go back in time, I'd ask, "Grandma, was it harder or easier for you to speak your history in Hebrew, a foreign language, and not Yiddish, your mother tongue?" Grandma's husband forbade her from speaking Yiddish to him or anyone ever. To Grandpa Simcha, it was diaspora speak, the language of the weak and oppressed. But in trying to form a newer, tougher Jewish identity – in shedding his victimised skin – Grandpa must have cut Grandma off from words, phrases, cultural connotations, even humour that had connected Grandma to her dead mother, murdered father and rich cultural ancestry. Rebirthing can be lifesaving, but not when it kills off the past.

Grandma Rivka's is an untold story. Unlike her husband, she didn't arrive in Palestine with Zionist ideals. She was brought there by a non-Jewish man who collected Jewish orphans and shipped them to a place he hoped was safe. And I pray that telling Grandma's story gives her peace in whatever beyond she resides, outer or inner.

Hey, it's my story. I haven't called on her, but little Talia emerges, anyway — eight years old, with a human bite on her ankle and our grandmother's words raw in her tummy.

"I didn't forget."

Sorry to have interrupted, she whispers, sounding more grown-up now, *but I could use a hug.*

The grand finale of third grade was a class trip to Trumpeldor's monument in Tel Hai, followed by a screening of a Nazi documentary film — footage the Nazis themselves took of medical experiments on Jewish prisoners with bald heads and skeletal frames.

What better, more efficient way to study the effects of hypothermia than dunking Jewish men, women and children into ice water? Test the toxicity of immunisation compounds for tuberculosis, malaria and other deadly infectious diseases by injections into their flesh? And why stop there? How about perfecting the art of bone-grafting and other surgeries, without wasting anesthesia? All that was missing from this reality horror show was a lively re-enactment of Chana and her seven sons, cabaret-style.

Imprisoned in her seat, Talia grew more and more nauseous, her face weak and numb. She turned to look for Mrs Hamorah, aching to be excused. But, when she spotted our teacher sitting a few rows behind, words got stuck in Talia's gut, rendering her mute. Mrs Hamorah was taking large, juicy bites from a homemade sandwich, her eyes transfixed on the big screen as if she were watching a Hollywood blockbuster.

Who shows this kind of imagery to children? And who eats a sandwich watching it? No wonder Talia had nightmares for decades, and no wonder I still do. These images are forever tattooed on our psyche. And our Jewish identity? It's racial, not religious. I could go on and on, but I'm running out of steam.

Still, before I call it a day, I have a confession to make. Something even more devastating happened to Talia than hearing Grandma Rivka's harrowing story, witnessing Noam's PTSD, or watching documentary footage the Nazis took of experimenting on, torturing, mutilating and murdering Jews.

It happened in Haifa, at our other grandparents' house, Dad's parents – Grandma Mami and . . . No, I can't, I won't. I admire Tarantino, I do, but it's time to pause.

7

FAKING MADNESS?[5]

In 1982 the then prime minister, Menachem Begin, egged on by his general, Ariel Sharon, lied to the Israeli people. It was a big lie. Under the guise of creating a security zone in northern Israel, the Israel Defense Forces crossed the border and invaded Southern Lebanon.

"Can you believe that Begin and those fascist murderers are calling this war Operation Peace for the Galilee?" Noam scoffed. "Can it get more Orwellian than that?"

"It's beyond disgusting. I'm going to the Peace Now rally tonight," Talia said. The event promised to be a massive protest against the IDF's role in the Sabra and Shatila massacres – the slaughtering of hundreds, some reports claimed thousands, of innocent Palestinian and Lebanese Shiite civilians.

"I'll see you there, little sister."

Like in the Vietnam War, TV coverage coupled with reports from soldiers at the front exposed the political lies in real-time, and for the first time in Israeli history, war did not have a uniting effect. Instead, loads of citizens turned against the government, disgusted by the deception and bloodshed.

One of 400,000 protestors (in a country of a mere four million people), Talia held an "Embarrassed to be an Israeli Jew" sign and chanted with the crowd for Begin and Sharon to resign until her throat got raw. Noam was on her right, holding a sign with "Shame!" printed in bright red letters. To her left, a man's placard read, "If I forget Sabra and Shatila, I shall forget Jerusalem." His was a reference to the biblical pledge that many, like Mrs Hamorah, held sacred: *If I forget thee O Jerusalem, let my right hand forget its cunning.*

First, the Yom Kippur War. Now, the Lebanon War. Talia went to funeral after funeral, refusing to cry. Precious lives lost, and for what? It was heartbreaking, but catharsis? Fuck that. Fuelled by righteous indignation, she took steps to renounce her Israeli citizenship, but the government denied her request.

About a year after the Lebanon War and just short of Talia's eighteenth birthday, our dreaded draft notice arrived in the mail. Talia's reaction was the ultimate *hell, no* – no way would she serve in the IDF and participate in its atrocities. But, despite the growing anti-government sentiments, military service was something people didn't question.

Enlisting in the IDF was like breathing – it kept the collective alive. Besides, it was compulsory. Even Tel Aviv's intellectual left-wing elites, the most anti-government activists Talia had gotten to know in the many grassroots gatherings and rallies, had or would soon be enlisting. She did not meet a single person who questioned that. Not one.

The options for women's dismissal from military service seemed impossible, especially on short notice: marriage, religious conversion, or being deemed mentally incompetent. Despite the country's democracy, marriage laws and rituals were the purview of the health ministry, run by the Orthodox Jews. Marriage itself was in rabbinical court and involved *tevilah* in a *mikveh* – an archaic and humiliating female "cleansing" – so even if Talia could find a guy who'd be willing to fake marry her, it was a hard no.

And if that option was distasteful, the second was worse. Becoming ultra-religious meant undergoing an official and proven conversion and then living in a ghetto of sorts where men woke up in the morning praying, *Blessed are you, lord, our god, ruler of the universe who has not created me a woman.* Yeah, right! She'd have rather died.

The third and final route was obtaining a psychiatric-based dismissal. That, too, seemed tricky. How could she face a committee of experts and prove she was too mad to enlist?

No matter. Whatever happened, Talia was clear. She would not cooperate with a corrupt political system and bow to its false idols. And if she failed to get a psychiatric profile warranting dismissal, then the scary as fuck Military Police Corps, the Mem Tzadik, would have to drag her kicking and screaming into a prison cell.

"Listen here, missy. You'll do no such thing as pretend you're mentally ill, or I'll report you to the Mem Tzadik," Dad said.

Talia's heart sank. *If Dad loved me* — No, it was better if she didn't go there.

Mom had a different tactic up her sleeve. She motioned for Talia to follow her into the basement and then proceeded to fish out her military uniform from a waterproof box, where it had been perfumed, pressed and stored with medicinal-smelling mothballs. When Mom was nineteen, she became one of the first female officers in the Paratroopers Brigade, or whatever they call it in IDF lingo – an unprecedented feat for a woman in her generation.

"Look at the hourglass figure I once had," Mom said, pressing the drab beige fabric against her large bosom. And even though this trophy no longer fitted, its message was clear – its wearer would've gladly died for her country, and her children, if raised properly, would have too.

Noam, who was as anti-military as they come, wasn't convinced that acting crazy was a good idea. "I'm worried you'd be dooming yourself, little sister."

"I can't believe that you, of all people—"

"Please, hear me out. I don't want you to serve; I don't. But no one will hire you with a mental health discharge." He pointed his index finger at her. "It would destroy your life."

"I will never ever wear that uniform."

"Not even if refusing it meant imprisonment? You're not thinking clearly." Noam shook his head. "You should enlist. Time will pass by more quickly than you think." Noam's arguments were very rational, but Talia was shocked. How could he have not supported her?

It was Gil who became Talia's single, unexpected ally. "You're not going to survive being in the IDF." He spoke from his traumatic experience with a sadistic seargent, who used her god-like power to torment him daily. "You're too outspoken. Sooner or later, you'd get in trouble anyway. So, yeah, faking madness is the only way to go."

"What if the committee sees right through my act?" Talia wailed.

"Don't invent anything. Exaggerate whatever you're feeling or doing. Trembling? Go into spasms. Whispering?

Become inaudible. Speaking? Shout." Gil seemed to be onto something. Wasn't the difference between normal and crazy a matter of degree? "One more thing. Don't sleep, eat, or shower for a few days before they call you in."

Right, but how the fuck would she manage to go that long without sleep?

"Talia Ben-Zeev, do you understand why you're here?"

Talia nodded yes. Noticing she had been tugging on her necklace, she yanked the leather strap again and again, then twisted it around her neck, abrading its sensitive skin.

The man was wearing a white lab coat. A psychiatrist? The other four had on green army uniforms heavy with insignia. Their badges of honour indicated what exactly? That they were superhumans?

"I need you to speak," the man in the white lab coat said. "Do you understand why you're here?"

"Yes, Sir," Talia yelled, as if they were sitting on opposite ends of a football stadium instead of across the table.

Screaming, is that all she could muster? She imagined herself on an audition tape, failing her life's biggest, most important role. Pathetic. A clown. A clown with a ruby-red nose. A joker of a clown with a ruby-red nose, smeared makeup, long green hair, cuts around the mouth and a maniacal cackle. Talia roared, her body convulsing, tears stinging her bruised neck.

"What's so funny?" It was one of the green uniforms, his face covered in puss-filled rosacea.

Talia used her bare hand to blow her nose and wiped the snot across her chest, leaving yellowish trails on the off-white fabric. What had she planned to do next? Yes, count silently till ten or something like that before answering a question, but she lost track of the count. She hadn't slept

124

a wink in what felt like forever. It wasn't easy, but thank goodness for endless pots of coffee, face dunks in ice-cold water and the terror of being locked up.

Talia's groin was on fire. No wonder! Her underwear was smelly and moist. She hadn't showered or changed her clothes for at least three days, or was it more? Wait, what day was it? Wednesday? Thursday? Wednesday. It was Wednesday. She reached her hand down her pants and scratched, but it only made the itch worse.

What a barbaric and uncouth creature Talia had become. A flea- and tick-infested monkey. A lonely monkey in need of a monkey friend — a kind soul who'd pick the blood-sucking critters lodged in her fur. She only had her clownish monkey self to save the day, and who that self was, was far from clear.

She closed her eyes and conjured a colony of black and red ants snaking in her sullied panties. An arachnid crept over the ants, tickling her sensitive down there. *It feels good, right?* The creeper asked in a gruff, alcoholic voice.

"Get off me," Talia yelled, clawing at her crotch, thighs, and belly, digging sharp, unkempt nails into soiled flesh. Had she fought against unwanted touch, maybe the world would have been . . . what? Safer? But there was no safety without *no*, and while this word was playing hide and seek, she had been seeking and seeking.

Screaming, Talia woke up from one nightmare into another. All five committee members were staring at her. Their heads were too large for their bodies, like the characters in Alice in Wonderland. Hadn't Alice said something about writing a book when she returned home, post-madness? Was there hope for redemption? Or had Talia been the Mad Hatter all along?

"Sorry, what did you say?" She tried steadying her

mouth, but her teeth kept knocking against each other. Had the uniforms dialled down the air-conditioning to its surgery-room setting? Did they plan to stick an icepick through her eye and into her frontal lobe?

There were whisperings. Questions, maybe? Something about what made her so special. Once upon a time, Talia was able to understand words, but she had lost her ears somewhere, like the antique teddy she found at a flea market that looked like an alien. Somehow, somewhere she had also shed the outer layers of her skin, reduced into a bundle of exposed nerve endings.

Can someone please, please see that she gets help? A motherly lap or a feathery bed? Sweet, soothing oblivion?

Waiting for the committee's verdict was nail-biting. Once delivered, Talia fell to her knees and wept. *Hallelujah*! The uniforms declared her psychiatrically unfit to serve in the IDF. It wasn't unanimous, but a majority vote, three to two. Still, this narrow escape was all she needed.

Talia's "shameful stunt", as Mom put it, placed Talia's relatives in a quandary. To disown or not to disown her? Had Grandpa Simcha been alive, they would have turned to him, but he had passed away from lung cancer. And Grandma Rivka? She was a shell of her former self. Having suffered a massive stroke, her speech was indecipherable.

So, the family at large turned to Uncle Benjamin for guidance. After all, he had shown leadership by taking over Grandpa Simcha's construction company and running for town mayor. But despite the relatives' prevailing sentiment that Talia should avoid showing her treacherous face at family gatherings, Uncle Benjamin's 50th birthday party was coming up and he invited Talia to attend.

On the day of the big bash, Talia felt torn. Mom had

all but commanded her to stay home, but Talia wanted to honour our uncle's milestone. Sure, their politics clashed, to put it mildly, but people aren't two dimensional, and besides, what about Grandma Rivka? Surely she'd need someone at the party who'd make an effort to understand her slurred speech?

Tel Aviv was only fourteen kilometres south of Herzliya, but with traffic, it took more than an hour to get to Uncle Benjamin and Auntie Tzipora's house on the humid, crowded bus. Once alighted, Talia straightened her crumpled dress, muttering, "that'll have to do," and entered the back patio.

"Hi, my child," Dad shouted in a surprisingly cheerful voice for someone who had recently threatened to turn his daughter into the authorities. He was wheeling Savta Rivka to a round table where Mom was already seated. In stark contrast to her husband's, Mom's expression was sour, impervious to the festive décor – tables with white linen, hydrangea with succulent centrepieces and white, black and silver balloons swaying in the warm breeze.

Talia kneeled by Savta Rivka's wheelchair and took her hand. "I've missed you, Grandma."

"*Talu*," Our grandmother mumbled with visible effort. This once vivacious woman had shrunk, and her smile was lopsided. Still, Grandma was in there somewhere.

"Yes, it's me, your Talusinka." Talia kissed the older woman's leathery cheek. "I'm sorry I haven't been able to visit, but I will come by soon, I promise." The thought that Grandma felt abandoned was harrowing.

"What are you doing here?" Mom hissed at her daughter.

Talia inclined her head in Grandma's direction as if to say, let's not distress her. "Where is everyone?"

Mom was about to say something when guests started

swarming in. And with one exception – Talia's cousin Efrat who gave Talia a bear hug – the family ignored her. It wasn't a silent treatment exactly; there was plenty of gawking and finger-pointing.

The chatter died when Uncle Benjamin entered the patio with Auntie Tzipora on his arm and his poodle, Lulu, trotting beside them, a pink ribbon in her hair. "It's an honour to be surrounded by family and friends," Uncle Benjamin raised a champagne glass. "Thank you all for being here."

Benji'le, as Mom called her younger brother, looked like Tony Soprano from *The Sopranos* – stocky and handsome in a brutish way. Like Tony, he had fast cars, friends with nicknames like "The Brain", and believed in the sanctity of the family. Our uncle loved babies and adored Lulu, who was shaved everywhere except for pompoms of fur on her face, paws and tail. "Lulu, you look like a French hooker," he'd tease.

"What's your birthday wish, Grandpa?" A little girl squeaked.

Uncle Benjamin scoured the room, then his gaze settled on Talia's face. "I want Talia to get married and have kids. It's about time, don't you think?"

"Hear, hear," the uncles cheered.

Talia didn't believe in marriage and Uncle Benjamin knew that. "You're such a silly girl," he once said after Talia had shared her fantasy of becoming a writer and travelling the world by herself.

"I don't know about a husband and kids, uncle, but how about a furry four-legged cousin for Lulu?" Talia asked, praying he'd ease up.

Uncle Benjamin glared. "What's wrong with you? The least you can do is find a man." He looked around the room.

"And if you don't find a husband soon, I will pay someone to rape you."

Had Talia heard him correctly? She looked at Mom for support, but our mother turned away.

Benji'le wasn't done. "Once you're pregnant, you'll thank me for it."

Talia felt sick to her stomach, and when no one came to her defence, she staggered outside for some fresh air.

Another claustrophobic bus ride and Talia was finally back at her flat. An ominous note was tucked under her door: "Your rent is late for the third and final time." Shit, if she didn't pull double shifts at The White Gallery restaurant, she'd get evicted.

As crazy as it sounds, servers at The White Gallery, like at most restaurants back then, weren't given salaries. Living off tips alone was unfair and, ultimately, unsustainable, but no one else would hire her. She tried and tried, but if a failing high school diploma weren't enough, the IDF's psychiatric profile was the last nail.

Noam was right. The powers that be might as well have branded a T on her forehead. T for Talia? T for Traitor? It wouldn't have mattered; they meant the same thing. No money. No education. No future.

"You forgot your change." Talia ran out of The White Gallery in pursuit of a group of women holding theatre tickets in their manicured hands. Talia had waited on them, hand, and foot, for over two hours, running back and forth at their every whim.

"It's your tip." The tall lady with the coiffed blonde hair and Gucci purse smirked. "Now excuse us; we must get to the show on time."

The few coins these women had tossed on the table as an after-thought? They added up to less than a one-percent tip instead of the customary ten percent Talia had come to rely on for barely making the rent.

"As regulars, you know us waiters live off the tips, right?" Talia's face sizzled. "So, how can you justify being so stingy, especially after treating me like your slave?" But her protest was an exercise in what exactly? Not empowerment, evidently, as the women responded with head shakes and eye rolls.

When 2 a.m. rolled by, Talia sighed in relief. She couldn't wait to get home, shower and fall on her bed, but her stomach was growling and her fridge was empty. Talia needed food and fast. Anything but The White Gallery's grub. Her clothes and bedsheets reeked from fish, garlic and grease mixed with body odour.

Walking on the dark, empty streets, Talia questioned her sanity. What if her outburst earlier was yet another indicator that she was truly mad, mad as a mad hatter? After all, the IDF committee that declared her to be mentally unfit was made of experts. There were also nightmares that left her in puddles of sweat. Blackouts.

If only Talia hadn't stopped writing to the drawer. Ugly, emo poetry would have been better than no poetry – words were a way to connect her heartbreak to the world's, a good enough reason to get up in the morning.

The all-night hummus dive by the Tel Aviv seaport was out of the way, but just the thought of the homemade dish made Talia's mouth water.

She wasn't aware of it then, but this late-night spot, with its dirty beige walls and two-and-a-half metred ceiling held another, more subconscious, appeal. Situated by the dark of the seaport, it was the regular hangout spot for the notorious "shemale whores" – that's how this group of trans women sex workers was labelled in lip-curled whispers – the lowest of the low, the dregs of society.

Occasionally, police officers would stop by for a bite or to amuse themselves by horsing around with the women. Sometimes these exchanges would escalate into bullying, even violence, like the other night when a cop punched one of the women in the face because she insisted he address her as Ma'am.

"Fucking faggot," the cop said, looking pleased with himself.

"Fancy her much?" One of the ladies yelled. She was older, with an ill-fitting wig and smeared lipstick.

The officer turned to his partner. "This ugly should watch itself, or I'll fuck it up too."

This brutality had escalated dizzyingly quickly. Seconds? Minutes? All Talia knew was that she needed to snap out of being frozen, say something. Anything. "Leave her alone. You should be ashamed of yourselves," Talia yelled.

"What's a real girl like you doing at a place like this?" The officer was muscular, pseudo handsome in a Jeffrey Dahmer-like way.

"What do you mean by real?" Talia countered.

"C'mon, let's go." The man's partner motioned towards the exit.

"*Yefhat-nefesh.*" The officer spat on his way out. But before Talia could respond, the lady with the smeared lipstick grabbed her arm. "It's not worth it, doll."

Yefeh-nefesh and its feminine counterpart, *yefhat-nefesh*, meant "beautiful-souled." On its surface, this adjective sounded positive, but it was meant as a derogation – a naïve "bleeding-heart liberal". Talia should have been used to

131

being called that by then, but in that setting it delivered an extra blow.

Thankfully, no boys in blue were present after tonight's shift, only a few of the ladies and a couple of truckers who tore into the warm pita bread with calloused hands and used it to shovel dollops of hummus into their gaping mouths. Starving, Talia ordered a dish with her favourite toppings – fava beans, olive oil and za'atar. Creamy and tangy, the Middle Eastern dip melted on her tongue.

"Long night, love?" It was the same lady who had confronted the cop the night before, but her makeup was freshly applied this time and her wig combed.

"Yes, and you?"

"Busy. Had an odd one today."

"Really?" Talia raised an eyebrow.

"Orthodox Jew with the yarmulke, tallit and everything. Prayed when he came." The woman grinned, exposing a gold tooth. "I'm Kiki, and what's your name, doll?"

"Talia."

"So, Talia, what *is* a nice girl like you doing at a place like this?"

Talia laughed. "Not sure that even my mom would call me nice, but hey, I'll take it."

"Why don't you tell mama Kiki what's going on. I can smell when something's not right."

"I—"

"Hey Dudu darling," Kiki shouted to the tattooed guy working the counter, "How about Turkish coffee for me and my friend here?" She turned back to Talia, "Sorry, you were saying."

"I met this guy at the restaurant I work at. A famous poet." Talia sipped the bitter brew and sputtered. "Anyway,

Eyal and I have been fucking for a couple of weeks now, and I asked him to read a poem I wrote. I mean, I'm not a poet or anything, I barely finished high school."

"Fancy poet man said, another time, didn't he?"

"How did you know?"

"And he keeps making excuses about why he's not introducing you to his friends."

"That's right."

"Honey, these players are the worst kind. At least I get paid for my services."

Talia smiled. "Point taken." But then her expression clouded. "Hey, Kiki, what gets you up in the morning?"

"Hope, doll. One day, I'll have the operation, a husband who adores the shit out of me and a house up in Teverya." She downed the rest of her coffee. "And what do you hope for, my lovely?"

Nothing came to Talia's mind, so she said nothing.

The Mediterranean Sea was calm, illuminated by a half-moon, and the shoreline was deserted. Talia should have been in bed, fast asleep, but instead of heading home after talking to Kiki, her feet brought her here.

She took off her shoes and walked along the water's edge, the soft sand tickling her toes, the balmy night breeze caressing her face. She was alone in a world that didn't want or need her, and walking untethered, she left footsteps for no one to trace.

When exhaustion finally hit full force, Talia stopped dead in her tracks, shed her clothes, lurkers-be-damned, and immersed her tight muscles in the warm waters. Who'd miss her if she'd let herself drift off like a love message in a bottle to a destination unknown?

*

Deus ex machina. Sometimes, god does jump from the machine, making real–life stories seem contrived. In Talia's case, our father landed a two-year part-governmental job in Milan, Italy.

Yes, Talia betrayed every value our parents held dear, but surely they could tell that their daughter was drowning? Joining Mom and Dad in Europe, even for a few months, would have been the perfect pause — an opportunity to regain ground and plan what to do next. Even if *next* was an abstract and empty concept.

Mom was still enraged at her daughter, but Dad had softened. "We all make mistakes," he said. Did it have something to do with that late-night incident? The one where Talia caught Dad making a surreptitious phone call at a public phone booth?

"Choose life," Talia heard herself pray. "Whatever happens next, please, choose life.

8

(I)TALIA[5]

In 1985, Talia arrived at our parents' two-year rental in Milan, Italy, waving a one way-ticket as a white flag. Mom and Dad barely held back from slamming the door shut on her treacherous face.

She was nineteen-going-on-twenty, but her transgressions could have filled a book. Taking first place, of course, was faking madness to avoid compulsory service in the Israel Defense Forces. Coming at a not-so-close second was her abysmal high school diploma. Or was it the affair with one of our teachers – a respectable, married man who, age-wise, could have been her grandfather?

The back cover of *Mea Culpa, A Memoir* by Talia Ben-Zeev would have boasted an impressive list of the author's accolades. Turncoat. Homewrecker. Slut. Ingrate. A where-did-we-go-wrong-with-you child.

Gil convinced our parents that welcoming Talia into their Italian sanctuary was a matter of life or death. "Talia is lost and despairing," he warned. "If you don't take her in, she might sink into a deep catatonic depression or kill herself."

Our brother's delivery proved effective. Guilt is the ultimate Jewish weapon.

Be kind, Talia says, hovering.

"What? I've barely begun the Italy chapter."

But I've seen how judgy you get, and anyway, I had to make a choice, so I did.

"Choice? I've been thinking a lot about this word lately. But wait, are you trying to stall?"

You need to get this one right.

I hear her. This is our life's next act, and it changes everything.

"If you're going to stay here for two years, you'll need a job," Mom exclaimed with a business-like expression. Was it masking resentment? Horror at being chained to a daughter who had brought her shame and grief? "Hopefully, you'll find something to help you get work once we're back to The Land." The Land, or *H'aretz* in Hebrew, was how Israelis referred to their homeland and still do.

Employment in a foreign country and with such a dismal record? It didn't seem possible at first, but after a month or so, thanks to Dad's new connections, Talia landed a temporary, part-time gig as a private tutor for the children of the Israeli consular community. It was a minor miracle no one had asked for a copy of her failing high school transcript.

The Assistant to the Consul General explained that Talia's would-be students had been missing out on Hebrew literature, history and secular Bible lessons back home. Upon the students' inevitable return to The Land, they'd need to be caught up with that material.

"Would you be able to bring the kids up to speed in weekly one-on-one tutoring sessions?" The woman asked.

"Absolutely," Talia answered, without an inkling about what this endeavour would have entailed.

"I'm so bored, I'm so bored, I'm so bored," Shira, the Israeli Consul General's seventeen-year-old daughter, chanted in her pink-gold-and-black-themed bedroom before Talia had a chance to open her mouth. Where was Shira's tiara?

"What kind of person do I see when I look at you?" Talia needed this job but had a thin reactivity filter for injustices, brattiness included.

"What? I don't understand," Shira said, lines forming between her perfectly plucked eyebrows.

"Pretend you're looking at yourself through my eyes. What kind of person is staring back?"

"Not a very nice one," Shira murmured.

"We're stuck with each other. It can be torture or fun. You choose."

"Fun with the Bible?"

Despite Talia's lousy education, she'd been fascinated with the Old Testament. Even her dreadful high school couldn't ruin its drama. "Homosexuality, prostitution, infidelity, even Satan, appear in the Bible."

Shira's eyes widened. "Really?"

"You'll need to be prepared to discuss the readings, but you won't have to memorise anything," Talia grinned. "Call me crazy, but I bet there's a rich world inside that stubborn head of yours."

Sure enough, Shira delivered. She relished exploring literature and poetry and became enamoured with the Israeli poet Dahlia Ravikovitch. "I love 'Clockwork Doll'," Shira said.

"How come?"

"My whole life, I've been treated like a doll with a

137

winding thingy on my back," Shira said, unbraiding her dark, wavy hair and shaking her mane. "From now on, I just want to be me."

Aspiring to self-actualisation was reserved for the privileged, those who envisioned futures. Talia? She convinced herself she had contracted HIV and had now developed full-blown AIDS – a ticking time bomb. After all, before leaving for Italy, she had rough, unprotected sex with Eyal and other men she had met at the White Gallery restaurant, leaving droplets of blood on her sheets and underwear.

It wasn't an overreaction. In the mid '80s, AIDS fatality was in the air. The posters and billboard signs around Milan were ominous, urging people to get tested. In one, a young, healthy-looking woman gazed coyly at the camera. "This is what someone with HIV looks like," the caption warned. And Ryan White, the American teenage boy who had contracted HIV from a blood transfusion, appeared on *Italia Sera*. Bony and winsome, he debunked myths about who could get the disease and how. AIDS was thought to be a gay man's disease, Ryan said, but heterosexual folks, including women, died from it too.

Talia had nothing to lose. Her philosophy, if you could have called it that, leaned towards fatalism. So, why not enjoy Milan, the now? Dealing with finality could wait until it came knocking. Besides, everyone had expiration dates.

But I wasn't as callous as you're making me out to be. Talia's manifested with a bang, even though I hadn't summoned her.

"That wasn't my intention."

Maybe you're just angry, then.

"Angry about what?"

You tell me.

"Alright. Maybe I am. You were so fucking self-centered even AIDS had to be about you."

Whoa, where is that coming from?

"Why didn't you say no?" I scream.

No?

"To Eyal, who was so clearly using you. To you know who. To all of them." It's back, the familiar constriction in my throat. "Most of all, I hate that you were so readily willing to die. What was that about?"

The bridge Talia had burnt to our motherland, its result-ant uncertainty and death's salience – they gave the now an urgency, made it that much more precious. Sure, Talia was plagued with bouts of despair, but she was breathing Milan's fresh air – exploring desire, art and even fashion. And Milan, in the mid '80s, exploded with a kooky, over-the-top clothing design.

The best runways were on the bus. At the Duomo stop near the Galleria, there'd be a flock of models tall and cool waiting to pounce onboard. These towering figures sported big platinum-blonde and rainbow-coloured hair. They wore dizzying garments and accessories – bright, neon-coloured, oversized dresses with padded shoulders in geometric silhouettes, bras on the outside of shirts, tight leather pants, humungous earrings made of glittering crys-tals, and gold and metallic pumps.

Talia didn't have the models' slender physique – her shoulders were broad and athletic, but she matched them in style. Her latest acquisition was a green neon, leopard-print coat from Fiorucci and a black, balloon mini skirt, which she wore with a tight-fitting blouse and men's suspenders flipped back to front.

"I want to feed them," Mom said, looking the models up

and down from the best viewing section on the bus – the middle section, facing its interior. "Don't you dare roll your eyes at me, missy! They're walking corpses."

"Morbid much? How about thinking of these ladies as walking modern art pieces?"

"Art, *shmart*. What's so chic about looking like a holocaust survivor?" But before Talia could protest, Mom followed up with a left-field question. "Why does Noam hate me?" Not only was this question abrupt, but it violated their unspoken agreement to stay away from explosive topics.

"Hate is such a strong word," Talia said, buying time. It was a hypocritical thing to say, as she was no stranger to strong words.

"Resents, then," Mom conceded.

"It's because you have a god complex."

"What does that mean?"

"You think everything bad that's happened to him is your fault. If only you said this or did that, he'd be okay." Talia was on a roll. "It's a wonder Noam can breathe on his own without you giving him mouth-to-mouth resuscitation, twenty-four seven."

"If he needed oxygen, I'd give him my lungs," Mom said, as though she were auditioning for the Israeli National Theatre.

"But what if he could breathe on his own? Would you force the lung transplant?"

"You're being cruel."

"How about you show some interest in Noam's life instead of trying to control his every move?"

"I resent that. I always ask him . . ."

Talia could no longer bear the stranger's stare and turned to get a good look at the guy. He had a mop of dark hair on top of what could have been a cherubic face, except for a potato-shaped nose reminiscent of a troll doll. Talia held the guy's gaze, but he wouldn't look away. What *chutzpah*!

"You've not been listening," Mom said.

"Sorry, there's this person; never mind, you were saying?"

"I always make a point to tell your brother—"

"Excuse me, ladies, but are you speaking Hebrew?" The stranger was looming over them now. His English had an Italian lilt.

"*Shalom*, young man! We talk Hebrew, yes." Mom wasn't comfortable speaking English but didn't let her embarrassment get in the way of a golden opportunity to educate a young and willing victim about the chosen people.

"Oh, how very beautiful! I was raised Catholic here, a Milano, but my beloved grandfather, you see, turns out he was Jewish. But my manners? I am Giovanni. *Un piacere conoscervi*, I mean, very nice to meet you both."

His handshake was soft. Was he gay? It was hard for Talia to tell when it came to Italian men. They were so damn dapper.

"You, how old?" Mom looked him up and down with the kind of stare Noam had once described as dagger-like sharp.

"I'm so sorry." Talia scowled at our mother. "We Israelis are known for being rude."

"No, but really, it is okay." Giovanni smiled at Mom. "I am seventeen and a half years of age, Madam, but an old soul."

At a sharp halt, the bus arrived at Talia and Mom's stop. How did time pass by so quickly? They blurted their goodbyes, hurrying to get out, but Giovanni followed, undeterred. "My stop, you see, has been a long ago," he said as the bus doors slammed shut behind them with a loud thud.

He seemed more charming than stalkerish. Italian men have a kind of magic, right?

Despite his youth, Giovanni courted Talia like an old-world gentleman. He gifted her his dog-eared copy of *Il Poeta è un Fingitore* (The Poet is a Pretender) by the Portuguese poet Fernando Pessoa and took her to the famous La Scala theatre.

For the occasion, Talia wore a men's top hat from the Rinascente department store. "Please take it off. It is ridiculous," Giovanni said. The more he implored, the more she resisted.

Later that night, in the dark of his bedroom, they had sex for the first time. Giovanni barely lasted a minute. She was underwhelmed — and tried to hide her disappointment — while he was beside himself with excitement. "I just lost my virginity to ... a woman," Giovanni tittered. He then confessed he'd only had sex with men but suspected he was bisexual.

Before Talia could say anything, the bedroom door flung open, and a shadowy figure turned on the lights. "Ma che' cazzo!" the elegant, middle-aged man yelled at the top of his lungs — which, translated into English, meant, "What the shit" — and exited with a puff, slamming the door shut.

Blinking, Talia and Giovanni saw each other naked for the first time. They covered their mouths and giggled like school children, eyes blaring from the interrogation-like brightness.

"I am sorry you had to meet Father this way," Giovanni whispered.

"I'm not." Talia convulsed with suppressed laughter.

Meanwhile, one of the nosier, impossibly loud consular moms decided to play matchmaker and set Talia up with Henry, a nice Jewish boy from New York City.

Neither was aware of the setup, and if they had been, both would have declined. But the meddling woman didn't ask. So, as "fate" would have it, Talia and Henry found themselves sharing a cab – two young puppets on a *yenta*'s string.

As the cabbie took off, Talia sized the stranger up – early twenties, dark hair and green eyes, his lower lip somewhat protruding, but otherwise, a pretty boy. "I'm Talia, by the way."

"Nice to meet you, I'm Henry." His voice was a pleasing baritone. "So, you're Israeli?"

"Guilty as charged."

"We could switch to Hebrew if you'd like. I went to *Ye'shiva* for high school."

"*Yeshiva*'?" Talia repeated this word, putting the emphasis on the last syllable like a Hebrew speaker would. She was surprised; Henry didn't look like a fanatic Jew.

"It's not like in Israel." He seemed to catch onto her disdain. "In New York City, *Ye'shiva* is just a fancy name for a Jewish high school."

"That's a relief. You don't strike me like the kind of guy who'd start his morning praying, 'Blessed are you, lord, our god, ruler of the universe who has not created me a woman'."

"I'd never. I'm conservative, not orthodox."

"I'm not sure I get the difference. Religious Jews in Israel are sexist, racist, political opportunists and right-wing fascists." In case she was being too subtle, she added, "especially the ones who come from the United States."

Henry roared. "But tell me what you really think."

"Sorry, I get too passionate sometimes for my own good. So, tell me, what was it like growing up in New York City?"

"The best. New York's exciting on so many levels, I wouldn't even know where to begin. How about you? What was it like growing up in Israel?"

"The worst. I hate my country."

Henry snorted. "How come?"

"How can the Jews treat the Palestinians so abhorrently when we know first-hand what it's like to have the Nazis put us in ovens?" Granted, it wasn't the conversational stuff of first meetings, but Talia could tell that Henry was more curious than taken aback, and that was a point in his favour.

"Speaking badly of Israel is a taboo in my family," he said.

"It's in mine, too." Emboldened, she added, "Hey, would you like to meet up sometime?"

"Sure, and sorry if I'm making unwarranted assumptions. I have a girlfriend back home."

Then and there, Talia made up her mind to seduce Henry. She didn't want to ruin his relationship or jeopardise her connection with Giovanni. Collecting men's hearts was a survival reflex. I've detested her for it, but maybe it's time I turned a gentler look inside.

It was only Talia's second time in Giovanni's bedroom, but instead of having sex, they lay in each other's arms, whispering. There was too much to talk about.

"I have something to confess." Talia was grateful for the dim lighting. "*The Poet is a Pretender* is a compelling title, but I don't like Pessoa's poems."

"Really?" Giovanni raised his voice. "But you must be joking."

"Tell me why you're so enamoured with him."

"It is all about the heteronyms, his alter egos. You see, Pessoa wrote about being empty, a nothingness, and at the same time, he was a multiplicity."

Talia laughed. "You're so pretentious."

"Shhhh, you will wake father up," Giovanni said, placing an index finger in front of his lips. "But of course, you are right. I, too, am a pretender."

"Tell me something that's moved you to tears," she whispered, running her fingers against his smooth chest.

"When I was ten, father took me on a trip to Rome. In the Galleria Borghese, he showed me a Caravaggio painting of John the Baptist. It was called *John in the Wilderness*. I saw myself in that painting – pale and sad." He paused for a moment. "I was too young to know Caravaggio was gay or that I was gay – I mean, bisexual."

"Have you ever been in love?"

"Yes. I still am, but he is dead."

"AIDS?"

Giovanni nodded his head, yes.

"How heartbreaking," Talia said, listening to Giovanni's heart pound against her ear as if she were a doctor. It was not the right time to share that she had gotten a negative HIV test after an excruciating two-week wait, convinced it would have come back positive.

"I am scared," he said, gripping her against his body.

"Of death?"

"No, of life and loss." Giovanni sighed. "Maybe that is why I like Pessoa. Nothingness is appealing."

"If you're gay, we don't have to be lovers." Talia kissed Giovanni's forehead. "I'd adore you just as much."

"I was terrible at making love to you," he mumbled.

"No, that's not what I meant—"

"I am in love with you too, but you are alive." Giovanni cupped Talia's face with both hands and looked into her eyes. "Give me time. I am – how you say it? Green."

How could she have not fallen for him? Like Milan,

Giovanni was romantic and existential. And, sure, Milan was not the prettiest city by tourist standards, but its destruction and rebirth offered freedom from imprisonment to the past.

As Talia drifted off, wrapped in Giovanni's arms, Henry's face popped in her mind. They had made plans to hang out the next day. It's not like she owed Giovanni an account of her hypothetical flings, or did she? Being futureless meant this was time for play, meaningful and open-hearted, yes, but not committed or exclusive.

In the morning, Talia stopped by our parents' flat, showered, and went on her friend-but-possibly-more date with Henry. They devoured the Pinacoteca di Brera and wandered around Centro Storico, spending hours talking over cappuccinos and gelato. Henry wanted to know all about Talia's childhood. What was it like growing up with Grandpa Simcha – a man who survived pogroms, constructed Talia's family home with his two hands and fixed his false teeth?

Curiosity unsated, Henry went the extra mile and asked to borrow Grandpa Simcha's memoir, *Chaii, Beiti, Artzi* (My Life, Home, and Country) that Mom had hauled from Herzliya to Milan. "It's impressive your grandfather wrote a book without having finished elementary school," Henry said.

Like it or not, our grandfather's autobiography was an impressive feat. He wrote it in Hebrew, a language he learned from a dictionary in the '20s upon arriving in Palestine from Russia, traumatised by anti-Semitism and disillusioned by the communist revolution.

"Yeah, I admired him, and at the same time, I couldn't stand his politics. Mind you, I used to jump to his defence when people who didn't know shit about being persecuted and killed for being Jewish critiqued his beliefs. Fuck that. But I baulked at the vile shit that came out of his mouth."

"Sounds complicated," Henry said.

Talia leaned to kiss him. "Don't." He pushed her away. "I'm dying to, but I can't do this to Shoshana."

"Of course! I respect that," she said, turned on by the challenge and his integrity.

"How about I walk you home?" Henry had that smitten glimmer in his eyes. "This way, I'll get to hear one more story."

Talia told Henry about how as a kid, she taught Grandma Rivka how to read and write. Once a week, our grand-mother would give up her precious afternoon rest while Talia donned an old pair of Mom's glasses, with no lenses, to appear more tutor-like. "I was so proud of her," Talia said.

"You were destined to become a tutor. I mean, how lucky are Shira and the other consular kids? I can't even begin to imagine how challenging it would be to subvert a bad education and always be only one step ahead of my students."

"Thanks, if only my high school grades reflected that."

"Fuck grades; you're brilliant."

Talia teared up. "You remind me of Grandma Rivka."

"Thanks. I think?"

"You're masculine and sexier, of course, more like the wolf dressed as grandma."

Henry chuckled. "I'm afraid I'm more like Little Red Riding Hood than the wolf. I've been a good boy all my life. Perhaps it's time to change that."

In the next couple of weeks, Talia saw Giovanni one day and Henry the next. She invited each of them over for dinner with Mom, who didn't condone Talia's behaviour but was curious to get to know the men who had captured her daughter's attention.

At first, Talia rationalised her behaviour — yes, she had flirted with Henry, but no, she hadn't done anything sexual with him, at least not yet. Still, as time went on, her secretiveness weighed on her conscience, and rightly so. She needed to come clean.

Mom agreed. "You should tell Henry about Giovanni before you break that boy's heart." She chewed on her nail for a moment, then added, "Maybe I shouldn't say this, but I like Henry better."

"That's because he's Jewish, speaks Hebrew and most importantly, asked to borrow Grandpa Simcha's memoir."

"Giovanni has a peacock's arrogance, but Henry, he is like a crane — not obsessed with looking grand because he knows he can fly," Mom said, like a diehard Aesop's fables fan.

Talia groaned. "Okay, Mommy dearest, I'm off to meet Giovanni."

"Where at?"

"Santa Maria delle Grazie. We're seeing *The Last Supper*."

Mom tsked. "Be careful. That boy is trouble."

"It's not like he's taking me gambling or to an opium den."

"Mark my words; the peacock looks swell but can't soar."

Talia arrived at the church with our mother's words still buzzing in her head. Giovanni was already there, scrutinising the fresco. He did look quite the dandy — what with his turquoise polo shirt's collar turned upwards and a pink sweater draped over his shoulders, its sleeves hanging in a studied knot around his chest.

148

"I see what you mean about faded glory," she said, examining the masterpiece. Its deterioration was heartbreaking. Giovanni explained that the fragility resulted from Leonardo da Vinci's short-sighted perfectionism – his insistence on forgoing quick painting with plaster and instead taking his sweet time instead of working quickly the way a mural demanded using paint that did not adhere well to the wall.

"He was gay, you know," Giovanni said.

"Leonardo?"

"Yes. Look how feminine John the Baptist is." Giovanni pointed at the figure adjacent to Jesus. "The one who looks like a fainting woman."

"I met someone." Admittedly, it was a non-sequitur, but Talia was afraid of losing her nerve.

"Sorry? I do not—"

"An American guy. We haven't kissed or done anything sexual, but I'm attracted to him." The look on Giovanni's face pained her, but she pushed on. "It's not a big deal, really. He has a girlfriend back home and is in Milan for only a few more months."

"If it is not, as you say, a big deal, why tell me?"

"Honesty is important, no?" She tried taking his hand, but he turned away. "Hey, we're too young to be exclusive, and besides, I can't stay in Italy either."

Giovanni turned to face her with a determined look. "Listen, we were brought together by fate."

"I don't believe in—"

"Israel is not far away. I will visit, *te lo prometto*." He looked desperate now. "And when I turn twenty-one, I will have access to my trust fund. I beg of you, wait for me and we will travel the world."

"It's a lovely fantasy, but I'd kill myself before going back to Israel, even for a little while."

149

"But tell me you are joking."

"It's hyperbole," she said. The truth was she did mean it, but it wasn't fair to dump such heaviness on him. "I promise to give your offer some thought, *te lo prometto*."

Telling Giovanni about Henry was a relief. The young Italian wasn't thrilled with a non-exclusive agreement, but he was more concerned about sharing a future.

And Henry? After eons, he finally made his move. In the elevator on their way up to our parents' flat, he nudged Talia against the wall and leaned in. The kiss was tentative, his tongue missing hers.

"I have something to tell you," he said.

"Me first. I have a lover, but we've been using condoms." Talia regretted her blunt delivery as soon as these words came out of her mouth.

Henry's face fell. "Why didn't you mention this before I broke up with Shoshana this morning?"

"Don't worry, it's not serious with this guy." She regretted the lie the moment it came out of her mouth, so she added, "And, anyway, you and I are passing ships, right? So why should it matter if there's someone else?" This part rang true.

"But don't you think you should have told me earlier?"

"Why?"

"Really? You have to ask?"

"Who you choose to be romantic or sexual with has everything to do with you and nothing to do with me." Talia was speaking from her gut. "I respect that you can only be with one person at a time, but it's not the case for me."

"I didn't think about it like that," Henry said.

"Kiss me again. I've been dreaming about it."

And even though the second kiss was just as awkward as the first and paled in comparison to Giovanni's, Henry wanted her in a way the young Italian couldn't muster – a saviour's passion that, warranted or not, gave Talia hope.

Naked, Henry looked like a porn star. His legs and butt were muscular from riding his bicycle from the East to the West Coast, and even though his humungous penis would have made many gay men swoon, it hurt like hell.

She would have been okay with mediocre sex, having taken vicarious pleasure in her partners' ecstasy – their turn-on was her turn-on. Besides, physical intimacy wasn't all that exciting with Giovanni either, but luckily, Giovanni's penis was smaller than average, so penetration didn't hurt as much.

But with Henry, the growing pain down there made it harder to zoom out and watch a sex scene as though she were a spectator. Once she learned Henry would orgasm quicker if he suckled her nipples, she'd stick her breasts out for him to nurse, praying for mercy when he jabbed her with his weapon of a cock.

"Are you okay?" Henry asked this one time when she tried to suppress wincing but couldn't.

"Penetration is painful sometimes," Talia whispered, shame stinging her skin. "I'll see a doctor."

A pelvic exam was a nightmare for all the reasons I now know. And I was and wasn't there when in a cold hospital room with pale green walls, the Italian physician, a thirty-something man, told Talia her pain was *un dolore psicosomatico*. There was that word again, the one the elementary school nurse had used to diagnose Talia's tummy pains in the third grade.

If only Talia had known she had VVS – an inflammation

of the vulva that was curable by surgery – her prolonged suffering could have been prevented.

"Psychosomatic pain? Does that ring true?" Henry asked.

"I dunno, maybe." She nuzzled her head against his chest. "I've had traumatic sexual experiences, so, yeah, it's possible."

"Oh no, how awful." Henry fell silent for a moment. "What happened? I mean, if you're okay talking about it."

"What if telling you changes how you feel about me?"

"It won't." He brushed her hair away from her face. "From the moment I get up, you're all I think about."

"I love you too," she said and meant it. It didn't invalidate her feelings for Giovanni. It was possible to love two men at once, right? "Here goes, then. In the third grade, my parents sent me to stay with Grandma Mami, Dad's mother, who lived in Haifa. Her bungalow was only a two-hour bus ride north, but by Israeli standards, it was the end of the world."

"The Carmel?" Henry asked.

"No, nothing fancy like that. Kiryat Bialik – a run-down neighbourhood where my father grew up in tin-roof poverty."

"Ah," Henry said, whatever that meant. His parents lived on New York City's Upper West Side, and his father co-owned a diamond-cutting business.

"I dreaded visiting Grandma Mami. She guilted me into eating her food and she spoke to her dolls in a creepy voice." Talia willed herself to go to that wounded spot that hadn't scabbed, much less healed. "But the real issue was that my Peruvian grandfather, Gershon, had just come home after being gone for over thirty years."

"What?" Henry looked horrified.

"Yeah, long story short, Gershon abandoned his family when Dad was only fourteen years old, leaving Dad to

152

provide for his mother and sisters. Dad found work as a porter on the docks, but that's a different story."

"So why did your grandfather come back?"

"Don't know, don't care. My question is why did Mami take him back?" Talia gazed somewhere to her left. "Grandpa Gershon would sit on the porch, morning to evening, with a beer in his hand. There were these big yellow spots on his white wifebeater under his armpits." She shuddered, then met Henry's eyes. "I was terrified by this man, repulsed, but he was family, and my parents told me to be nice to him and do as he said." She was speaking so softly now, she was barely audible. "He offered me sweets – blue and red fruit candies in a tin can, covered in white powder – but I could only suck on them if I sat on his lap." There it was. That familiar, crawling sensation under her skin. "Sorry, I can't."

"If it's too painful, then—"

"He tickled me down there, asking if that felt good."

At first, Henry didn't say anything. Was she too much? Did she scare him away? But then he took her hand. "You didn't deserve that."

"There's a collection."

"Of what?"

"Unwanted touches from him and other men." She was feeling too many things at once. "I'm damaged goods."

Henry's body shook once, like a dog releasing tension. "Come to America with me."

"What will I do there?"

"Go to college."

"But I barely made it through high school." Talia reached her hand to her throbbing down there and pressed. It usually eased the burn, but this time the friction left blisters that bloodied her fingers.

153

"Don't worry. I'll teach you everything you need to know."

From that point on, Talia continued to confide in Henry – the kind of stuff she hadn't even dared utter to herself. These secrets were painful and embarrassing, not the easy-to-shock revelations that sounded intimate because they were intense. Looking in his mirror, she seemed less broken.

The predictable thing about being alive is that time moves forward non-consensually. *Boom*, only two weeks were left till Henry's departure and three months before Talia's visa was set to expire.

"I told my parents about you," Henry said.

"Really? What did you say?"

"That I fell in love with an Israeli woman, and if she needed more time to decide about coming to America with me, I'd stay in Italy and defer my studies."

"Wait—"

"Mom and Dad are flying over this weekend. They want to meet you."

Talia didn't know what to say, so she nodded her head. When she later shared the news with Giovanni, the young Italian exclaimed, "*Dio mio*, but are his parents mad?"

"Imagining saying goodbye to you – it kills me."

"Then, do not. *Ti prego*, say yes to my offer."

"I'm not ruling it out quite yet," Talia said.

In the little time they had left, Giovanni continued to charm and dazzle. He was irresistibly European, cloudy, intellectual, grandiose, with bouts of vulnerability and tenderness. Henry, too, was brilliant and worldly but his American, brave-new-world exoticism was sunnier, more naïve and reassuring.

Henry's parents on the other hand? Well, that was an altogether different story.

"So, Henry, what are your plans for your senior year?" Ruth, Henry's mom, asked. A tall woman with coiffed silver hair and bright-red lipstick, she towered over her husband, Jacob.

"Same as they've always been." Henry stuffed a large piece of ossobuco into his mouth.

The restaurant's Michelin-star menu was outrageously expensive, so Talia settled on a modest risotto. She ate in silence, as did Jacob, bearing witness to the sparring mother-son show.

"You must graduate on time. You realise that, yes?"

"Mom, let's shift topics, okay?"

After the main course and before dessert, Ruth got up and signalled for Talia to follow. "Excuse us while we ladies go powder our noses," she said.

The sound of Ruth's urine stream in the adjacent stall was, well, awkward. Talia's discomfort intensified when they stood side-by-side washing their hands, their strained faces reflected from the bathroom mirror. Ruth's lower lip protruded. So that's where Henry got it from.

Ruth cleared her throat. "I don't want a shotgun wedding," she said.

"I don't understand." Talia had never heard that phrase before.

"How will you live with yourself knowing you destroyed Henry's career?" Ruth wiped her hands on fine linen and applied a fresh coat of lipstick. "Go ahead and name your price."

"You're misjudging me, Ma'am."

"Think about it."

Later that evening, Talia asked Mom, "Is Ruth right? Am I bad for Henry?"

"The way I see it, there's only one way forward," Mom said. It was apparent she deemed Henry as the ideal son-in-law. And Dad? He was too busy trying to sell the Milanese on the idea of an avocado gelato to form any opinion about his daughter's romantic prospects.

Falling asleep on Henry's chest, Talia wondered if she, Talia, was toxic. And how had she become such an anti-feminist cliché, a woman in need of saving?

It was excruciating, Talia says, materialising on a whim. Again.

"What was?" I ask.

Choosing between Henry and Giovanni, of course.

"But that was never the question, was it?" I confront her.

Then what was?

"You chose life – to fly on Henry's wings to the land of the free, the home of the brave. And deciding between life and death, well, in the end, that's a choiceless choice, right?"

9

THE AMERICAN DREAM[5]

"But a wedding will kill the romance," Talia protested.

"I don't understand," Henry said, still jetlagged after arriving in America from Italy.

"Signing a contract will make me feel trapped." She could tell her sentiments hurt him. "Think about it, living together in sin," she winked, "means choosing each other daily." Choice. There was that loaded word again.

"I respect that." Henry looked older than his twenty-one years. "Then let's get you into college on a student visa before your six months are up."

Academia was a path Henry had envisioned for her anyway, but Talia's abysmal high school diploma didn't qualify her for college. Still, Henry persisted. He made call after call, filled out forms for admission exceptions and edited Talia's personal statement, deleting the part where she had reflected on her ambivalence towards pursuing academia. ("University might not be a good fit for people like me.")

In the end, Henry's hard work paid off. Rhode Island

College, or RIC as the locals called it – a modest four-year institution on the other side of the tracks from Brown – offered conditional acceptance. Talia had to pass elementary English and maths courses to stay enrolled.

At RIC, students took on second jobs to pay the $5,000 undergraduate tuition, compared to Brown's $50,000. They wore colourful outfits, ate Velveeta and Hostess Ding Dongs, and their dialects were wild and exciting – the letter "r" materialised at the end of some words (*idea* was *idear*) or went MIA from others (*car* was *cah*). When it snowed and slushed in the dead of winter, Talia's peers would say that it was *wicked cold*. Talia liked the word wicked.

Social categories, like race, had a different flavour too. At Brown, white students were white. At RIC, Italian Americans were thought of as vastly different from Irish Americans. To an outsider like Talia, this intersectionality between class and ethnicity was challenging to understand, especially given the general culture's "myth of meritocracy" – that anyone could become president of the United States of America.

Mostly, RIC was a far cry from Brown in intellectual stimulation. Most of Talia's professors were frustrated academics, irritated by teaching too much and for too little pay. Still, Professor Vanessa Frith talked about something called "mindsets" in her developmental psychology class that blew Talia's mind.

"You're lucky you're RIC and not Brown students," Professor Frith said to a room full of students with slacked jaws. "Professor Carol Dweck's research shows that when kids are repeatedly told that they're brilliant, they develop a 'fixed mindset'. A bad grade becomes a threat to their identity, so they get fixated on their grades at the expense of taking intellectual risks." Frith spoke with fervour. "But you, who have not been expected to pursue academia as a natural next step, have the opportunity to develop a 'growth mindset' – treat your mistakes as empowering, an opportunity to deepen your knowledge and thinking."

One of Dweck's research findings was especially gasp-worthy. Dweck gave fifth graders a set of problems to solve. She praised half of the students on their intelligence and the other half on their effort, and guess what? When she then offered these students a choice – a new problem set with the same difficulty level or a more challenging set – the fifth graders who had been praised on their intelligence played it safe and stuck with the less challenging option. (Dweck referred to this predicament as being stuck in "the tyranny of now".)

The labels "smart" and "brilliant" had their drawbacks too. Who knew? And how could praising effort versus intelligence be harnessed to help all students, especially those who were never groomed to pursue higher education?

For the first time, Talia couldn't wait to write her midterm paper, and for the first time, Talia dared think of herself as having scholarly potential.

Talia's emerging sense of belonging was cut short when RIC's departmental chair summoned her for an urgent talk.

"Professor Frith is accusing you of plagiarism," he said, waving a piece of paper. She claims you couldn't have written the midterm by yourself." He then read Frith's note verbatim, "How would this student know how to use words like 'uncouth', 'non-plussed', and 'disinterest'? This student's college admission is pending on passing elementary English, so it doesn't add up."

There was no evidence of plagiarism because there was none. Granted, Talia could be a pain in the ass, but presenting someone else's work as her own was something she would have detested. Professor Frith was relying on what she called intuition. Others might have called it bias.

"Books," Talia said, her face flushed. "I've learned words like uncouth by being a bookworm."

"You're saying it wrong. It's not kauth like MOUTH, but kooth like BOOTH," the man said.

"Sorry," Talia whispered with a thicker accent than usual.

"So, you were in the middle of telling me about being a bookworm."

"Yes. I learned English early on in life." She mustered the energy to convince the Chair of her sincerity. "My father got a job in Sweden when I was four years old, and I spent kindergarten through second grade in an Anglo-American school in Stockholm."

"Second-grade English isn't very advanced." The Chair looked sceptical again.

"I assure you I kept reading and reading."

Admittedly, Talia's self-education was fragmented. She had mainly read novels, plays and philosophical treatises in no apparent order and only lingered on works she found compelling. She had huge holes in her science education unless you counted Encyclopedia Britannica's entries on diseases. And when she later happened upon Jerome K. Jerome's *Three Men in a Boat*, she laughed out loud. She too imagined having had every disease she had ever read about, from A to Z.

"What's your favourite novel?" the Chair asked.

"*The Master and Margarita*." The title had instinctively blurted itself out of Talia's mouth, or else she would have had difficulty deciding. There were too many great options to choose from!

"What part?"

"I love how Bulgakov describes The Devil as a middle-aged, dark-haired guy with different coloured eyes, and then adds, 'In sum, a foreigner'."

"It's pronounced fo-rhe-ner, not fo-rhegh-ner," the Chair said.

"Sorry, I have a problem enunciating words I've only read but haven't heard," Talia said, questioning, yet again, whether she belonged at a university or anywhere.

"I believe you." The man ripped up Professor Frith's note and threw it into the trash. "Keep up the good work."

Besides the Chair's support, RIC offered an additional surprise. Talia's math-for-dummies teacher, this geek of a man, with his sizeable bald spot, overbite and sports jacket covered in white chalk, turned pre-calculus into poetry. Math was about concepts, not inane formulas. Who knew?

Muttering "growth mindset" like a mantra, Talia placed her maths errors under a psychological microscope. From badges of shame, they turned into valuable specimens. Were mistakes based on an internally consistent logic? Could they provide a backdoor into understanding learning? Thinking about thinking was exhilarating. Perhaps there was a place for people like her in the inaccessible halls of the academe, after all.

The possibility of success induced more panic than experiencing failure ever did. Come exam time, Talia would break into cold sweats that erupted from her armpits, the palms of her hands and sometimes the soles of her feet, leaving her skin clammy and cold. She was shedding her skin, readying to rebirth into an academic, something she had never thought possible or even desirable.

College presented a third surprise. Professor Collin

O'Doherty, Talia's social psychology teacher, suggested she volunteer in his research lab. Talia didn't deem herself research assistant material. "Nonsense." Henry wagged his finger at her. "Of course, you'll say yes!"

Professor O'Doherty's work centred on what was known as a "partner effect" – an individual's unique and consistent impact on a large group of diverse people. And while this topic had nothing to do with how mistakes illuminated learning – it, too, proved fascinating.

Come to think of it, was Talia's partner effect that people who loved her felt (or would soon feel) betrayed?

Is this an actual dig, or are you looking for validation? There Talia goes again, interrupting my narrative.

"Validation? From you?"

Why not me?

"Go away," I command, and wait, where was I? Ah, yes, Talia's research assistantship.

Professor O'Doherty encouraged Talia to present a first-authored poster at a conference and write an award-winning honour's thesis. She reciprocated with dedication, spending countless hours running participants, analysing data and devouring academic publications. Mastering *academese* meant a taste of empowerment – developing tools to evaluate research findings instead of accepting or rejecting them based on faith or emotion alone.

Late one night, smelling of coffee and cigarettes, Talia gulped when she stumbled on Professor Robert Sternberg's articles in the library's smoking section. The Yale scholar had radical ideas on who succeeded in academia – a mismatch between teachers' and students' values predicted whether students performed to their potential. Students who thought more creatively and promised to change existing paradigms were often left behind.

"I'm thinking of applying to Yale for the combined master's and PhD programme in cognitive psychology," Talia confided in Professor O'Doherty. Henry had suggested she apply, and after a heavy dose of prodding, she finally warmed up to the idea.

"Yale?" her mentor scoffed. "Don't bother. It's best if you remember where you came from." Perhaps he was trying to spare Talia what he believed would be the inevitable pain of rejection. Or maybe he was threatened by her budding ambition. Who the hell knows?

At first, Talia was taken aback, but ultimately, O'Doherty's reaction lit a fire under her behind. She wrote a letter to Professor Sternberg, explaining how his work had impacted her thinking and resonated with her lived experiences. Henry asked to edit it, and for the first time, Talia rejected his help. "This letter needs to be in my words, and anyway, it's not like he'll respond," she said.

There goes nothing. She slipped the envelope into a blue US Mail collection box. Shockingly, the eminent scholar wrote back, and, as unimaginable as it sounded, their back-and-forth resulted in a full scholarship offer from Yale for its doctoral programme in cognitive psychology. Who would have thought? Not Mrs Hamorah, Talia's third-grade teacher, that's for sure, nor Mom or Dad, and definitely not Ruth, Henry's mom. It was Henry who had believed in her all along, and he felt vindicated.

"Of course, we'll move to New Haven," he said.

"But what about your job offer in Los Angeles?" Talia protested.

"Yeah, Pixar is a dream come true, but there's no way you can turn down Yale. We've been working so hard to get you to this point." Henry's face glowed. "I'm incredibly proud of you."

"I couldn't have done it without you," she said.

"Hey," Henry patted Talia's head. "I told you from the moment we met that you had it in you. So, I taught you a few things, big deal." Then, when she didn't respond, he asked, "Why don't you look happier?"

"I am; it's just that I'd hate for you to turn down such an amazing opportunity. How about," she chewed on her lip, "we separate for a while? You could move to LA, and I could live in New Haven."

Did she really voice something so heretic? Henry was the closest she'd ever had to an ally, to home, even though they avoided talking about avoiding sex. It was a sensitive subject. The pain in her down there had progressed and they hadn't been physically intimate in well over a year. It was a snake eating its tail situation — avoidance bred avoidance.

"I could get work at Yale. There's an opening in Professor Benoit Mandelbrot's lab."

"The fractal genius?"

"Yeah, him." Henry's expression changed. "Marry me."

"But—"

"You don't have to answer now. Think about it, okay?"

How could Henry ignore how lonely they had become together? He must have known they'd keep pushing a heavy boulder up a never-ending hill. Ages ago, they chatted non-stop, but now, on weekly dinner dates, they eavesdropped on other people's conversations.

And their domestic routine? Henry cooked, Talia did the dishes, and before going to bed, Henry asked Talia to show him her work. "Great job, but here's how you could improve," he'd say, offering pointers. He did everything for

164

her, even filing down the verrucae spreading on her feet with a Swiss army knife.

"Yes," Talia murmured one night after they had brushed their teeth and were curled up in bed. She was resting her head on that spot on his chest that held an illusion of refuge.

"Yes? So, you'll marry me?" Henry howled.

She let him insert his tongue into her gullet, his mouth reeking of toothpaste and garlic. "But I don't want a white wedding or a Rabbi," she said, wiping her face.

To Henry's mom's chagrin, who demanded both, they married at a Justice of the Peace office in downtown Providence. Henry wore a white suit, and Talia, a black-and-white polka dot dress that ballooned at the hips, her nails painted emerald-green like Liza Minnelli's in *Cabaret*.

So, what are you writing next? Talia is loitering again.

"About Yale, of course."

Everything?

"I can't possibly cover every . . . wait, what are you worried about?"

You have the luxury of hindsight, but I didn't know that—

"And what if you had known?"

I would have pushed Henry to take the Pixar job. It kills me to think he could have had generous shares in a company—

"That became a billion-dollar Disney subsidiary," I finish her sentence. I cried in *Toy Story* when the toys bid Andy goodbye, and granted, it was an emotional scene, but mostly, I thought of Henry's sacrifice and was flooded with guilt.

The trip from Providence, Rhode Island, to New Haven, Connecticut, took less than two hours on the I-95 heading south. To Henry, it was a shift from one Ivy League to another, but, to Talia, a change in planets.

"Welcome to Yale," Professor Robert Sternberg said. His office smelled musty, like an old library – books fighting for space on the wooden racks. His publications alone filled a few shelves. They had impressive titles, like *Beyond IQ: A Triarchic Theory of Human Intelligence* and *Metaphors of Mind*. But, hiding amongst them was an oddity, *Love the Way You Want It*. What prompted the eminent scholar to write a popular psychology book? Perhaps one day Talia would dare ask, but for now, she needed to be on her best behaviour.

"I'm honoured to be here," Talia said, hoping she didn't sound as petrified as she felt. "You had a choice between top candidates. So, why me?" Damn, that came out as fishing, which wasn't her intention.

"Why not you?" Instead of a suit and tie as she had expected, Professor Sternberg wore a pair of blue jeans and a white button-down shirt. Did that mean he was approachable?

"I don't have an Ivy League background."

Talia's new mentor laughed. "I got a C in Introduction to Psychology when I was an undergraduate student here at Yale and failed an IQ test in elementary school."

"Is that why you study intelligence?"

"We're all drawn to researching our so-called limitations, don't you think?" The man's expression was hard to read. "Listen, I was impressed by your statement of purpose and have high expectations of you. Impactful scholarship goes beyond analytical ability; it requires creativity, practical intelligence and attunement to the greater good. The first is a common commodity around here, but the latter are rare."

How could Talia possibly live up to Professor Sternberg's

standards? She, who had failed arithmetic in the third grade and barely finished high school, was fuck-worthy but not date-worthy for the Israeli intellectual elites, a wild, lost soul.

Why hadn't she listened to our undergraduate adviser, Professor Collin O'Doherty, and spared herself from inevitable humiliation? Or to Mom, for that matter? *Better to be the head of the foxes than the tail of the lions*, our mother's voice echoed in Talia's head.

Entering the Sterling Memorial Library through its main entrance, the nave, was like stepping inside a Gothic cathedral. The high-relief stone ornament and eighty stained glass panels were a far cry from RIC's rundown buildings.

With no time to dawdle, Talia headed to the Starr Reading Room — a cloistered frater house with a curved ceiling and tracery windows. Perhaps it was inevitable that she wrote her first paper in this imposing architecture the way she had imagined a Yale psychology doctoral student should sound. She had accrued a large vocabulary from extensive reading, so why not use it?

But when Talia received her assignment back, Professor Sternberg's comments leaped from the page in angry red ink and smacked her hard across the face.

UGH.

Muddy!

What are you trying to say???

Worse still, halfway through, was a particularly gut-wrenching comment. *I can't stomach reading more of this rubbish*, the famous scholar wrote, leaving the rest of the manuscript's pages humbled by their nakedness.

It took a whole week before Talia could bring herself to revisit her scorned work. The sight of the red markings alone made her heave. But with every reread, it became more apparent that her mentor was right. Talia's paper was a piece of crap. She was trying too hard to impress, to prove she belonged, and it cost her her authentic voice. Still, seeing the work for what it was – separate from who she was – brought a smidgen of relief. Just enough ventilation to keep going.

Determined to do better, Talia started from scratch, asking herself how she might convey the main ideas to Grandma Rivka. After all, our beloved grandmother was wiser than most folks at Yale despite her impoverished formal education.

Talusinka, my sweet, what's your paper about? Grandma Rivka asked, with curiosity and love that reached beyond the grave.

"Remember how I flunked arithmetic in the third grade, Grandma? Well, now I wonder if I had learned the material too well."

Too well? What do you mean?

"There was a logic to little Talia's mistakes, to many of our arithmetic errors, that could be traced to how we were taught." How could she give Grandma an example without getting tedious? "Okay, so with numbers between one and nine, we always subtract the smaller from the larger, right Grandma? Like, 8 minus 2 equals 6."

Grandma bobbed her head up and down as though death were an illusion.

"So, when Mrs Hamorah asked what 12 minus 8 was, I said—"

Sixteen? Despite being forced to leave elementary school, Grandma was quick on her feet.

"Yes, my very wrong answer was 16. Bravo, Grandma!"

168

Many of us kids gave this exact answer. We simply did what we had been taught, subtracting the smaller from the larger number, in this case, $8 - 2 = 6$, and then mindlessly dragging down the 1. Without being taught conceptual understanding of base ten or what negative numbers meant, of course $12 - 8 = 16$! *Duh!* Professor Kurt VanLehn wrote a whole book about this topic. *Mind Bugs.*

But Talusinka, my sweet, you're getting a bit too riled up, and about what, arithmetic? Have you been getting enough sleep? Food?

"I don't care about arithmetic per se, Grandma. What upsets me, even now, is that kids like me were told we were stupid. Meanwhile, our mistakes reflected our bad education, not our so-called internal deficits."

I'll leave you to write that down, my sweet.

Emboldened by Grandma's spirit, Talia distilled her main ideas into questions and replaced big words with simpler, more exacting ones. "Could students' all-too-common arithmetic errors be an over-learning, a mirror to rote teaching? Should we reform the teachers before we correct the students?"

Now, you're onto something, Professor Sternberg wrote in blue pen.

One of the advantages of coming from a working-class background was that the people she grew up with used words to get to the point. It was a habit that could sharpen Talia's thinking if she remembered to turn to her past for inspiration and meaning.

During her first year, Talia had a choice between a dizzying number of electives. Despite exhortations from her new friend, Miriam, to avoid taking Professor Thomas Brown's Physiological Psychology course – "He's brilliant, but he'll make you read physics" – Talia decided to sign up for it, anyway. The mysteries of the human brain? Bring it on!

Professor Brown's teaching assistant started us off with anatomy and colouring books, but then she surprised every-one. "Enough with the diagrams; today, we're going to dissect human brains." How cool was that?

The brain nestling in Talia's hands made her fingers tingle. This incredible biological machine, the stuff of con-sciousness, empathy and self, was an ugly shade of grey – a far cry from the textbooks' neat and colourful illustrations.

Who had this brain belonged to? Better not to go there, or she'd lose her nerve. "Yum! Looks like goat brain," one of the students exclaimed. He was wearing a *dastār* and had an Indian accent. Everyone laughed, and Talia relaxed a little.

Searching for the amygdala, she cut into the mush using a scalpel, her mind exploding with questions. If a brain injury can change personality, who are we except for our biology? How do our senses trick us into thinking colour exists in the world when it doesn't? Should we be trusting the mind to study the mind?

She imagined a group of adolescents passing a joint, asking these same questions. *Whoa, dude, that's so groovy;* they'd snicker, high as kites. Social science required sober stamina, persistence and exactitude. Still, it had a macabre romanticism, the stuff of teenage angst.

While classwork was intense, the real challenge was gen-erating a dissertation proposal. With too many research questions to choose from, Talia settled on the one that kept her up at night – in what ways could mistakes be a window into learning?

At Henry's urging, she started a collection of common mathematical errors, from arithmetic to calculus, and could barely contain her excitement – so many of these mistakes had an internal logic, and in that way, they were rational. But the scope of her query went beyond learning mathematics. It touched on a fundamental aspect of agency – the only way to have choice in life was to reckon with the unconscious mind's tyranny, its tendency to over-generalise and jump to conclusions.

Professor Sternberg was pleased with Talia's progress. At the tail end of her second year, she published her research in a respectable journal and gave her first departmental colloquium on the topic of "rational errors".

At a place like Yale, treating mistakes as invaluable was an ironic endeavour. Errors were anathema. People didn't share their false starts, journeys into rabbit holes, initial holes in theorising, or clunky experiments. Miriam, and other women who ended their sentences with upward inflections, were directed to speak in exclamation points.

The working-class world Talia came from taught her that the higher one climbs, the harder one falls. "Don't be the worst or the best," Grandpa Simcha advised when she had failed arithmetic in the third grade. The upper-class world she was now trying to inhabit despised the middle ground. Go big or go home.

This intellectual machismo was a shame – it halted innovation and bred impostor feelings in most people, except true narcissists. Professor Dweck was right about the elite's fixed mindset. If the overshadowing goal was to be deemed successful and smart, then people plateaued early, getting stuck in initial accomplishments, without reaching their potential.

Midway through Talia's PhD programme, Professor Jehoram Drek left a handwritten note in her school mailbox, inviting her for coffee. After deciphering his spidery script, Talia dashed to the bathroom, locked herself in a stall and burst into joyous tears. Professor Drek – the man whose work had changed the field of psychology – was interested in knowing more about *her* dissertation and discussing *her* scholarly ideas. No fucking way!

Even at Yale, Drek was considered a god amongst mortals. At the cusp of turning sixty, he was still going strong, despite battling a vicious form of cancer. Scholarship aside, he was involved in politics and the arts and volunteered in the community by teaching local school children how to play the piano. A renaissance man with a heart of gold, or so it was said.

Talia had a week to prepare for their so-called informal chat. What if the venerable professor started their meeting with a pop quiz, a smouldering redder-than-red pen in hand? Readying herself, she delved into his latest publication and reread his seminal book, *Drek on the Human Conundrum*.

"It's an honour," Talia said, shaking Professor Drek's hand.

"The pleasure's all mine." He looked emaciated yet dapper in his tailored grey suit.

Talia asked a question about Drek's research, and when that attempt failed to elicit meaningful conversation, she shared her thesis findings, hoping for feedback. Alas, that attempt, too, proved disappointing – Professor Drek suggested an idea that Professor Sternberg had already brought up.

They sat in silence. She – sipping on a tepid cappuccino and eating a sugary jelly donut that made her teeth hurt. He – studying her face.

"You seem uncomfortable," Drek said.

"I'm sorry if I've been asking too many questions." Talia glanced at her shirt. Had she spilled coffee or jelly on her chest?

"I've mentored many young women over the decades, but few have been as beguiling."

A prickling sensation crept over Talia's skin. Not knowing what to say, she said nothing.

"I confess. It's been hard for me to focus on our conversation." He was staring at her chest openly this time. "What is it about you that makes men so distracted, do you think?"

Was her shirt on too tight? Had she been smiling too much? "I'm late for class." Talia snatched her backpack from the floor and hurried out of the door.

"Wait for me," Drek said.

Talia could have said no, but Drek's illness made him seem vulnerable, and, besides, the word no was playing hide and seek again like it did when she was a child.

In the alleyway behind the psychology building, Talia didn't return Drek's kiss, but she didn't push him away either. When, finally, her numbness thawed, she took off running.

I'm such an idiot. Why the hell would Professor Drek care about what someone like me has to say?

A week later, Talia screamed in her dream – an ear-shattering shriek that woke her in a jolt of adrenaline and cold sweat. It awakened Henry too, but he dozed off again after she reassured him it had only been a nightmare. Falling asleep at the drop of a hat was one of his superpowers.

Talia had survived worse, so why was she so upset over one smooch from a horny old goat? Big deal! Still, the kiss's saliva had hardened on her teeth like plaque, tinging everything she consumed with a foul aftertaste.

In the morning, while brushing her teeth more vigorously than usual, an image of Drek's face appeared in her mind. *You were flirting with me*, the apparition said.

"Stop it," Talia yelled.

"You okay?" Henry shouted from the other side of the door.

"Yes, sorry." She was determined to put the Drek incident behind her and move on.

In the next few weeks, Talia tried her best to repress what happened, but failing to, she decided to talk to Miriam. Our friend was training to become a therapist and had become a trusted confidant.

"What a vile man," Miriam said after Talia had divulged what happened.

"What should I do?"

"Report him," Miriam scowled.

"But that means telling Henry."

"You mean you haven't?"

The surprise in Miriam's voice caught Talia off guard. "No, I didn't want to upset him."

"But doesn't that create a distance between you guys?" Miriam insisted.

"I dunno, I'm already a such a burden on him. He's constantly helping with my research, even when . . ."

"You don't want his help," Miriam finished Talia's thought.

"That's right." Voicing the unspeakable was terrifying. "And, Miriam, there's something else."

"You can tell me anything; you know that."

"I'm such a horrible romantic partner." Wrapped in shame, Talia disclosed the ever-growing pain in her down there. How it made her a sham of a wife.

"Seek couple's counselling before it's too late."

"You're right."

"And you must report Professor Drek. What if he accosts another woman?"

"I hear that, I do."

"And—"

"Please, I can't handle more advice right now." Talia flashed back to Grandpa Gershon's alcohol breath. To Gil's friend, who opened her bedroom door at night and let himself into her body. To all the unwanted touch that she, that too many women and girls get subjected to, where *please, stop* is muffled by a hairy hand over the mouth.

"Sorry, you'll have to deal with one more piece." Miriam grabbed Talia's wrists. "Seek medical help. Obviously, I'm not a physician, but your pain doesn't sound psychosomatic."

The problem with burying unprocessed trauma is that at some point, it re-rears its head.

The following year, Talia heard through the grapevine that a new student, Ella, had a shady encounter with Professor Drek. She asked Ella for coffee, and they shared an almost identical script – an invitation to intellectual exchange that ended with groping. Bewildered, they knocked on Professor Macher Mooglev's door. As a senior staff member, he had administrative know-how and importantly, he had a reputation as an ally, a feminist, even.

"He kissed each of you?" Professor Mooglev asked.

"Yes," Talia and Ella said in unison.

"The buffoon!" The man exclaimed.

Talia tried explaining that even though Professor Drek's unwanted physical touch was violating, its main harm was in its message – the esteemed professor pursued Talia and Ella for their body, not minds.

"I'm not justifying what Drek did, but I don't get why

his behaviour had anything to do with disrespecting your intelligence."

Was Professor Mooglev incapable of understanding that for women, especially those from underrepresented backgrounds, sexual harassment was a message that they could never be taken seriously? Or did he willingly bury his head in the sand?

Still, Mooglev promised to take action. "I'll talk to Jehoram, and in the meantime, how about we keep your complaint internal?"

A week later, he offered an update. "I met with Professor Drek and explained the gravity of the situation. I told him in no uncertain terms to never behave like this again."

"Did he own up to what he did?" Ella's tone was sceptical.

"I'll admit, at first, Jehoram became slightly defensive. He said he was being chivalrous, avuncular, that you both misunderstood. But after I pressed him, he confessed that he behaved like a romantic fool."

A predator, Talia thought. *He behaved like a predator.* Why didn't she say it out loud?

"Jehoram feels humiliated, so I'm confident he won't do this again," Professor Mooglev said, getting up. "And there's also the matter of his illness to consider. It has progressed considerably, and he doesn't have much time left. If we exposed him publicly, think what this would do to his family." Mooglev's expression was grave. "Are we agreed that the matter's resolved, then?"

Talia and Ella thanked Mooglev. What else could they have done without risking their careers and reputations? It was 1995, and Mooglev's gesture was considered a victory for women.

*

Talia's graduation from Yale was a big to-do affair. Mom and Dad travelled all the way from Israel, accompanied by Uncle Benjamin and Auntie Tzipora. Henry took lots of photos and bought a Ben and Jerry's ice cream cake. *Hurray, Dr. Talia!* it said in bright red icing.

"Congrats," our family yelled when she marched up the stage, receiving her diploma to the sound of "Pomp and Circumstance". Luckily, they didn't question why she was part of the smaller group of students wearing darker, flimsier robes. Cap and gown rentals had different colours than those for sale, differentiating haves from have-nots. But never mind the robes! Talia had come a long way from being a failing student and a military defector.

"*L'chaim!* We're in awe of you, my child!" Dad made a toast over a fancy dinner at a seafood restaurant renowned for its New England clam chowder, his famous smile as wide as the Atlantic Ocean.

Mom joined in, "Here's also toasting to Henry. After all, at least half of Talia's Ph.D. belongs to him." Henry seemed delighted. Everyone knew he had been grooming Talia for this moment. And Talia? She didn't have the emotional vocabulary yet to understand why Mom's comment was a stab to that softest of spots.

That night, Talia thanked Henry by offering her body for sex – letting him seed her in whatever holes he wanted. She had consented, initiated, even, so why did she feel betrayed?

The pain in Talia's down there only seemed to increase over time. But that wasn't the reason she couldn't stomach his ... everything; feathery touch, bloated lower lip, and body that reeked of home-cooked food. She hated herself for feeling this way. Henry was beautiful, inside and out, and she? An emotional basket case. An unworthy wife.

Looking in the mirror didn't feel good, but she needed

to steel herself. The night was young, and there was still dancing and merriment to be had at a nightclub Talia and her classmates rented for the big occasion.

"We've made it, class of 1997!" Carlos yelled into the microphone. This hunk of a gay man wore glittery, over-the-top female drag. Not just any drag – he had asked to borrow one of Talia's outfits and settled on one of her favourites – a retro disco number in pink sequins.

"Let's Dance!" Carlos moved his muscular body to David Bowie's sonorous voice. And dance Talia did. She swayed her hips and arms to the rhythm, thrusting them in all directions, shuffling her feet inwards and out.

Talia hadn't told anyone yet, not even Henry or Miriam, that she had gotten several interviews lined up for faculty positions, and one was at Brown. Imagine coming full circle from RIC to Brown, Henry's alma mater? Now, that would have made Henry proud.

But here's the deal, when the saved do not admit to resenting the saviour – not even to themselves – then the saved commit an unforgivable act to break free.

10

STEREOTYPE THREAT[5]

Fully erect, the anti-Henry's dick was five inches long. That part of the sordid affair was a blessing. The man shoved it down Talia's throat, as deep as it would go, rubbing against tender tissues. She gagged on his salty mucous once a week, sometimes more.

Hardly anyone dared venture into that dark, dank basement at Brown University, where old computers and other to-be-recycled or thrown-out items collected dust. Still, Talia and that narcissist, her senior colleague, could have been caught, sparking disaster.

She had come full circle, having accepted a visiting assistant professorship at Brown University's Cognitive and Linguistic Sciences Department. It took immense effort and vulnerability to get to this point, and her new post demanded (even more) sacrifice from Henry, who was now commuting from Providence to yet another new job in Boston, Massachusetts.

So, what the fuck was she doing fucking it all up?

*

Talia called Miriam to ask if our friend could recommend a therapist in Rhode Island.

"What's going on?" Miriam asked. She lived in Cambridge, Massachusetts, doing an internship at Harvard.

"Nothing major, just the stress of starting a new job." Talia couldn't bring herself to confess that she had been sneaking behind Henry's back. She, who had prided herself on loyalty and truthfulness. It was sickening.

"Believe me, I get the pressure of adulting," Miriam said and recommended a therapist, Ms Linda Starr, who was "really, really good with work–life stress."

As luck would have it, Talia was able to book a consult with Ms Starr the next day.

"So, what brings you here?" The therapist asked. Her chair was positioned at a slight angle to Talia's, but her stare was aggressive.

Talia gazed at her lap. "I've been cheating on my husband, and I want to stop, but I need help."

The woman smirked. "And what kind of help do you expect me to offer?" Was it Talia's confession that put her off, or was there something about Talia's looks, accent maybe, that raised a red flag?

"I love my husband, and this is really hard for me to say," Talia paused, overcome by a sea of guilt, "but he repulses me physically. Something's terribly wrong with me." What she didn't say was, *If I knew what kind of help I needed, I wouldn't be here.*

"Would you describe your relationship as being emotionally intimate?"

"Yes." Talia should have hesitated, but she didn't.

"So, is it possible you're compartmentalising sex and intimacy?"

"I guess so." The smear of pink lipstick on the therapist's

front teeth was distracting. Should Talia have pointed it out?

"Alright." The woman scribbled something on her pad. "Let's talk about your childhood. What was your relationship with your mother or primary caregiver like growing up?"

"Why?" Talia cringed. Not that our mother wouldn't have made for a fascinating analysis, but more than anything, Talia craved concrete guidance on how to stop her self-destructive behaviours – the compulsive sexual liaisons in the basement with that lecherous asshole.

"What do you mean, *why*?" The therapist did not sound pleased.

"Won't talking about my childhood derail us from the present?"

The therapist scrutinised Talia's face. "You seem exhausted. How many hours did you sleep last night?"

"About five."

"And the night before?"

"Same. Wait, maybe less."

"I don't know how to say this without being blunt." The woman's voice was shrill, her face bird-like. "We're not a good fit."

"A therapy reject? How low can one go?" Talia said, but when Ms Starr remained poker-faced, she muttered, "So, what do I do now?"

"I can give you a referral to a psychiatrist."

"I don't have anything against meds, but I'd rather have talk therapy."

"Then, I wish you all the best," Ms Starr said, and that was that.

At home, Talia might have failed as a wife, but at work, she aspired to become a rigorous researcher and affecting instructor. Thankfully, she had some experience lecturing as a teaching assistant at Yale. Still, Brown was a new ball game. Here, she was responsible for designing and delivering a whole course from scratch. And of all subject matters she could have been handed, it was statistics. (Or *sadistics,* as students nicknamed it.) A math heavy course? Ha! Take that and shove it where the sun don't shine, Mrs Hamorah!

Armed with an arsenal of multi-coloured chalk and an alleged quote from Mark Twain – "There are three kinds of lies: lies, damned lies, and statistics" – Talia was determined to ignite in her new students an unbridled passion for means, medians and standard deviations. After all, statistics were in service of exploring meaningful psychological questions, were they not?

Her first class started smoothly, but fifteen minutes or so into her lecture, a student raised his hand.

"Go ahead," Talia said in a voice she hoped conveyed confidence and enthusiasm.

"You might want to visit the restroom," he said.

The face that looked back at Talia in the ladies' bathroom mirror made her gasp. It was covered with red, yellow and blue chalk marks. Not an auspicious beginning, exactly.

If looking the clown wasn't bad enough, midway through the semester, she somehow managed to make a group of female students cry. Of course, the women didn't outright wail or beat their chests. It was more a case of moistened eyes and tears rolling down a few cheeks. Still, that was not the pedagogical effect Talia had been shooting for.

True, she had given her students a challenging midterm exam, but surely, they could have handled it. Not only were they Ivy League students, the crème de la crème, but their majors were quantitative, like neuroscience and computer science. So, what the hell happened?

As luck or fate would have it Michael, an energetic doctoral student at Brown's Psychology Department, asked if Talia would supervise his Ph.D. thesis. It was on "stereotype threat", a recent discovery by Professor Claude Steele. Folks who pursued careers in which "people like them" weren't expected to succeed had to contend with a unique worry – that what they said or did would confirm negative stereotypes about the group or groups they belonged to.

Stereotype threat went beyond the usual impostor syndrome. In a culture of always sounding smart no matter what, almost everyone who cared about doing well was afraid of being found out as not good enough (except for the true narcissists), but those with stigma about their intellectual abilities worried that any hiccup in their performance would also confirm the belief that people in their racial, gender, social class, or other socially devalued groups, were not up to par, that they didn't belong.

Did the women in Talia's statistics class experience stereotype threat? Did the stress of having to prove themselves equal to men explain why they were so upset on the midterm? If stereotypes about women's math and science ability were hurting her students, Talia needed to investigate this situation pronto and do something to level the playing field.

Talia, too, was in a similar predicament. Despite her Yale PhD, her social-class background was non-traditional at best.

Come to think of it, did stereotype threat make Talia erupt into cold sweat during exams at Rhode Island College? It was a reasonable conjecture. Her anxiety began in earnest the moment she started embracing an intellectual identity, questioning if she could ever belong.

The burgeoning studies on stereotype threat impacted the way Talia understood her life. If she believed Brown was Henry's world, not hers – and that eventually, she'd be exposed as someone who had infiltrated its ranks – could the affair with the loathsome senior colleague be "protective" self-sabotage? Or was she trying to succeed by ingratiating herself to a senior colleague, the power of the powerless? Then again, maybe the affair had everything to do with needing to break free from Henry's tentacles? All these possibilities churned her stomach, but I'll give Talia this – tossing rationalisations and denials to the wayside, she didn't hesitate about what to do next – be as honest with herself and Henry, best she knew how.

Driving in a frenzy, Talia swerved, barely missing a tree. Home in record speed, she careened into the parking spot and slammed on the brakes, bringing the wheels to a screeching halt. She then sprinted into the house, forgetting to lock the car.

"You okay?" Henry asked. He was in the kitchen wearing a red, white and green apron, smelling of sauteed garlic and roasted chicken. Talia came clean about the affair, her coat and gloves still on. "We can work this out," Henry said. Why did he have to be so goddamn noble? Why didn't he kick her to the curb?

Taking a shower didn't make Talia feel any cleaner, but the scalding water slowed down her breathing.

"I want to know everything," Henry said. He was in bed, a thick down comforter covering his body and half his face.

"Everything?" Talia gulped. She stood by the bed, a damp towel wrapped around her torso, beads of water dripping from her long hair onto the floor.

"Yes, every gory detail and start from the beginning."

★

"Whatever you do, stay away from stereotype threat research," Professor Ike Arrtay said. He was trying to be helpful, a mentor of sorts. After all, he had been one of Talia's professors at Yale and now her senior colleague at Brown.

"You know I have tremendous respect for you, Ike." His first name didn't roll off Talia's tongue, but she reminded herself they were colleagues now. "But, why?"

"Cognitive psychology is about studying the mind, its architecture – nuts and bolts. Leave social justice to educators." Ike gave her a knowing look, befitting a tier-one intellectual.

"I still don't get it. Why can't we study both basic and applied aspects of—"

"Talk to Neven." Ike looked at his watch. "He does cutting-edge research on thinking. The two of you should collaborate."

She found Professor Neven La-Mons seated at a bewilderingly tidy desk. "Have you read 'A rational analysis of the selection task as optimal data selection'?" he asked in a nasal voice.

"Not yet," she muttered.

"Well, that's disappointing." Neven's face was ugly as an orc's. Well, perhaps not that ugly, but I can't bring myself to look at his then photos, or his current ones, for that matter.

"Your wife and daughter?" Talia pointed to a framed photograph on Neven's desk. The woman was handsome – dark hair, blue eyes and a squarish jaw – and luckily for the girl, she resembled her mother.

"Yes, and how about you? Married? Kids?" He twisted his wedding ring as if he were contemplating taking it off.

"A husband, no kids." A rush of adrenaline surged through Talia's body like a flirtation junkie. Sure, she hadn't said anything suggestive, but come on – hadn't she already transgressed by sweeping her hair to expose her neck, leaning forward to show off her cleavage and crossing and uncrossing her legs to draw attention to her slutty down there?

Stop, Talia commands. *You're not being fair.*

"Ungrateful whore." I'm seeing red. "What possessed you to seduce this man? Risk your career? Stab Henry in the heart?"

You know it's not that simple.

"Do I?" I can't stand her right now. "Go away, or I won't get back to your story."

Our story, you mean.

★

"You're beating around the bush," Henry said, propping himself on the bed and leaning against a stack of pillows. "Where did Neven fuck you for the first time?"

"Please, I can't." Talia was ready to swap the wet towel around her torso with warm pajamas, but she continued standing there, shivering.

"Tell me," Henry said.

She collapsed on the armchair facing the bed. "I don't see the point of—"

"Your first kiss, then. Where was it?"

"In Neven's office."

"Was he hard?"

"Don't."

"Was he?"

"I don't know. Maybe."

"He fucked you on his desk?"

Talia smiled like a hyena. The image of having sex on Neven's sterile table was hysterical. It wasn't funny, more *ha ha stop*, as though someone had bound her and was now wriggling their fingers under her armpits. "No, not on his desk," she said, lowering her chin to her chest.

"Where then?"

"On a couch in the basement, and –" she paused, it was excruciating to talk about this, "– we didn't fuck exactly."

"Did he suck your tits?"

"Why are you doing this?"

"Did he?"

Was Henry touching himself under the blanket, or had she imagined it? "What are you doing?" She asked, reality disintegrating into horror.

"Show me your tits."

"No," she mumbled. The word that had evaded her childhood found its way through her throat and out her mouth.

"And how is that fair to me?" Henry kicked the blanket off, exposing his erection. "Take off the towel and tell me everything. Make it juicy; I want to feel and smell every detail," he said, stroking his dick.

Shivering, Talia recounted the first time she and Neven got naked, her tears forging trails of shame on her chest and belly. When she described Neven's mouth on her down there, Henry erupted, seeding the barren bed.

"I'm so sorry," he sobbed, naked and sticky.

"No, I'm sorry." She tried hugging him, but he pushed her off.

"So, what brings you here?" The marriage and family counsellor asked. She was a middle-aged, plain Jane.

"We're trying to save our marriage," Henry said.

"Do you agree?" The woman's gaze shifted to Talia's face.

"I'm not sure that's possible," Talia murmured, distracted

by the floral rug. Its pastel shades matched the room's peppermint and lilac colour scheme. What if this woman decided to reject Talia too?

"If anyone should be sceptical, it's me." Henry swallowed hard. "She's the one who cheated."

"What happened?" The counsellor asked.

"I had sex with a married colleague," Talia whispered. "I can't explain it. I can't even stand the guy." She looked at Henry. "You don't deserve this," but Henry didn't return her gaze.

"Is it possible you're going through a hypomanic episode?" The counsellor asked.

"I don't know what that is." This term rang a bell, but Talia had taken only one abnormal psychology course at Yale.

"How's your sleep been?"

"Five hours a night if I'm lucky."

"It could be hypomania. It makes people behave differently than they normally do – become impulsive, take risks, go from feeling on top of the world to being irritable and ashamed."

"Sounds about right." Talia would have signed up for a lobotomy, anything, to stop her madness.

"What triggers it?" Henry asked.

"Trauma. It's not my area of expertise, so I can't give Talia an official diagnosis or suggest treatment. What I can do is recommend a psychiatrist." She sounded like a kind kindergarten teacher. "In the meantime, do something as a couple to ignite some romance. A relationship is like the ocean; there are stormy days and calm days."

Once outside and out of earshot, they burst out laughing. "An ocean? Really?" Henry chuckled.

"An ocean of pastels," Talia said, welcoming Henry's smile like a long-lost friend.

"Being a Brown academic is hard. Maybe all the work stress you've been under has re-opened an old wound?" He put his arm around her. "Meds might be the way to go."

"You're not angry?" Talia didn't know what to feel. There was gratitude, of course — there have always been loads and loads of gratitude — but something else was bubbling under the surface.

"I love you. That's what's important, right? We'll get over this hump," Henry said.

That night Talia slept for seven hours; her head nestled in Henry's chest. In the morning, she made an appointment to see the psychiatrist and broke off the affair. "You're a liar, and your research is a bunch of bull," Neven said, twisting the knife he had rammed into her soft underbelly, but at least what was done was done. It was time to move on.

Over the next month, Talia waited for a mood stabiliser to kick in. "This might or might not help," the psychiatrist had said. She tried to muster her desire for her handsome, doting husband — she wanted to want Henry more than she wanted to want anything ever, but her body was a mess. She had been battling bouts of acid reflux, and the scarring had become so severe her esophagus required dilation.

The pre-operative sedative made Talia weep. "It's normal," the nurse told Henry. "Don't worry; she won't remember much."

"Why aren't you walking away?" Talia mumbled on the car ride home, still half-sedated.

"You make me feel alive," he said, squeezing her hand. *Stop suffocating me*; Talia screamed in her head but told herself she was too drugged to think clearly.

Henry made an elaborate French meal to celebrate Talia's first publication on stereotype threat. The sauces, alone, took a few days to prepare. It was a celebration-worthy event; the article, co-authored with her student, Michael, was published in *Psychological Science*, a high-impact journal. And I'm not one to brag – no, really – but it's been cited widely since.

"How about we invite Kiefer to join us?" Henry asked.

Kiefer was a post-doctoral fellow who looked like George Clooney. Talia met him during her faculty orientation, and they liked each other right off the bat. He reminded her of Henry – a sincere, edgy geek with a touch of melancholy.

"Great idea. I'll see if he wants to bring a date."

Kiefer came solo, bearing a fancy bottle of pinot noir. They talked about *Sensation*, Charles Saatchi's infamous show. It had travelled from London to Berlin to New York and featured provocative British artists like Damien Hirst, Mark Quinn, Rachel Whiteread and Chris Ofili.

Talia and Henry had recently seen the show at the Brooklyn Museum of Art, where it had created quite the stir – Mayor Rudy Giuliani called it "sick", but his attempts to shut down the exhibit proved futile.

Ofili's painting, *The Holy Virgin Mary*, stood out as especially sacrilegious. The Black Virgin Mary was surrounded by what looked from a distance like fluttering angels or butterflies but turned out to be cutouts from pornographic photographs. To add that sense of *je ne sais quoi*, Ofili placed a ball of dried elephant faeces ("dung", the press called it) on the Madonna's chest.

"It's cool Ofiili's Madonna is a woman of colour, and I'm okay with porn, but why feces?" Henry asked.

"It's supposedly an earth element that makes her more relatable, or so I've read," Talia said. "Didn't he travel to Africa to collect it?"

"You're both full of crap," Kiefer said, gulping the rest of his wine. "Do Jews even get to comment on the Madonna?"

"Does a White Anglo dude get to comment at all?" Talia retorted.

"Fuck you," Kiefer said, raising both eyebrows at once.

"In your dreams," Talia winked.

After dinner, the threesome retired to the living room. Talia and Henry sank into the white sofa while Kiefer kept shifting in his seat. The red Italian armchair was designed for guests who didn't intend to stay long. Wine glasses empty, they moved to whiskey on the rocks.

"Are you attracted to my wife?" Henry asked point-blank.

"I'm sorry if I—"

"Yes or no?"

"Yes."

"Stop it, the both of you," Talia yelled. They were talking about her like she was a prop. "Henry, what do you think you're doing?"

"She doesn't want me anymore," Henry said, ignoring her.

"I should leave." Kiefer got up.

"No, don't go." Henry gestured to the sofa. "Please, take my seat."

The rest of the evening unfolded like a French New Wave film, *Jules and Jim* perhaps, or maybe something darker? If, in *Sensations*, Mark Quinn used his blood to make art, why couldn't they have used body fluids to create an installation? *The Last Sex Act in Twelve Years of Marriage.*

"I'm coming," Kiefer yelled, ramming Talia from behind.

"Hold on," Henry screamed, stroking his dick with a death grip.

Kiefer exploded in her ass, Henry on her face. Her eyes and anus should have stung, but Talia was too numb to notice.

*

It was the end of Talia's two-year stint at Brown and the end of the world. Divorce. How does a long-time couple divide sentimental possessions? A painting by a street artist they had fallen in love with walking hand-in-hand on the streets of New York City, or a fragile Italian fruit bowl that miraculously survived the transatlantic voyage from Milan to Providence intact? What belongings should go to whom was like asking which memories belonged to whom – it was an impossible task.

"Tell me you don't love me, or I won't leave," Henry said. When she summoned these loathsome words, he collapsed on the sofa, his body convulsing in epileptic-like fits. "What about our kids?" he wailed. He was mourning the children that would have never been born. Had he not believed her when she said she didn't want to have any? Did it matter anymore? Henry's pain engulfed her, seeping into her pores.

The next day, Henry's mother called. Ruth accused Talia of being evil, a cold and calculating user. The insufferable woman was right. After all the things he had done for her, Talia paid Henry back in suffering and betrayal.

Am I being too harsh again?
I deserve much of the blame, but not all of it, right?
"I'll rephrase."

People say that it's easier to leave than to be left, but that's not always true, is it? Talia did a bad thing, and I sure as hell don't condone it, but she wasn't a bad person. And she paid dearly, deservedly, for the harm she inflicted.

My hated-beloved, only I know what happened next. The panic attacks. Problems swallowing liquids, even water. Dissociation. Blackouts. How excruciating to sever your umbilical cord from Henry's fatherly womb and become once again a persona non-grata. I understand, but I do not forgive you. Not yet. Perhaps, never.

Tempted by the call of that gentle night, Talia wrote a goodbye letter and made her way out of the door. She planned to head to the tallest bridge in Providence, but Mom emerged from the ether, filling up the apartment complex and blocking the front gate.

Had Talia exited that gate, it would have been the first domino, setting in motion the rest of the steps Talia had diagramed and rehearsed.

Don't you dare; the apparition roared as only a Mother Spider could. *I'll die if you die.*

"But I don't want you to die."

Then don't do this to me.

"I'm tainted, Mom. Admit it; I'm your biggest disappointment."

Look at how well you've done at Yale.

"But you said yourself that Henry earned half my degree."

I love you, my child.

"You never say that." Talia was fighting back the tears. She needed to stay strong, dissociated, and crying would have ruined her plan.

Go back inside and call Miriam, okay?

"Mom, I can't stand being in my skin. I can't—"

Call Miriam. Now.

Miriam answered the phone on the first ring. "Stay with me until you get on your feet," she offered.

Cambridge was only an hour away by train. She could do this!

Talia filled a large suitcase with books and clothes, snatched the stuffed gorilla Henry had gifted her on her 30th birthday from his perch on the bed and hopped the train to Massachusetts. She sat the 50-inch beast on the empty seat beside her – a perfect, silent companion.

On Miriam's advice, Talia enrolled in Jon Kabat-Zinn's Mindfulness-Based Stress Reduction (MBSR) programme at the University of Massachusetts Medical Center. The teacher, Jim, started the sessions with a guided body scan – students lay on yoga mats, closed their eyes and followed Jim's instructions to focus attention on different parts, toes to head.

At first, other people existed too loudly. Their mouth noises were the worst – throat clearing, gurgling, coughing, wheezing. And when Talia's mind wasn't hijacked by external noise, stray thoughts would interrupt her concentration, again and again. Her mind was a tyrant.

"Remember, relaxation isn't the goal," Jim said. "Thoughts come and go like the weather. Don't judge your thoughts or mistake them for truth." Talia's throat softened. It helped to witness her mind's catastrophes and not take her self-criticisms too personally.

In the third week, Jim announced that he had a surprise exercise. "I'll reveal it mid-class," he said, clapping his hands. Midway through the body scan, Talia relaxed into this now-familiar ritual. Our peers were no longer obstacles to overcome but a community, fellow travellers on life's journey. We were an eclectic bunch, too many to mention, but two come to mind – the young mother with terminal cancer who wanted to meet her twin daughters' grief with an open heart, and the middle-aged man, barely recovered from open-heart surgery, who realised that treating his anger was a matter of life and death.

"It's time for the new exercise," Jim said with childlike glee. "Ready? Good. Now, close your eyes and think of someone you love or loved."

Talia conjured an image of Mom, but loving thoughts turned complex, and some resentment seeped in. And if that wasn't bothersome enough, her mind started crooning the song about that thin line between love and hate. Undeterred, Talia tried manifesting other beloved faces, including Grandma Rivka's, and eventually settled on our childhood dog, Mickey.

"Zoom in on this person's face," Jim said.

Mickey looked at her with innocent, puppy-dog eyes, the ghost of his chin resting on her knee.

"Thank this cherished person," Jim said.

Thank you, Mickey, for always being happy to see me.

"Express your love and affection in whatever way feels right."

I miss you, my sweet boy.

"Good, that's very good," Jim said encouragingly. "Now, replace this person's image with your own face."

What kind of devilish trickery was this?

"Now, zoom in on your face."

The face that looked back at her in the mirror that morning got distorted as though she had been in an accident – raw meat, like a Francis Bacon portrait.

"Thank yourself for showing up," Jim said.

Thank you, Talia hissed at the person she despised most. Still, she bawled her eyes out in cathartic relief, aching to be kinder to herself, without having the first clue how.

Encouraged by Talia's progress, Miriam suggested she apply for a job at Williams College. "It'd be perfect for you," Miriam said.

"Do you even know me?" Talia snorted. "I've heard that it's harder for students to get into Williams than Harvard or Yale. I'd stick out like a sore thumb among the one percent of the one percent."

"And you'd love that. Think about it – it's a fresh start, gorgeous location and an opportunity to immerse yourself in a rigorous liberal arts culture that respects teaching as much as research."

"I do love teaching." It was bizarre how devalued teaching was at universities like Yale and Brown. They were all about research and grants. "But I'm worried my panic attacks will get in the way."

"I believe in you," Miriam said.

Sometimes a good word from a friend is all it takes to put one's foot in front of the other, especially when one's vision is cloudy and one's heart raw.

11

ADONIS[5]

Williams College was nestled in glorious isolation in the scenic mountains of Northwestern Massachusetts. It was as though Talia had entered a blinding-white sanitorium. The snow was white. The lights on the Christmas trees were white. Students were overwhelmingly white – curated and cultivated to be the "right stuff". They sported flattering, neat haircuts, monochromatic clothing that fitted their athletic and toned bodies just so, and cardigans draped over their shoulders in effortless chic.

The one percent of the one percent did not rest. In the mornings and evenings, students took challenging seminars. In the afternoons, they played sports or had Oxford-like tutorials. No wonder the Williams proud had rejected acceptances from the likes of Harvard and Yale – they were positioned to become America's future political leaders, investment bankers, NASA scientists, big pharma CEOs, and those behind the scenes who bent socio-economic reality into their vision and goals.

In the hallways, Talia heard whispers about ski vacations

in St. Moritz or the Klosters. Parents picked up their kids in private planes. She might as well have chosen a faculty position in a different solar system. Who lived like that? Not even most Brown or Yale students.

But Talia was used to being an outsider and, as such, enjoyed adding a tawdry colour to Williams' muted luxury tones. She paraded about in post-apocalyptic meets drag-queen outfits, an African grey parrot on her shoulder, and her pitbull mix, Eli, by her side. All that was missing from this walking circus act was an eye patch and cries of, *Land, ahoy.*

The parrot's name was Tukey. Tukey meant "parrot" in Hebrew. Parrot, the parrot. As it happened, Tukey was also the name of a famous statistician. Talia's new colleagues thought it a clever reference, befitting an elite institution rivalling the Ivy Leagues.

And Talia's eccentricity? It was welcomed, celebrated even. Old money's appearance was understated, but its personality was self-assured – it was intrigued instead of threatened by the unexpected. Couldn't her new colleagues have feigned some shock and disapproval? What was the fun of being a tame, loveable pirate?

The glorious isolation would last for two years and eventually become too insulating. But in 1999 and at the age of 34, Talia still suffered from panic attacks that came from left field, and Williams was an ideal place to heal.

She took Eli (or was it the other way around?) on woodsy trails – lush green in spring and summer, fiery red-orange-and-yellow in fall, and treacherous, icy white in winter. The duo summited Mount Greylock – that same mountain that was said to inspire Herman Melville's *Moby Dick* – crossing paths with hardcore, single-minded hikers trekking the Appalachian Trail from Springer Mountain in Georgia to Mount Katahdin in Maine. The scenery was breathtaking, but what was it exactly that spurred people to spend five to seven months of their lives hiking this trail? Were they running away from life or towards it? Could one do both at the same time?

Despite being high up in the mountains where Massachusetts meets New York meets Vermont, the region exploded with theatre, art and music. The Williamstown Theatre Festival drew the likes of Gwyneth Paltrow, who killed it in *As You Like It*. The much grittier Patti Smith delivered a gut-punching concert in the newly opened MASS MOCA – a 100,000 square feet museum that featured provocative, large-scale pieces that couldn't fit in smaller, more urban spaces.

For classical music, Talia ventured to nearby Tanglewood. Listening to the Boston Symphony Orchestra perform Berlioz's "Requiem" while sprawled on a blanket surrounded by sycamores? Not too shabby for a sanitarium.

And when she was in the mood for sex and romance? There was Kiefer. He spent every other weekend with her, and sometimes she'd visit him in Providence, a five-hour drive and a world away. Kiefer sang to her – folksy sentimental tunes about bittersweet goodbyes to fading lovers and crumbling hometowns – while strumming his acoustic guitar. They had anal sex and explored kink-light, using DIY blindfolds and wrist restraints.

Unlike Henry, Kiefer challenged her. He called her out on her bossiness: "You have no right to criticise my choice of clothing," he once said, when she suggested he might want to change out of a banana, pink and green striped T-shirt. He also demanded Talia snap out of punitive silences. "Use your words; I'm not a mind reader," he'd say.

It was a rude but necessary awakening. Talia needed to grow emotionally, not just intellectually, and that meant reckoning with her many unskilful behaviours. But as good as Kiefer was for her, he was tainted by our ex-husband's ghost, a reminder of how she had stabbed our saviour in the back.

"You're right; I've become a cliché of the passive-aggressive nag. I don't know how Henry put up with me," she admitted late one night, curled up in Kiefer's arms, Eli nestling against their feet.

"More like aggressive–aggressive," he said, and they both laughed. "I've been meaning to ask; do you miss Henry?"

"He came by with divorce papers the other day."

"How was it? Seeing him, I mean."

"It was . . . weird. He wore this striped cashmere sweater he bought in Paris." She paused, but then completed her thought. "It could have looked chic, but the sleeves were two inches short of his wrists."

"There you go again, criticising."

"No, that came out wrong," Talia sighed. "I'm not being mean, I swear, it's just that, I dunno why, but the short sleeves made me sad." It's like she had failed to appreciate Henry, again.

"Goodbyes *are* sad." Kiefer patted her arm. "I get it. I should feel happy that I got the girl, but I also feel guilty, you know?" He sat up and leaned against the bedframe. The movement woke up Eli, who yawned, then curled back into a snoring fuzzball. "Does Henry know we're seeing each other?"

"I don't think so. We didn't talk about our personal lives. Hell, we barely talked at all." Talia reached for her favourite short story collection, Grace Paley's *Enormous Changes at the Last Minute*. "Are you familiar with this book?"

"I'm not, but the title, wow."

She read him the first two lines of the short story bearing that title. The protagonist, a Jewish New Yorker, runs into her ex-husband of twenty-seven years. "Hello, my life," she says.

In the new millennium, and about a year after she arrived in Williamstown, Talia's panic attacks got more and more infrequent. She gradually got off the anti-anxiety meds and slept better.

One morning during winter break, her metaphorical fever broke. She leaped out of bed and made a mad dash out the door, screeching Abba's "Dancing Queen" at the top of her lungs. Eli darted along, his body wagging from head to tail.

The abandoned lot across the street was covered in virginal snow, the skies were blue and the sun's rays stung like jellyfish. But who cared about freezing one's ass off when all was right with the world? Talia went flying through frosty flurry clouds, swinging her arms and singing off-key. Her loyal backup singer howled away, smiling like dogs do with eyes squinting and ears back.

Talia's happiness abated when a lone spectator made his way towards them. From a distance, the intruder looked like a typical Williams athlete – clean-cut, swimmer's build, about 6 feet tall. Nothing special. But when he got closer, Talia's face turned tomato red. Captain America wasn't her usual type, but this guy was gorgeous – an Adonis.

Eli sprinted towards Adonis. He was a scary-looking dog – muscular, with a broad snout and large, sharp teeth. Even the most ardent of canine lovers would have thought twice about welcoming this bounding hound of the Baskervilles, but Adonis kneeled to greet Eli. It was a Kodak moment. They were both so handsome and gentlemanly.

If only Talia was more dog-like, she would have joined the stranger with unabashed curiosity and a wagging tail, but she was self-conscious about her zebra-patterned pajamas. Had Adonis seen her prancing around like a mad woman, or worse, heard her singing? No one should listen to such a cacophony, especially not someone this breathtaking.

So, she kept her distance and waved. Adonis waved back, flashing a heart-piercing smile, and continued down the deserted road, likely heading to the only worthwhile destination in that part of town – the Sterling and Francine Clark Art Institute.

If Talia had done a quick outfit change and headed to the Clark, she could have "run into" the captivating stranger. Surely, he would have deemed it a coincidence. After all, the museum was worth a visit. Its permanent collection boasted *A Street in Venice* by John Singer Sargent, which, like Williamstown, was beautiful and claustrophobic.

Tempting, but Talia decided against this plan. She had too much work to do, and besides, being a stalker wasn't her style.

Still, she second-guessed herself. Adonis' face kept popping up in her mind, quickening her pulse. What kind of spell had he cast?

The phone's ringing interrupted Talia's daydreaming. It was Estelle – a friend Talia met during orientation, and even though the two only hung out a couple of times a month, they shared an ease that makes a new connection feel old.

"Why aren't you at my going away party?" Estelle asked.

"Sorry, I'm on my way," Talia said, cursing herself for having forgotten. She threw on a black dress and hurried out the door. Article revisions would have to wait.

She found the party in full swing – women flirting, dancing to k.d. lang and Melissa Etheridge – a Williamstown queerness reserved for private venues. Estelle was in the kitchen, pouring vodka into a cherry-smelling fruit punch.

"Are you sad about leaving?" Talia asked.

"No, *The Stepford Wives* vibe here has become too creepy." Estelle turned her attention to a party-size bag of Doritos and dumped its cheesy-orange contents into a rainbow bowl.

"I hear you. I applied for a job in San Francisco," Talia said, reaching for a Dorito. The crunch was satisfying, but it left a residue on her upper lip.

"The West Coast? Damn!"

"Yeah. I'm dying to be in a more diverse place." San Francisco State University had an impressive legacy of political activism. In the late '60s, the Black Student Union, Third World Liberation Front and Students for a Democratic Society organised sit-ins, teach-ins and strikes to end the Vietnam war.

"An orange moustache looks cute on you." Estelle handed Talia a glass of fruit punch and a napkin. "I get why San Francisco's a better fit for researching stereotype threat."

Talia rubbed her face with the napkin, feeling self-conscious. "Yeah, I bet you're not feeling too inspired here either."

"True. Besides, I keep meeting the wrong women."

Was that a dig about the night they had too much to drink? If so, Talia deserved it. On that unfortunate occasion, Talia flirted with Estelle in the careless way she often did with people she wasn't all that attracted to. They ended up kissing, but when Estelle reached for Talia's breasts, Talia apologised for not being able to take it any further. Estelle didn't seem to take the rejection personally. "You're still dating this guy, Kiefer?"

"Yeah, but we're not monogamous, and he's seeing this woman he seems to be getting serious about." Talia scolded herself for her thoughtlessness. "Sorry, Estelle, if I were batting for the other team, I'd be all over you, but I'm—"

"Straight?" Estelle asked.

Talia nodded, yes, and that was that.

After a couple of hours of dancing and chit-chat, it was time to go home. Poor Eli, he needed his last walk of the night. And Tukey couldn't fall asleep unless she covered his cage with a blanket.

Talia hugged Estelle goodbye, wishing our friend good luck and saying how much she'd miss her. Heading out the door, the unimaginable happened – who brushed against her on his way in but Adonis? Twice in one day! What were the chances? At least this time, Talia wasn't wearing her silly pajamas.

"You said hi to my dog today." Talia rubbed her face with her hand. Cute or not, the remnant of an orange moustache was the last thing she wanted.

"The two of you were adorable." Adonis was even more attractive up close, but his voice was higher than she had expected.

"Oh no, how much of the madness did you witness?"

"Enough to make me distracted at work."

What a night! As it turned out, Adonis' was a butch lesbian and her name was Theodora, or Teddy for short. She was a descendent of Bostonian merchants traced back to the Mayflower, a competitive athlete on Williams' water polo team and an up-and-coming fine arts painter, working on a series of self-portraits for a gallery exhibit in New York City.

Even though Talia had not been attracted to women before, she was smitten and when Teddy asked for her number, Talia didn't hesitate.

Talia and Teddy had been talking and kissing on Teddy's grey mid-century sofa in first-base heat for almost an hour until Talia could no longer bear it and reached for her new lover's pants.

"Don't, I'm stone," Teddy said.

"I'm sorry, I don't know what that means."

"You can touch my chest, but not my genitals," Teddy explained, and after looking at Talia's face, added, "I like being the person who gives pleasure, receiving feels ... too feminising. Does that make sense?"

It didn't, and it did, so Talia said nothing.

"Go back to making out?" Teddy asked.

Talia had been aching to explore Teddy's body. All of it. Disappointed, she settled for exploding in her lover's mouth.

Here, this will explain stone and such." Teddy fished a dogeared copy of Leslie Feinberg's *Stone Butch Blues* from the stack of books on the end table. "You're welcome to keep it. I'd imagine this book will come in handy in San Francisco."

"They called me for an interview, but I don't have an offer yet."

"They'll love you." It was nice to hear, but why didn't Teddy sound sad?

That night, Talia stayed awake, reading Feinberg's book. Its protagonist, Jess Goldberg, was a gender non-conforming butch dyke whose pronouns were *zie* and *hir* – combinations of "he and she" and "him and her". (Today's non-binary equivalent would have been *they*.) And Jess's life story? Well, it was heartbreaking. Zie was institutionalised in a mental ward by hir parents because zie refused to act feminine.

This narrative rang familiar, if less extreme. Neighbours would harangue Mom about Talia's choice of clothing. How could Rina Ben-Zeev let her eight-year-old daughter dress like a boy in mismatched plaids?

It wasn't just Talia's choice of clothing that raised eyebrows. "I beg you, be more lady-like," Dad would plead with her time and again. Normally, he stayed out of family dynamics – this was his wife's domain – but Talia's tomboy tendencies worried him. Would Talia be teased or, worse, shunned?

Otherwise, the book felt foreign. Talia had mostly lived in the heterosexual world and, as such, had minimal exposure to women who identified as lesbians or dykes – Estelle, and now Teddy, excepted. Perhaps if Feinberg's Jess discovered he was a gay trans man, Talia would have had a gender Eureka moment, and I could have been rebirthed earlier. But, alas, it was not to be. Not yet.

"Do you want to go by *zie*?" Talia asked.

"Not now, but maybe one day," Teddy said, and Talia didn't push this issue any further.

"Where to?" the taxi driver asked.

This was Talia's first time in San Francisco, but instead of opting for a blockbuster attraction, like the Painted Ladies or the Golden Gate Bridge, she said, "Anywhere in the Castro."

"Here okay?" The man asked, slowing down by the Castro Theatre, an early '20s historical landmark with a Spanish Colonial Revival facade.

"Perfect," Talia said. It wasn't a nicety or hyperbole. She fell in love with Gay Mecca's queerest neighbourhood at first sight. Its colourful Victorian houses were adorned with rainbow flags and gaggles of men were strutting their stuff on the sidewalks in tight-fitting clothes. How could she not have?

What if she choked on the interview? Never got to explore finding herself, the way only this city could offer? The stakes had become higher than ever.

A beer sounded good, but the barhopping options made Talia's head spin – Daddy's? Midnight Sun? Moby Dick? (The double entendre would have amused Melville.) Peeking in, she saw seas of men, some with their hands down each other's pants. Was this a place she'd be welcome?

Dazed, Talia settled on Does Your Mother Know, a touristy store selling a hodgepodge of souvenirs, sex toys, T-shirts printed with sayings like, "Sounds gay, I'm in", and rainbow-coloured knickknacks. She was a tourist, why pretend otherwise?

Behind the counter, on a shelf, was a Barbie dressed in a dominatrix outfit, holding a tiny but mean-looking whip. "Isn't she fabulous, darling?" The shopkeeper asked in a sing-song voice. "A local guy makes these petite leather outfits."

"Subversive Barbie? That's an omen I belong here," Talia said.

San Francisco State University lay southwest of the city, near the San Francisco Zoo and Fort Funston.

Talia arrived on the main green just as the early morning classes were letting out, and hordes of students swarmed the campus, scurrying to their next destination. In stark contrast to Williams' muted homogeneity, San Francisco State University's diversity was intoxicating – an eclectic mix of ages, ethnicities, body shapes and gender presentations.

The Amazonian, blue-haired barista at the Cesar Chavez Student Center had a T-shirt with "genderfluid" printed on it. Talia couldn't wait to tell Teddy about that.

Over-caffeinated, she marched into the Psychology building's largest lecture hall, having rehearsed her stereotype threat talk so many times she knew it by heart. Professor Jones, the Chair of the Search Committee, was already there, waiting for her. "Not the fanciest of rooms; we're a state school, after all," he said, balding and fidgety.

"I like it here," Talia said. Was she already failing an unnamable test? True, the chairs were a bit shabby, but the walls were recently painted white and the projection system seemed adequate.

"I'll be blunt. Many of my colleagues favour you for the job, and I'm the one holding out."

"May I ask why?"

"If we extended you an offer, I bet you'd turn around and use it as leverage to get a promotion at Williams." The man was avoiding eye contact. "I don't see why you'd leave an elite private school to come here. We've been burned like this before."

"The best students I've mentored at Yale, Brown and Williams came from non-traditional academic backgrounds," Talia said, trying to catch Professor Jones' gaze. She hoped he'd ask why, but he muttered, "Right," whatever that meant.

At this point, faculty and students streamed in, and within minutes, the room was teaming with life. All these people were here to see her! Better push the conversation with Professor Jones out of her mind; she was here for a reason.

On a hunch, she started the presentation by sharing a slide with a photo of an eight-year-old Talia and Grandma

Rivka. "This is my grandmother, who only had an elementary school education and was the wisest and kindest person I've known. And this is little me. I was never expected to pursue a university degree, much less obtain a PhD and become a professor." Students nodded. After all, most were the first in their families to go to college.

Judging by the numerous questions Talia received, her talk was well received. And if that wasn't affirming enough, a line of people waited to speak with her afterwards.

On the long plane ride back to Massachusetts, Talia replayed the incident with Professor Jones in her head. Had she shown enough enthusiasm? Or had the Ivy League's aloofness somehow rubbed off on her? At Yale, Brown and Williams, she had to prove she was worthy of the elite; at SF State – that she wasn't an elitist.

A week after she returned to the Northeast, the Dean called with a job offer. "We're no Yale, Brown or Williams," he said, warning that Talia's salary would be lower, her lab space smaller and there'd be no paid research assistants.

"Thank you, I'm honoured to accept," Talia said. She put down the phone and broke into a happy dance, cheered on by Tukey's squawking and Eli's woof, woof, woofing. Was she really moving to San Francisco? It wasn't a dream, right?

Instinctively, she called Kiefer. "I have big news to share."

"You got the job?"

"I did!"

"Congrats, that's great!"

"There's still plenty of time before I leave, and you can always visit me in San Francisco." Was Kiefer silent or did the line go cold? "You still with me?"

"I don't think I can do this anymore," he mumbled.

"You're falling in love with this woman?"

"I am."

"I'm happy for you," Talia said. It hurt but she meant it.

The rest of Talia's Yale and Brown friends were less than supportive about her new job. "Why are you throwing your career away?" Miriam asked. She had stopped by for an impromptu coffee on her way to the chi-chi Kripalu Center for Yoga and Health in nearby Stockbridge.

"What are you talking about?" Talia protested.

Miriam removed her large Hollywoodian shades. The specks in her eyes were *Saba* Simcha green, a reminder of what moons ago had been home. "Let's not pretend you're not downgrading."

"Alright, let me ask you this – what do you think is a successful career for someone like me?" Talia's tone had an edge.

"That's easy. Doing what you love, research and teaching, at a university with exceptional students and the highest standards for intellectual rigour."

"And by intellectual rigour, you mean what?" Talia was channelling, in part, Professor Sternberg's teachings. "Educated language can be taught. But let's face it, psychology needs insights from people with rich lived experiences, emotional maturity and grit. Those who ask authentic versus look-at-how-smart-I-am questions, who desire, dare I say it, to make social change." Damn, that came out as a sermon.

"Whoa, are you saying—"

"Yes," Talia cut Miriam off. "With some exceptions, faculty and students at elite institutions hold onto their smart cards so tightly they become self-immersed, one-trick ponies."

"I'm a Dweck fan, so believe me, I get it." Miriam dipped

a freshly made shortbread cookie into her pour-over coffee and took a bite. She had a hedonic side and usually made sounds while consuming baked goods, but not this time. "But as someone who grew up wealthy and being told how brilliant I was, it's hard not to feel defensive."

"My dear friend," Talia touched Miriam's shoulder. "I didn't mean to insult you, but your attitude towards San Francisco State University is biased and condescending."

Miriam laughed. "I could always count on your honesty." She took another bite of coffee-soaked shortbread, sighing this time. "So, let's start again. Tell me what excites you about this position."

"As corny as it sounds, I want to make a difference in communities that society neglects. Besides, it's a win-win. My intuition is that once San Francisco State students learn to translate 'academese' into accessible English, some will surpass the most talented Yale, Brown and Williams students."

"I love your optimism, and hey, San Francisco itself has a lot to offer."

"Yup. It's an ideal place for reinvention."

Miriam put her hand on Talia's shoulder. "An existential crisis? Is that what's going on with you?"

"Well, I need to grow up, and sheltered places like Williams aren't good for that. I hate to admit this, but I didn't mature much during my marriage. Henry was a father figure."

Miriam smiled. "More like a Jewish Mama."

"Well speaking of, guess who's coming to town soon and bringing Dad with her?"

"Your mom and dad are arriving on the scene?"

"Yup, they insisted on helping me pack up and move across the country."

"Say a warm hello from me." Miriam put her shades back on. "I hate that you're moving all the way to the West Coast. I'm going to miss the hell out of you."

"Ditto," Talia said, and the two friends held each other like only chosen family can.

Mom and Dad arrived in Williamstown a month before Talia was slated to leave. "We know you're busy, so don't worry about showing us a good time," Dad said. Our parents had a full agenda: taking day trips in nearby leafy Vermont, assisting Talia with packing and other moving logistics, and flying to San Francisco to help her settle in.

Talia didn't need Mom and Dad's help, but it was kind of them to have offered. Dad was 76 and in top shape, but at 69, Mom's body had become feeble. Still, she refused to acknowledge any signs of what would later be diagnosed as Parkinson's.

"Let's have a garage sale." Mom's voice trembled with excitement. She had learned about this tradition from watching American TV shows and thought it exotic.

Her idea proved brilliant. People came in droves and everyone, including Dad, had a blast. Instead of retiring to the guest bedroom in his usual introverted style, Dad was tickled when potential buyers seemed to fancy . . . anything. "For you, no money. Enjoy!" he said to anyone and everyone. When people begged to pay, he relented. "Okay, for you, a quarter."

A lamp was a quarter, a stack of books was a quarter, and even the washing machine was a quarter. It was the only garage sale Talia had been to where people insisted on haggling up. Over the course of five hours, everything went, including the stuffed gorilla Henry had gifted Talia on her 30th birthday.

Starving, the trio spent their modest earnings at Friendly's Diner, gobbling tuna melts with french fries and downing them with thick, creamy milkshakes.

"What's happening with the dog and parrot?" Mom asked.

"You mean your grandkids, Eli and Tukey?"

"Jeez, I'll never understand why you and Henry didn't have—" Mom started saying, but Dad shushed her.

"I'm taking Eli with me to San Francisco and Tukey will stay here with a park ranger who has other parrots Tukey can bond with."

"Does that make you sad, *chabibti*?" Dad asked. Like Talia, he loved pets.

"What fuss; it's just a bird," Mom said, but before Talia had a chance to respond, Teddy arrived at their table.

"May I join?" Teddy asked.

"I thought you said a female friend was coming," Mom whispered in Hebrew.

"Correct," Talia hissed in our mother tongue, then switched to English. "Mom and Dad, meet Teddy."

"Nice to meet you," Teddy said, looking dapper in a blue button-down over a white T-shirt. "So, Mrs and Mr Ben-Zeev, how are you finding Williamstown?"

"You girl or boy?" Mom asked.

Talia clutched her forehead. "Sorry, Teddy."

"I get asked that a lot, Mrs Ben-Zeev, especially by little kids. Some days I'm a masculine woman, other days, I'm just me."

The hush that followed made Talia squirm, but Teddy seemed unaffected. "I'm curious, what was Talia like as a kid?"

"A tomboy. When Talia was three, I told my wife that instead of having a girl, we ended up with a third boy."

"A tomboy, really? I would have never guessed." Teddy's smile was as wide as Dad's.

It was an icy-cold spring. While the rest of Massachusetts' snow had already thawed, being high up at the tip of the Berkshires, where Massachusetts meets New York State meets Vermont, meant some icicles didn't defrost until May. Talia would miss the beauty of the mountains, but not the chill or isolation. She'd also miss her students — these clean-cut kiddos had been growing on her.

On the last day of her Controversial Topics in Psychology seminar, Talia entered an empty classroom and looked around in disbelief. Where were her students? When the clock struck ten minutes after class was supposed to start and no one had shown up, Talia felt a wave of panic. Had they abandoned her? Was this a goodbye and good riddance?

"Surprise!" students yelled, waltzing in, one by one, as though on an '80s Milan runway. They were dressed like mini-Talias, even the guys, in animal prints, bright colours, platform shoes and leather.

"Where did you find this kind of stuff in Williamstown? A store called Mirror Land?" Talia roared with delight. "You guys, this is the best gift ever."

"We're not done," a woman wearing a pink wig said. "This is a small token of our appreciation, Professor." She handed Talia a flower bouquet and a thank you card shaped like a motorcycle jacket. *Thank you for challenging us to relish our mistakes. Striving for so-called perfection is a life of fragility.*

"Thank you for being you," Talia said. Perhaps she could have offered something more original or profound, but her heart was too full.

"Flowers?" Teddy had been waiting in the quad,

kitty-corner to the classroom. "Do you have an admirer I should know about?"

"I will miss you terribly," Talia said, holding Teddy close.

It's excruciating to say goodbye to those we love, even when parting ways is right. But I admit – I haven't thought of Teddy much over the years. She was tied to a time and place, unlike rare and enduring connections that seem to transcend those. And, yes, I could Google Teddy now, perhaps even email her (them? him?); Remember that straight femme professor in Williamstown with the pitbull and parrot who had a massive crush on you back in the day? I'd rather continue to centre Talia's story, though, as I've almost arrived at its end.

Having packed up Talia's apartment, the trio spent their last night in Williamstown in a hotel suite. While Mom skimmed *Soap Opera Digest* and Talia gun glued tiger-print fabric on black sneakers, Dad boiled a Frankensteinian tea blend from his newly acquired collection of natural medicinals.

"Would either of you lovely ladies fancy a cup of tea?" It was generous of Dad to offer, but the smell was less than appealing.

"Is Teddy a mistake of nature?" Mom blurted out, the magazine covering half her face.

"What did you say?" Talia had been hyper-focused on her fashion misadventure, and Mom's left-field question made her jump and mess up her creation.

"I mean, I could've sworn she was a man. There's nothing normal about that. Unnatural, even, if you ask me," Mom said.

Nobody's asking you was about to roll off Talia's tongue, but she thought better of it. Instead, she rubbed her cheek with sticky fingers, trying to ease the pain surging through her jaw. "Was Einstein a mistake of nature? He wasn't normal either."

Mom contorted her mouth into an ugly smirk, an expression more like the siren of war than a drill.

"My Rina," Dad called out in time to nip the attack. "You love tulips, right? Isn't the tiger tulip your favourite flower?"

"Yes." Mom's tone had a hint of suspicion. "They're blooming right now in Haifa, on the Carmel."

"It's a rare flower, right?"

"Correct."

"Then why isn't Teddy a rare flower, a tiger tulip, say? Not something defective, but a natural marvel."

How had Dad come up with this enlightened gem?

Talia vowed to remember our father's wisdom and kindness, to use them as antidotes to difficult times. She didn't know it yet, but she was ready to mature into the rare flower he was meant to become. Avi. Me.

3.

Synthesis

Transition: The Following Five Years

(San Francisco, California, 2009–2014)

12

BLAST FROM THE PAST[6]

Yes, I know – I shouldn't drive and talk on my phone at the same time. It's just that my phone's been barking, and the mystery caller refuses to give up.

"Hello?" I cave to the temptation.

"Avi?" a familiar voice asks.

"Who is this?"

"It is me, Giovanni."

"Giovanni, Giovanni, from Milano?" My voice cracks like a teenage boy's.

"But, certainly, it is me."

The car engine growls as I take Portola Drive's sharp, windy turns, heading towards the Castro. The panoramic view of Twin Peaks rushes by in a flurry.

"Hello, you still with me?" Giovanni's voice comes from far away. Damn, somehow the phone got wedged in the crack between the driver's seat and the cup holder.

I slalom downhill, my left hand barely holding onto the steering wheel, the right trying to dislodge the blasted phone.

"Hello?" Giovanni yells from the abyss. "Hello, Avi. Are you still there?"

I pass the Harvey Milk Plaza with its 30-by-20 foot, iconic rainbow flag. Success! I put the phone to my ear.

"I have so many questions," I say.

"Dinner tonight? My place?"

"Are you kidding me?"

"I've been in San Francisco for three months now."

I slam on the brakes, defying a yellow *No Stopping* sign-post. My past has come crashing into the present. I need a moment.

Giovanni opens the door, looking like his father – a bear-ish, middle-aged professor with white-grey streaks in his thick, curly hair. His clothing is unassuming, but his round tortoiseshell glasses have that unmistakable, chic Italian flair.

We exchange two light cheek kisses, one on each side, our lips not quite touching each other's skin.

"You smell exactly the same," he says.

What is he talking about? Six years into gender transi-tion, my scent has changed dramatically with testosterone, and, anyway, what is he doing in San Francisco?

By local standards, his apartment is enormous, the design out of Italian *Vogue* – clean, modern lines in black, grey-brown and white shades. A Le Corbusier leather lounge chair is positioned by the fireplace, just so. An invitation to recline and devour one of the multitudes of books lining the floor-to-ceiling bookshelves? Or a state-ment piece to rarely, if ever, use?

"Follow me, please." Giovanni sprints across the spacious dining room, passing an antique table that could comfortably seat eight, and into a white kitchen.

Simmering on the stovetop is a reddish-orange risotto a la Milanese, filling the room with a sweet saffron aroma.

Images from a different lifetime – Milan in the mid '80s – bubble to my mind's surface, vivid and haunting. Impossibly tall and emaciated fashion models wearing over-the-top '80s clothing. Gay men, skin-and-bones, ravished by red, brown and purple tumour-like clumps. Giovanni – boyish, pretentious and charming. Our fateful meeting on a bus. I can taste it, the freedom to be so young and adrift that there's nothing to lose.

Dinner time, and Giovanni's transformed the dining room into a fancy *ristorante*, with white linen and fine china. The spread of appetisers is dizzying – prosciutto with melon, bites of grilled bread topped with pâté, and thinly cut marinated slices of zucchini, eggplant and red peppers.

"Thank you for the wine and the company. Salute," Giovanni raises a glass of barolo. I had purchased this bottle in 1987, twenty-three years ago and a few days after telling Giovanni I had chosen Henry, that ours was a final goodbye.

"To life." I clink my glass to his. The wine has aged superbly, hitting my taste buds with licorice, chocolate and leather explosions.

"Eat, *mangia*, or should I say *be'teavon*? We can speak in English, Italian or Hebrew, whatever language you choose," he says.

Hebrew? Could this night get more surreal? "Let's stick with English," I say. English doesn't have as many misgendering pitfalls. Why risk ruining this reunion before it begins? "Wait, how on earth do you speak Hebrew?"

"I will save that very long story for later."

"At the very least, tell me what brings you to San Francisco."

"But surely your life is more interesting than mine." He takes a sip of wine. "I thought you would have become an artist, but a psychology professor?"

"Henry encouraged me to go to university; the rest is history." Am I imagining it, or has Giovanni winced at Henry's name?

"And you tied the knot, as you say?"

"We did."

"But when we met, you did not believe in marriage."

"It's more accurate to say I didn't consider marriage romantic."

"So why the wedding?"

"Henry was the closest I felt to having a home, even though—" I stop mid-sentence. What am I doing? This conversation has turned into a one-sided confessional. "How about we shift to a different topic? We have so many things to catch up on."

"But, certainly."

"What do you do for a living?" it's high time he shares something. Anything.

"I, too, am an academic."

"Music-related? You used to be a huge opera fan."

"Good guess, but no, my Ph.D. is in Jewish Studies."

"Fascinating. What's your specialty?"

"Modern Jewish identity."

"Ah, so, you've learned Hebrew as part of your scholarship?"

"*Nachon aval lo rak bizchoot ze*," Giovanni says in perfect Hebrew and with a passing Israeli accent.

"So, you've lived in Israel?" I ask.

"I confess to having read some of your publications," Giovanni pivots again. "Did marrying Henry protect you from stereotype threat?"

I cover my mouth with a napkin and cough out a piece of courgette. Granted, it's not an elegant operation, but I try my best to be polite. "What do you mean?"

"Henry was *un prince charmant sur son cheval blanc*."

I don't speak French, but I'm pretty sure I can decipher the meaning. "I don't like where this conversation is going."

"My deep apologies; I do not mean to offend." Giovanni runs his fingers through his thick hair. "Remember that night when my father caught us having sex?"

"Of course. It was mortifying." I take another sip, a burn spreading across my face. "When your dad switched the lights on, I felt terribly exposed."

"You were the most captivating woman I had ever met."

"You mean Talia was." Giovanni makes a face, but I push on, "She was a fabulous drag queen, and I had fun dressing her in kooky '80s fashion, but it's such a relief to be me."

Giovanni looks me up and down. "So now, you're playing dress-up with your father's clothes."

"What a cruel thing to say." My tongue is tingling from salt and vinegar. I can barely taste the barolo.

"Please excuse me. I meant it as a joke."

"This reunion was a mistake," I say, getting up.

"Please do not go." Giovanni downs the rest of his wine in one gulp. "It will kill me."

"What do you want from me?"

"To reconnect." He presses his palms together in front of his chest. "Please, forgive me. It is hard to let Talia go." Giovanni gushes about her as though it's her wake. Was she really like that, the way he remembers? Has my memory changed her beyond recognition? And, yes, his put-down is still raw, but an apology goes a long way, and there's something in my gut telling me to sit down, see this through.

223

"You still haven't told me what you're doing in San Francisco."

"But it is time for risotto." Giovanni heaps a large serving on my plate, but as I reach for my fork, he gestures, no. "First this," he says and opens a bottle of a crisp California chardonnay.

Should I surrender myself to Giovanni's elaborate eulogy, or whatever this is, and brush off the ache in my stomach? I'm envious of how much he seems to remember about Talia, how much he liked her. Will seeing her from his viewpoint help me connect with my past, or will it distort her even more?

The room is too warm, or maybe it's the second bottle of wine. I should ask Giovanni to open a window, but whatever.

"This is my favourite spot," he says. We sit cross-legged on the shaggy carpet, the fireplace adding a glow to Giovanni's cheeks. "May I offer you port and dark chocolate truffles?"

"Thank you, but I can't have another bite," I say, tapping my belly.

Giovanni stretches out on the rug. "I want to make love to you. Properly, this time, to make up for having been such a horrible lover."

I feel a laugh coming on like a viral cough on a crowded train – convulsions in my belly that threaten to erupt into my throat. There's only one trick that stops the madness. I think of the holocaust – withered Jews in black-and-white stripes. Blame Mrs Hamorah for schooling us Israeli kids on how to use this macabre last-resort measure against impending social inappropriateness.

It doesn't work this time. A chuckle turns into a titter, a titter into a giggle, a giggle into a chortle, a chortle into a cackle, a cackle into a belly laugh, the belly laugh combusts into sputtering hysteria. I'm on my back, snorting.

"What is wrong with you?" Giovanni yells.

"With me? You're the one who waltzed into my life after all these years, being so mysterious and dramatic. You haven't shared anything about what you're doing here. *Niente.*"

"You left me. I do not owe you anything," he shouts.

"That was decades ago. We were kids."

"It was the biggest trauma of my life."

Talia's ghost is dancing in the fire's flames, casting shadows on our bodies. I take off my shirt, exposing the surgery scars under my pecs. They've become faint, almost invisible in this dim lighting.

"Feel my scars." I take Giovanni's hand and place it on my chest.

"You are beautiful," he says, tracing his delicate fingers under my pecs.

We hug, our bare chests touching in perfect alignment. Is this what it would have felt like if Talia's breasts weren't in the way? If I had met him then as me?

"I'm sorry for laughing. I'm not sure what came over me. It's—"

"It is okay. I understand." Giovanni slides onto his back and motions for me to lay on top.

I straddle Giovanni and cup his cheeks with my palms. Looking into his eyes, I slide my hands down his face and contract them into a light chokehold on his throat. He lets out a gasp, his dick protruding from the fine linen, pushing against my groin.

"You make me crazy," he mumbles.

I grind myself against him and reach to unbutton his pants.

"No, wait," Giovanni says, pushing my hand away. "I want to make you come."

I don't like the rush, but I recognise the look on his face, the longing. In a different lifetime, we cried our young hearts out, desperate for salvation. Giovanni, from the roaring AIDS epidemic that killed his first boyfriend. Me, from the dire consequences of having refused to serve in the Israel Defense Forces – forever homeless.

"Sit on my face. I beg of you," Giovanni urges and I relent.

He keeps moaning as he blows me, alternating between flicking his tongue up and down my dick's shaft and sticking it inside my front hole, until my body erupts into a rhythm of contractions.

"Did I redeem myself?" Giovanni asks.

Gasping for breath, I reach for his erection.

He flashes his palm. "No, I am okay."

"Espresso?" The alcohol has worn off; the fire reduced to embers.

I wait till Giovanni's out of sight to put my clothes back on. Before I can even begin to process what's happened, he reappears with a small cup that packs a big punch.

"I kept abreast of your whereabouts for the past fifteen years. It was not always easy," he says.

"Why didn't you reach out?" The bitter roast burns the roof of my mouth.

"You had your life with Henry, and I was already with someone else when I found out about your divorce."

"A man?"

"No, a Jewish-American woman. I met her in Israel, in the *ulpan* where I had been studying Hebrew."

"In Israel? How surreal."

226

"I wanted to learn Hebrew there, to get closer to my Jewish roots."

"So, what happened with the Jewish-American woman?"

"I married her."

I let this information sink in. "Does she know?

"Know?—"

"About me coming over tonight?"

"No, she does not."

"You're monogamous?"

"Yes, but—"

"You just cheated."

"It does not count."

"Because you didn't let me touch your cock? Because you didn't come?"

"Because you were my true love, the one who got away."

"You mean, Talia?"

"No, I mean, you."

Yawning, eyes sticky, I reach for my phone and blink. So, I've slept for five hours and change? Not as bad as I feared.

Jon emailed back. I can see you at noon. The note I had sent him last night asking for an emergency therapy session is a cruel reality check. Did I really have sex with Giovanni? Not a dream, right? In the sober light of day, there's some reckoning to do. But first, coffee.

"So, Giovanni from Milan?" Jon's wearing his famous black leather jacket. His stare is intense. Shouldn't I be used to it by now?

"Yup, in some mysterious twist of fate, he's materialised in San Francisco speaking fluent Hebrew." I spill all the details about last night's experience ending with the big reveal about Giovanni's cheating.

"And?" Jon looks unimpressed.

"What do you mean, and?"

"What's the problem?"

"I can't believe you're asking me that. Giovanni betrayed his wife."

"True, but we're not here to talk about him. So, let's try again — what's so urgent you needed to see me today?"

It's hard looking in Jon's mirror, even though that's what I'm here for. "I betrayed myself. I should have left after he ridiculed me, and I definitely should not have had sex with him."

"So, why did you?"

"I'm not sure."

"Alright, let's take it one step at a time. What kept you from leaving after he insulted you about dressing up in your dad's clothing?"

"He remembered vivid details about Talia, way more than I did."

"So, you wanted to learn more about Talia?"

"Yes, that was part of it, I think, but mostly, I wanted closure. When Giovanni and I met, he had only been with men. I was his first woman. How frickin' ironic is that?"

"Now we're getting somewhere," Jon says.

"So, I guess I wanted to come full circle, have sex as two men, the way it should have been back in the day."

"And did Giovanni see you as a man during sex?"

"I don't think so. He was too busy making love to Talia."

"Ah," Jon says in universal therapist speak and jots stuff on his pad.

"While I was trying to rewrite the past — force homoeroticism on what we shared in Italy and for what? A contrived continuity? A more coherent narrative? — Giovanni was holding onto his incipient bisexuality for dear life." Has Jon's statue of the goddess Tara always been

228

this red? "Humbling, but what I'm really furious about is that he didn't just violate his wife's trust; he robbed me of making an informed, consensual decision, and now I'm complicit in his lying."

★

When Talia – I mean, when I – was sixteen years old, I spotted Dad at a public phone booth late one night, and for a moment, our eyes locked. Our home phone turned out to be in perfect working order, so I chose a romanticised explanation for Dad's behaviour. He must be a Mossad agent, a spy. It was a story my brothers had made up about our father, and maybe, just maybe, they were right.

Israel Ben-Zeev managed to get himself through high school despite growing up in abject poverty with a drunk Peruvian dad who had left him at the tender age of fourteen to become the "the man" of the family. Dad was charming in a quiet, unobtrusive way and spoke multiple languages. He was often out of town and country – a perfect profile of a would-be-spy.

Dad's alleged secret life would have also explained his intentional psychological distancing from us kids – his philosophy of not getting too close to anybody and always being prepared for the worst.

I confronted him once about never asking how I was doing. "You could've been the neighbour's dad," I said. Dad responded that Mom had kept him informed about everything that went on with us kids. As such, there was no need to talk. Surely, I could understand that.

A few days after the telephone booth sighting, Dad asked to speak in private. "Let's go to a restaurant in Tel Aviv," he offered.

"Anything but Italian." I loved this cuisine, but I was

craving a new culinary adventure. Dining out was an unusual proposition back then. I'd never eaten out with Dad's side of the family. But, on Mom's side, we frequented a restaurant once a year to celebrate Grandpa Simcha's birthday. It was always the same Italian restaurant in Tel Aviv, year after year, and Grandpa Simcha ordered the same dish, spaghetti Bolognese.

"This isn't going to be easy, but I have something to ask you," Dad said.

"Does Mom know about our dinner?" It was the first time I had tasted sushi and my tongue was tangy.

"No, and let's keep it that way." Dad had never sounded this stern. "So, the phone booth you saw me at that night? I was talking to my secretary, Sarah. We've been—" He took a gulp of water, "—romantic for two years now." Dad looked somewhere to his right, as though he was choosing his words carefully. "I know it's wrong, but please understand, your mother is frigid."

I chased the raw fish with sake. Sarah with the gross body odour? Stinking ashtray mouth, Sarah?

"Boy, does it feel good to get this off my chest." Dad heaved a loud sigh. "Listen, it'd be better for everyone if you didn't mention the phone booth or this conversation."

"How can you do this to Mom?" I asked when what I should have said was, *How can you do this to me? How dare you? I'm not the person that should be hearing this.*

And, no, I didn't tell Mom about Dad's affair. Instead, I turned my anger inwards and hated myself for becoming complicit in his deception.

Has protecting Mom with my silence (have I?) been worth the permanent barrier it has erected between us? And how do I reconcile my two fathers – the open-hearted, gentle version who fought to welcome me back into the family, with Gershon's son, who betrayed Mom and forever changed my relationship with her?

Now, Dad is struggling with dementia and Mom is frail with worry and Parkinson's. That ship has sailed, but should I tell Giovanni's wife what happened?

What's the right thing to do?

★

I don't usually find myself at a Purim warehouse party or any Jewish event, but my date suggested this venue for our first hangout, and I said yes. David has an endearing geekiness about him, a vibe I'm choosing to trust. Besides, maybe it's time I gave another Jewish-American man a chance.

An hour in, I spot them across the room, Giovanni and a thin, curly-haired woman. He waves hello, and queasy, I wave back. The evening won't be completely ruined if we make sure to avoid crossing paths. It shouldn't be too hard. This venue is large and busy enough for such an unspoken arrangement to work.

Giovanni doesn't cooperate. He grabs the woman's hand and barrels his way towards us.

"Friends of yours?" David whispers.

"He's somebody I used to know," I mumble. How gross to subject a man I'm on a first date with to who knows what's coming.

"Avi, meet my wife, Raquel," Giovanni says.

She's pretty in an affluent, yoga, *namaste* kind of way, her handshake firm for someone so petite. "How do you and Giovanni know each other?" she asks.

"Avi is an academic colleague." There's no hint of hesitation in Giovanni's voice.

"Wonderful. You should come over to dinner sometime. My hubby is famous for his *risotto a la Milanese*."

I had a taste, I almost say, but hold back. As tempting as it is, it would be unfair to ambush this woman with news of her husband's cheating and cause a scene.

"This is David," I introduce my date.

"David, the second king of Israel?" Giovanni exclaims. His wife and I roll our eyes in a moment of unexpected bonding, but David is a good sport. "My mom chose this name for its Hebrew origin, beloved."

"So, let me guess, you are a doctor or lawyer."

"A doctor."

Giovanni opens his mouth, but Raquel intercedes. "Don't," she says, smacking him on the arm.

"You know me too well, *carissima*. I cannot resist making jokes, especially in such charming company."

"It was a pleasure meeting you, but please excuse us; we need to get back to our friends," Raquel says, as though she's read my mind.

"Is it me, or was something off with those two?" David asks when the duo is out of earshot.

"Yup, something was off, alright."

The rest of the night is pleasant enough. David and I play Hit the Hamantasch and take photobooth pics using Purim props, play-fighting over Esther's crown. But it's hard to relax with Giovanni hovering about. Seeing him dance with Raquel makes me sick to my stomach. I hate how he plays her for a fool.

"You seem preoccupied. Tell me," David says.

"Dating terrifies me, you know, this whole trusting-my-heart-to-a-man business."

"Same here, but what's the alternative?"

"You're right, I needed to hear that."

"Happy Purim!" David raises his glass.

"Happy Purim, handsome!" I clink my wine with his club soda. "*L'chaim.*"

I won't let Giovanni ruin what's left of the evening. And, no, I'm not going to tell his wife anything. It's their business, not mine.

"So, the good doctor is your new boyfriend?" Giovanni asks over the phone.

"Did you get some kind of sick pleasure in introducing me to your wife?" And what is he doing calling me, anyway? "Wait, don't answer. I don't want to know, and I thought I made it clear – I don't want any contact with you."

"If that is your true wish, I will have to accept it, but I have one last question, if I may."

"And you'll leave me alone?"

"*Te lo prometto.*"

"Go on then."

"You and I were in love, yes? So why choose Henry and not me?"

"Choice? This word is loaded with privilege."

"I do not understand."

"Goodbye," I say, touching into a new kind of freedom Talia never dreamed she'd have – not having to explain yourself, defend, or pacify. Fuck that.

13

IT'S YOU, IT'S NOT ME![6]

"Sorry, what?" I can't make out what David's been trying to say.

We're at Gracias Madre, a vegan Mexican restaurant in the Mission, sitting at a communal table squeezed between San Francisco hipsters. The salsa music blaring from the restaurant speakers is deafening, and our table mates are laughing their lungs out and pantomiming with long, slender arms.

I'd suggest we cut our losses and head over to Taqueria Vallarta — it's quieter, and the meat options are to die for — but David's vegan, and besides, it was his idea to meet up here.

Cupping my ear? Not sexy, but it'll work for now. And truth be told, the Portobello mushroom fajitas aren't too bad.

"Amazing food, right?" David asks as we step out into Mission Street. At 5'5", he's shorter than me, which is nice for a change.

It's our third date. Should I lean in for a kiss? This

stretch of the Mission neighbourhood might not be the most romantic of settings, though. It reeks from urine and ammonia.

Fuck it, he's too cute!

"Wait." David takes off his glasses and wipes them on his sleeve. "There's something I need to disclose first."

"Go on." If he has HIV, it's a non-issue. There's been hype around a soon-to-be-released treatment for preventing HIV infection, PrEP or something like that, and besides I'm okay using condoms.

"I'm in recovery. I got my second-year AA chip today," David says.

"Congrats!" He's only been drinking soft drinks so far, so I had a hunch, and, anyway, I've dated sober guys before.

"The thorny issue is that I've never had sex sober."

"Ah," is all I can muster.

"Well, here's the deal. My sponsor wants me to wait to have sex. Date a guy for at least a month, maybe two, before doing anything physical."

"An old-world courtship sounds refreshing." I hear the words topple off my tongue when what I should say is that I need time to think about this. How can I trust that David will be into my body, or for that matter, I'd be into his? Erotic chemistry isn't intellectual; it's a sacred animal body thing, an integral part of embodied romantic exploration.

"Great, I realise it's a few weeks from now, but how about joining me for a sober Passover Seder?" David asks.

"Thanks, the thing is—"

"You're not into the sober part?"

"I'm not into the Passover part." It's one thing to go to a random Purim party, a whole other thing to commit to celebrating Jewish holidays.

"Don't worry. We're low-key queers reading from a

235

feminist *Haggadah* and eating yummy vegan food. Nothing too religious, I promise."

It's my first sober vegan feminist Passover Seder, and so far, I'm digging it. We yell out the name of each plague, dip our index fingers in grape juice, then sprinkle a drop on the tablecloth. Shouting out victimhood brings back childhood memories, but the grape juice lacks a certain edge.

When I was a kid, we flicked red wine on white linen. "Blood, frogs, insects, wild animals, pestilence, boils, hail, locust, darkness and the death of the first-born son." Ten flicks apiece and the white tablecloth got splattered with blood-red spots. Now, that's more like it.

David's friends delight in my Israeli accent. "Read some more from the *Haggadah*," they say. I'm the exotic pet for the night, representing who exactly? The people I betrayed and ran far, far away from?

"Happy to read some more, but please don't ask me to open the door for Elijah."

"Not a fan of the prophet?" David asks.

"More like Passover PTSD. When I was six, I was tasked with opening the door for Elijah's ghost. I was terrified of ghosts, so, I only half-opened the door, expecting a translucent Elijah to slip through the crack and gently graze against my skin," I close my eyes and whisper, "It was horrible, just horrible."

David chortles. "What happened?"

"A flesh-and-blood monster came bounding through the crack! I screamed and hid under the table. The ghoul cackled and took off his blood-curdling face. It was my beloved older brother, Noam. And that betrayal of trust, my friends, was the end of innocence."

Who would have thought I'd enjoy an American

Passover? I hated celebrating this holiday (or any holiday, really) with Henry's family. They were Jewish; Passover's gist was the same, so why did theirs feel so foreign? To add insult to injury, Henry's folks would end the dinner with the traditional blessing, "Next year in Jerusalem". They were comfortable in Manhattan. Why pretend otherwise?

"My friends loved you," David says as we head out into the crisp San Francisco night.

"They're delightful. I haven't felt this connected with fellow heebs for a long time."

"I'm in love with you," David exclaims without warning.

Run, a voice in my head yells. Is that Elijah's prophetic whispering or my fear of intimacy masquerading as wisdom?

"It's okay; you don't have to say it back, but would you do me the great honour of joining me for the opening night of *Uncovered, The Diary Project*, this weekend?"

"You kidding? How did you score these tickets?"

"I've been a Sean Dorsey Dance sponsor for a while."

"Thanks, I'd love to go. I've been dying to see *Lou*, Sean's tribute to—"

"Lou Sullivan, I know," David says.

It blows my mind that David supports trans arts and knows gay trans male history. Wow, just, wow. Way too often, my mere existence as a trans man who loves men raises eyebrows. *Why did you transition if you've always liked men?* people ask. It's as though what gender people identify with and who they're attracted to aren't separate things.

I wonder if that question is, at its core, sexist – this idea that as a once-woman, I could "get the guy" and in this way be "normal". If so, this heteronormative logic goes, why would I have opted to change into two abnormal identities?

So, yeah, I love that David doesn't question that we,

gay trans men, exist, and I can't wait to experience Sean's *Uncovered* together. Still, his "I'm in love with you" hangs in the air, sucking its oxygen.

Sean Dorsey and Company are gyrating to spoken excerpts from Lou Sullivan's diaries. ". . . what can become of a girl whose real desire and passion is with male homosexuals? That I want to be one."

Lou's words, Sean's movements, and I'm back to the re-birthing mirror, terrified of being unlovable, but determined to follow my truth. I don't want this performance to end, and when the curtain falls, David and I rise from our seats and clap. "Bravo," we yell at the top of our lungs, "Bravo."

"Hey Avi," a familiar voice says. It's Angel. Of course, he's here! Angel is good friends with Sean Dorsey and Sean's partner, Shawna Virago. Wait, does this also mean that Camilla's around? Whatever. My heart's too full to care.

"Angel, this is David."

"Nice to meet you," David says, reaching his hand to shake Angel's. "I'm embarrassed about bawling my eyes out."

"No need to apologise. Sean gets me every time," Angel says, as sexy and charming as ever. He must have seen the dress rehearsals, lucky man. "Do you guys wanna join us for a bite to eat?" By us, Angel means himself, Sean, Sean's partner Shawna and, of course, Camilla.

Sparky's, the all-night diner in the Castro, is the perfect rendezvous spot. It has vintage '50s Americana décor – neon signs, chrome counters, a checkered floor and even a jukebox.

The six of us – Sean, Shawna, Angel, Camilla, David

and me – are huddled at a corner table, arguing over the word "tranny". Empowering or degrading? It's a complicated issue, and what tickles me isn't any single viewpoint but how different our opinions are. Agreeing to disagree, Shawna raises her milkshake and toasts Lou's legacy. "Hear, hear," we say.

"So, what do you think empowered Lou to come out to himself as a gay man in the '70s with zero role models?" I ask Sean. I can't imagine how Lou did it. Ozzie was Talia's proof that men like us existed. Lou only had himself, and the word "transgender" didn't exist yet.

"Based on his diaries, it was a process that took grit. And I've read somewhere that Lou was inspired by Billy Tipton, you know the—"

"Stealth jazz musician from the '30s?" Camilla cuts Sean off. Of course, she knows all about Billy Tipton.

"Yup, him," Sean says.

"Sorry, stealth?" David chimes in.

"Under the radar," Sean explains. "Billy identified and lived as a man, and no one knew until his death he was trans. My sense is that Lou saw Billy as ancestral: 'our grandfather', I believed he called him."

Angel grins. "We've always existed."

"Amen to that," Shawna raises her milkshake again, only this time it's empty.

"Amen." I clink my glass with hers. The thought that Lou felt he had roots – that our trans identities are transcendent – is comforting. Dad was right. We are rare flowers, not nature's mistake but part of its glorious biopsychosocial diversity.

Still, something's been nagging me. "I love that Lou expressed so much joy in living and loving authentically; that's radical."

"I sense a 'but' coming," Angel says.

"*But* how sad that he felt like he gained gay male credibility by dying from AIDS." In saying this, I realise that to the outside world, we look like a group of three non-trans couples, two straight and one gay – David and me. In reality, I'm the only gay trans guy at the table, the only Lou.

"Lou being denied gender-confirming treatment because he was attracted to men is all kinds of fucked up," Angel says. The way he looks at me is distracting. I'm still attracted to him, but no, I don't want to flash back to fighting, then ravaging each other.

"I can relate to how an HIV diagnosis might feel affirming," I say, refocusing on the present.

"Really?" David looks puzzled.

I share what happened with Sammy less than a year into my transition. "I had to wait two weeks for the RNA test. And, sure, having HIV wouldn't have been as devastating as it was for Lou, but still, it would have sucked." What's left of my chocolate milkshake leaves a sugary taste on my tongue. "I admit, if I had gotten a positive test, a part of me would have felt validated as a gay man. Does that sound ludicrous?"

"No, it makes perfect sense," Angel says.

We debate what belonging means to trans folks who are marginalised within marginalised communities and our freedom to be ourselves. "Thank you for making trans histories visible, Sean Dorsey," Angel says. As though on cue, we all yell our variations on, *yes, thank you, Sean*, and this brilliant, big-hearted artist's dapper smile fills this queer diner with hope.

David walks me to my car, animated despite the late hour.

"As the only cis man in the group, I hope I didn't

embarrass myself. I wasn't sure it was my place to contribute to the Lou Sullivan discussion or t-word debate."

"The what word?"

"Tra—," David stops mid utterance. "Is this a trap?"

"You were great," I say. I wouldn't have been offended if he said "tranny", but his conscientiousness is admirable.

"I love that underneath the cool exterior, you're a bunch of nerds."

What does he mean by this collective use of *you*? "Sean does a shitload of research for his pieces. I guess you could call that nerdy. But Shawna is full-on punk." Whoa, my tone is a bit too biting.

"Sorry. I should have said that you're all very passionate people."

There's that *you* again. "I only know Sean and Shawna through Angel. We're not close friends, so I can't promise more hangouts with them. In any case, I'm a me, not a you."

"You're adorable," David says, as though I'm a puppy in a window. "Come over for a little bit?"

"No sex, right?"

"No sex, but you'll finally see my apartment, even sleep over if you'd like."

Why not? The drive from the Castro to the Outer Richmond will be quick at this time of night and I'm curious to see his place. Not so sure about cuddling, though. I love being physically affectionate, but let's face it – cuddling instead of having sex is weird. It's not a question of pushing David to be sexual when he's not ready. That'd be gross. But I need to decide if I want to bow out and soon.

"Wow, you're really into taxidermy for a vegan." I hope my tone sounds non-judgmental.

"Well, I wasn't into it until I met my AA sponsor." David

takes his shoes off and lines them up with his other foot-wear, like soldiers. "She has them all over her flat."

"The animal skulls, gothic art, faux-fur throws?"

"She's inspired that too."

"What did your place look like before you met her?"

"It was nice. Nothing out of the ordinary, really."

Having adapted to the visual cacophony, I take another look around the room and settle on a relatively muted piece. It's a framed photograph of a dingy alleyway filled with garbage and graffiti. A peculiar detail stands out – someone had left a shiny red vase with a fancy bouquet by the bins – orange and gold roses strewn with grey-blue thistle thorns.

"I was raped on this side street," David says, dabbing his eyes with his fingers. "I have this vague memory of stumbling drunk in the dark trying to find my way home. The next thing I knew, it was morning, and I was face-down in the dirt, my jeans and underwear wrapped around my ankles."

"How horrible," I say, jolted wide awake. "Did you have any recollection of the guy? Of what happened?"

"No, none of that. There was this piercing pain in my rectum, so I guessed what must have happened. But let me tell you, it was quite the shock when my hand got covered in blood and dried sperm."

"I'm so sorry to hear that," I say, stroking his arm. "And the flowers?"

"They're a thank you to my rapist."

"Not sure I get it."

"I wouldn't have got sober if this hadn't happened."

We cuddle on his bed, talk about *Lou* again, and even share a few laughs, but there's a new heaviness in my chest. "I don't know how to say this—"

"Just speak your mind, hon."

242

"It's one thing to be an ally; it's another to have sex with a trans guy. Are you nervous at all about that?" I want the truth. It'd be a relief if David shared concerns about being attracted to my body, not knowing what to do, or whatever's come up for him.

"You're being silly," David says and opens his arms for a hug. I'm not convinced, but I lay on top of him, and we kiss, our bodies pressing against each other.

"Take our shirts off and cuddle?" I ask.

"Sounds great."

Torsos bare, I bury my face in David's neck and kiss his warm skin. "Stop," he yells, shoving me.

I bolt up. "What happened?

David props himself against the headboard. "Sorry, hon, I got triggered. Sobriety and the aftermath of the rape, it's a lot for one person to carry."

I care about what's happened to him, of course I do, but in his sea of hurt, is there space for how I feel? "It's late, so how about I head home?" I want to sound friendly, but I can hear the distance in my tone.

"So, what? Now you're mad at me when I've been nothing but vulnerable with you?"

"Have you been, though?"

"How much more exposed can it get than telling you about being raped?"

I believe he believes that. And I'm moved he trusts me enough to open up about something so personal and painful. But, to me, vulnerability involves reciprocity – sharing something that's hard to talk about while considering its impact on the person one's disclosing to. Otherwise, doesn't it risk becoming a self-centered puking of hurt? But I don't say any of this because my thoughts sound extreme, and I'm not sure if I can trust this rawness.

"What if what triggered you had something to do with my body?" I ask.

"Look, hon, I don't want to fight." David puts his shirt back on. "And I really don't care that you're trans."

"But I want you to care," I say as I gather my things.

On the drive home, I turn my playlist's volume up, up, up, but my brain is louder. I want to be desired, not tolerated, and I'm sick of second-guessing my intuition. Enough is enough.

"I have something exciting to tell you." David pre-empts my breakup call. Apparently, his AA sponsor has given him the green light. "She believes I'm ready to have sex. Isn't that great news?"

I'm ambivalent, at best, but I decide to go for it. Perhaps it's "sunk cost" – having invested so much emotion and effort into this connection already that I don't want to risk regret – or maybe it's that I don't want to be the bad guy. Besides, I should be the first to understand and honour sexual trauma. Didn't I deserve Henry's patience and love? Doesn't David deserve mine?

David suggests a romantic weekend getaway to a rustic cabin in the Russian River, and as advertised, the place turns out to be charming and secluded. It's situated on a quarter-acre of land, with no neighbours in sight. There's a fireplace, a small but well-equipped kitchen, and an outdoor hot tub nestled under the shade of a giant Redwood.

We've brought so much food it could feed a small army. "That's being Jewish, for ya," David says. While he takes over the kitchen prep, I sneak into the bedroom. The king-sized bed is covered by a floral duvet, more retro than sexy den. Will we be having sex in this room tonight? I'm touched that David wants to lose his sober virginity to me, but is he forcing himself to or am I imagining it?

I should get back to David, but even a few minutes of meditation could centre me. *Being present with your thoughts right now will be hell*, the devil on my left shoulder whispers, but a mini-Pema Chödrön on my right tells me to *just fucking do it*, so I do.

I find David undressing by the hot tub. "Hey, hon," he says.

He leaves his clothes in a neat pile on a bright-yellow Adirondack chair. The last thing to go is his glasses. "I'm blind without them," he says and dunks into the steaming, bubbling water.

Thankful that David can't see me too clearly, I throw my clothes on the Adirondack's twin and join him.

We hug, our naked bodies touching for the first time after two months of dating. "It's too hot, hon," David says, his arms falling to his sides. "Sorry, I need a breather," He climbs out and sits on a plastic stool, dripping water on the mowed grass.

Alone in the hot tub, I dip my shoulders into the scorching swirls, begging them to give a little.

"I trim my chest hair," David says as if I can't see that.

"I, on the other hand, am a hairy bear."

"Speaking of bears." He grabs his belly. "How gross is this?"

"Why are you doing this?"

"Doing what? I'm just being real. Have you considered shaving your chest and shoulders?"

I'm flooded by shame and shame about my shame. "I like being hairy. Is that a problem?"

"It might have been before I got sober, but my sponsor keeps telling me that looks aren't important."

"But attraction is, right?"

"I'm sorry if I'm making you uncomfortable. You're handsome, I don't mean to imply otherwise."

"Thanks, but I'm not looking for compliments. I'm attracted to you, and if we're doing this, I'd want you to feel the same about me." I need David to hear me. "If you don't, I'd rather know now. It's not too late."

"You're stressing me out," he says.

We spend the rest of the afternoon hiking in beautiful Redwoods and share dinner in what might seem to an onlooker like mindful, blissful silence that is anything but.

"What movie do you want to watch tonight, hon?" David asks.

"Please, watch whatever you'd like. I'll be in bed, reading."

"Enjoy. I'll join you soon enough."

The writing's on the wall. David and I will not be intimate tonight, and while nothing about this situation feels good, I'm relieved we're not forcing sex when it's so clearly not right for us.

I wake up with a jolt to a pitch-dark room. It takes me a second to get my bearings. David's spooning me from behind, his arms wrapped around my chest. But, wait — is he?

"David—"

"Shhh." I hear the snap of his boxers as he pulls them down. "Stay still," he mumbles, rubbing what feels like a hard dick against my briefs.

"Don't you fucking dare." I sit up and turn on the lights. "What's going on? One moment you're rejecting me, hating your body, and now you're humping me like a dog."

"Sorry, I'm damaged goods," he says, inching towards me. "Hold me?"

I don't know why I let him crawl into my arms, but I do.

"Thank you for being patient," he whispers.

Bellies touching, I stroke David's shaved back. His skin prickles like sandpaper. David moans and reaches his hand into my underwear. Wriggling his fingers against my crotch, he shoves them with sudden force inside my front hole. "I can't do this," he cries, jerking his hand and wiping it on the bedsheets.

I leap out of bed and throw stuff into my backpack.

"It's me, not you." David's voice cracks. "I'm not ready for a relationship."

"You'll be pleased to know that it took six years, but a *Crying Game* moment finally happened."

"With David, I presume?" Jon looks at me with what I've come to think of as his resting therapy face. "Did he throw up after seeing you naked?"

"No, but he came close." I tell Jon everything that's happened and how David yanked his hand in disgust.

"How did that make you feel?"

"Humiliated. It's also hard to stomach the thought that, in retrospect, David was vomiting in his mouth a little every time he touched me; that he forced himself to be attracted to me."

"Are you repulsive?" Jon asks.

"Jon—"

"Answer the question please."

"No, I'm not."

"Did every man you've ever slept with resort to using a barf bag?"

I laugh despite myself. "Of course not."

"What was it that Sammy called you back in the day?"

"A sexy, furry daddy."

"You're a what?"

"Ugh, do I have to repeat this?"

Jon grins. "It's a command."

"Alright, I'm a sexy, furry daddy, goddammit."

"Next time, let's talk about why you didn't trust yourself to walk away earlier and what you can learn from what happened. But, for now, be kind to yourself, okay?"

"I'll try."

"One last thing. Are you still a man even if a non-trans guy gets disgusted by your genitals?"

"Yes, I am."

"It was him, not you. Remember that, brave warrior."

"I wish Lou had access to allies like you," I say. If it was okay to hug Jon, I would. I so would.

It's almost Yom Kippur when David surprises me with a phone call. It's been a couple of months since we called it quits at the heels of the messy affair at the cabin, and I never expected to hear from him again.

"Come to synagogue, as friends? I have an extra ticket," he offers. I don't want to go to synagogue or be friends, so I decline. "I have wonderful news to share." David seems oblivious to my not-so-subtle lets-end-this-conversation-now hints. "I'm in love."

I don't ask who the guy is, but David tells me anyway, "Joey is twenty-two but very mature for his age."

"Congrats," I say and make an excuse to get off the phone.

Scrolling my Facebook feed, David's relationship status leaps from the screen and slaps me in the face. Engaged? Already? There's a picture of the happy duo – David's arm draped around the shoulder of a silky-smooth teenage-looking twink.

I dial his number on impulse. "I need closure," I say.

"Go for it."

"Did you want to want me out of some kind of ideology?" Please, please let him be honest. However brutal reality is, it's better than a mindfuck.

"What?"

"With your new fiancé – did you jerk your hand away during sex, explain it's your traumas, say you're not ready for intimacy?"

"No."

"So what? I was an experiment in how enlightened you had become?"

"I'm sorry you feel hurt."

"A pseudo apology? Really?" At this point, I realise I'm coming across as the angry minority – the fragile, sensitive trans guy who can't control his emotions – but I don't give a shit. "If you want to apologise, try again and own it."

"You're right. I thought I could make myself want you," he says. There it is; validation that I should have trusted my intuition.

"Thanks for being real," I say. Even though David's confession doesn't feel good, exactly, at least I no longer feel crazy. And what was it that Jon told me? Ah yes, "From now on focus on what you want, not what you think the men you date want."

14

PLAYER[8]

"You're a player," Jon says, leaning into his therapist armchair.

"I'm anything but." I've learned to trust Jon's tough love. It's been life-changing, but this statement of his is total bullshit and, besides, what the fuck? Eight years into gender transition and all of a sudden a weird diagnosis out of left field?

"I don't mean that you're a cold, calculating guy who ensnares innocent men in his web of manipulation." Jon points his index finger at me. "No, you're a very different kind of player."

Ouch, that p-word again. What the hell is going on here?

"You should see the look on your face. It's precious."

"Glad to entertain."

"Let me explain. You know how to listen and make a man feel good about himself. These are great skills if you're in a healthy, reciprocal relationship. But, for some reason, you're drawn to navel-gazing, dare I say it, narcissistic guys." Jon is on fire. "You listen, support and clap. They feel on top of the world. The bottom line? You get stuck with guys that aren't good for you."

"So wait, if I'm not cold and calculating, I'm what? A snake oil salesman?"

"Not at all. What I'm saying is that you contort yourself to satisfy men's needs."

"How, exactly?"

"Becoming overly attuned to what you think a lover wants and not asking yourself, first and foremost, what you want."

"I'll think about it," I say, a childhood pain brewing in my stomach.

"Don't be disheartened; I believe in you."

Very few people pay top dollar for this destroy-to-reconstruct mental-health treatment. Who wants to be yanked from a comforting, hot sauna of delusion and dunked into the cold plunge of reality, head held under ice water, lungs gagging for air? Masochists, that's who.

But what if Jon's right? He usually is, goddammit.

On the way home, I blast my loudest playlist on my noise-cancelling headphones, skipping public transport in favour of a brisk walk. But where's the endorphin high? Calm for my monkey mind?

Player, player, player, Jon's image chants at me, sticking its tongue out.

Crossroads Café is an ideal place for a first date, or any date really. The garden is tended with love. Beds of colourful flowers surround the weeping evergreens, competing for sun, yet somehow, they all seem to thrive.

I'm early, but not early-early. And yes, I'll admit, online dating is hell. Sitting interview style, trying to make a beguiling impression on a stranger who could be "the one" but probably isn't? ranks up there with a dentist's drill. Still, I'm looking forward to meeting up with this guy, Steven. His pics are handsome, and if there's no physical chemistry, we could always talk about Buddhism or writing. I'm curious about his nomad's debut novel, as he put it.

A tap on the shoulder interrupts my overthinking. It takes me a moment to recognise the guy. Steven's at least a decade and a half older than his photos.

"The ATM swallowed my card," he says, without sounding terribly upset. "Any chance you'd pay?"

"Sure." I mean, what else can I say? I gesture for him to take a seat at an outdoor table for two. "We need to order at the counter, so let me know what you'd like." Steven smirks from hairy ear to hairier ear as he picks up a menu and chooses the most expensive item.

Waiting to place our order, I'm tempted to make my escape. I don't owe this dude anything. But a move like that would be chicken shit and unkind. We'll share some food and conversation, then I'm outta here.

"Tell me about your novel," I say, setting a tray heaping with foodstuff on the table.

Steven scoops his grilled-salmon sandwich with both hands. "It's about my spiritual journey." He tears into his dish, garlic lemon-butter sauce dripping from his wispy salt-and-pepper moustache onto his shirt. "I've decided to let go of as many earthly possessions as possible."

"Marie Kondo-ing your life?" I attempt a nicety. By nomad, did he mean houseless? If that's true, he deserves some sympathy, but I didn't sign on for feeding him or being catfished.

"Listen," Steven says, chunks of salmon stuck between his yellowed front teeth, "I'm an expert on making a penis explode into a tantric, soul-shattering orgasm, but I don't know how to bring that kind of ecstasy to a trans man."

It's a shame to let my food go to waste, but I can't stomach taking even the smallest of bites. "Let's talk more about your book."

"Don't worry; I'm not propositioning you yet." Steven's spitting as he speaks. "It's just my inexperience with trans men's bodies is something I want to rectify. You see, before I came out as a gay man, I was married to a woman, but I didn't learn how to pleasure her."

"If you're looking for tips about how to have sex with trans men, I'm not your guy. There are multiple resources on the web."

"Gosh, somehow, in my quest to choose bravery over trepidation, you got offended."

"Enjoy the rest of your meal," I say, getting up.

"Holding onto anger is like drinking poison and expecting the other person to die." Steven downs the rest of his freshly squeezed orange juice and slams the glass on the table. "That's a quote from the Buddha. May it serve you well."

I don't wish him physical harm, but I wouldn't mind if a bird shat on his head. *Namaste.*

I run to today's therapy, a spring in my step and tell Jon all about Steven and how I didn't give him what he wanted. Not even close. "See, I'm not a player."

"This creepy date of yours doesn't count," Jon huffs. "Let's see what happens when a charming, eligible guy crosses your path."

"What about Luke?"

"Remind me."

"Luke, the guy that couldn't touch himself. Remember?

He was a great match in so many ways, but to get off, he had to get his dick sucked every night by some random dude at a bar. No judgment, but I walked away."

"Avi, Avi, what am I going to do with you? It's not that you're not discerning or can't say no. The problem is that when you get excited over someone, you feed him the fantasy he's been dreaming about."

Jon's words deliver a gut punch to that soft spot. "Do I? That's gross."

"Feeling disgusted can be a useful first step. Over time, you'll recognise it as a signal for, don't go there."

"I have a promising date coming up, so I'll keep your disturbing analysis in mind."

"Whatever you do, be kind to yourself. This seduction ritual of yours has been Talia's survival strategy. You don't need it anymore."

I almost suggested that my new date, Wolfie, meet me at Crossroads Café, but then Steven came to mind, and I felt a bit queasy. Besides, the weather's turned chilly, so an outdoor patio with heaters is a better choice anyway. Lone Star Saloon, AKA Bear Bar Central, it is.

Sitting on a bench, I sip a cold brew and admire the random hodgepodge of retro metal signs hanging on the fence. *Drink Coca-Cola*, *Chamber of Commerce*, *Flood*, and *Dope*, among others. This courtyard is quiet during the week, and there's enough privacy for making out, should the mood strike.

Wolfie arrives on the dot, looking like his photos – a handsome bear with a firm, thick belly, long beard, and a chest tattoo peeking out of his plaid flannel shirt.

"Your timeliness is sexy," I say.

"Sorry, what?" He tilts his head. "I can't hear out of my left ear. The perils of my profession."

"Construction?" I yell.

"No, drag. A year ago, performing to a full house no less, I fell off my stilettos and smashed my head on the concrete."

"Ouch." I gesture for Wolfie to sit to my left. "Is that a Southern accent?" I ask, leaning closer to his right ear.

"*There's no place like home,*" he says, in a falsetto, clicking the heels of his motorcycle boots three times.

"Kansas? My ex-husband made me watch *The Wizard of Oz*, or I would've missed this cultural reference."

"Made you? I thought you were the dominant one."

"I'll have you know that outside the bedroom, I'm a very nice and somewhat flexible guy." I cup my hand on the back of Wolfie's beefy neck. His posture slackens to my touch, chin lowering to his chest. "You're sexy," I say, sliding my hand down his muscular torso and resting it on his lower back.

"Look what you've made me do, Dad," Wolfie whispers, a wet spot forming on his beige cargo pants. His use of "Dad" versus the usual "Daddy" is wrong and exciting.

"Dirty boy." I reach for his muscular thigh and knead it, inching closer but not touching his dick. "Look at me," I say. Holding his gaze, I hover my hand over his bulge, then give it a gentle but firm press, feeling his dick swell against my grip. "Tell me what you want."

"To please you," Wolfie says.

"Congrats, you just earned a spanking."

"I'm a lucky bear boy." Wolfie's cheeks are red.

"Have you been with a trans man before?"

"Yes, in a threesome."

"How was it?"

"I was jealous of his, wait, I don't want to use a term that will turn you off."

I'm rarely triggered by words these days. It's more about

the energy in which they're spoken. Still, I appreciate Wolfie's thoughtfulness. "The word you were going to use — do you find it sexy?"

"Yes, very."

"Then say it."

"I was jealous of his pussy, Dad."

"Hot! Head over to my place?"

"Yes, please."

Wolfie's body is covered in thick, curly hair, like a were-wolf. I bury my head between his shaggy man mounds and squeeze them against my cheeks. We've been in bed for a couple of hours now, fucking, talking and cud-dling. Orgasming more than once in such a short time? Who knew?

"Can I ask you for something?" I'd swear his expression was coy if I didn't know any better.

"Go for it," I say.

"Call me girl?"

Not what I expected, but I roll with it. "Hello, my lovely girl."

"Hello, Dad," she snickers.

"Do you want me to tell you a bedtime story?"

"Yes, please."

"Very few people know the secret story of Snow White and the prince." I hear the words improvising out of my mouth, and as ludicrous as they sound, I can't help myself. Shit, what's come over me?

"I love secrets, Dad."

"Remember how the prince kissed Snow White awake?"

"Kissing? But that's so embarrassing." Wolfie covers her mouth with her hand.

"There's nothing to feel ashamed about," I say, fondling

Wolfie's hairy chest. "Now, let's pretend you're Snow White, and I'll show you what the prince did before he woke her up. But, you can't tell anyone, okay?"

"Okay," Wolfie whispers.

"Close your eyes and make-believe you're asleep."

"I'm sleeping," Wolfie says, half-shutting her eyelids.

"I'll try to be gentle." I straddle Wolfie's hips and slide her erection into my front hole. Claiming it as my cock, I ram her, slowly at first, then gaining momentum, harder and harder.

"Okay, if I—" Wolfie cries.

"Come for me," I say, gasping for air.

"Fuck," Wolfie yells, her body convulsing. I stick my hand in the viscous liquid and rub it on my cock, exploding into a shattering quake.

"I've always known I was a princess," Wolfie pants, "but, wow, Snow White? Who woulda thunk?"

"Kind of humbling for me too," I manage to utter between bursts of laughter. "Wait, does this mean I'm straight?"

Wolfie roars. "No, honey, it means you're twisted as fuck."

"How about ordering pizza and watching RuPaul's Drag Race?" Wolfie asks. He's wrapped my faux-fur blanket around his chest and is strutting around the living room in this improvised gown as if he's a contestant on the show.

"This is usually the time when my date orders an Uber," I say.

"Now, that's what I call a subtle sendoff."

"Damn, that came out wrong. Take two. I'd love for you to stay, and you should take it as a big compliment."

"So, you like me?" Wolfie bats his eyelashes.

"You're freakin' fabulous." I shake my head in disbelief at the glittery grizzly creature that's materialised into my life. "What kind of pizza would you like?"

"I'll have to consult with your dog first," he says.

Wolfie and Amos cuddle on the purple sofa, looking pleased with themselves. "Squirrel pizza, please."

"It's San Francisco, so I'm sure they've heard worse." I dial Tony's Pizza Napoletana. "I'd like to order your gorgonzola, figs and prosciutto pizza."

"No problem; anything else?" The man's voice is gruff.

"Do you have any ..." I cough into my hand, "dog treats?"

He laughs like a heavy smoker, wheezing and crackling. "*Dio mio*, I can throw in some bacon on the side."

"Make room," I say, sandwiching myself between my two furry creatures. Who knew that a recipe for happiness could be so simple? Step one, watch a drag queen show. Step two, add a diva of a hirsute drag queen, a cuddly brindle dog and smouldering hot pizza slices dripping melted gorgonzola.

It's date number two and Wolfie is hard to miss, even from across the street. His flannel shirt and motorcycle boots are gone in favour of a fuzzy pink sweater with black and white pandas, banana-coloured shorts and open-toe sandals.

"*The Lobster* got rave reviews," he says, handing me a ticket.

The newly opened Alamo Drafthouse movie theatre has a full bar and multiple auditoriums that allow guests to order food and drink to their seats. Best of all, there's an enforced no talking, no texting, no latecomers or else off-with-your-head policy.

The lights dim, the curtain parts; I lean against Wolfie's muscular shoulder, his beard tickling my face. It's showtime!

Ten minutes into the movie, our waiter tip-toes in with our order. Dark Belgian beers and jalapeno poppers. Can it get more perfect?

And just like that, two hours pass by in a flurry.

"I have two things to say," Wolfie declares after the curtain falls. "First, Colin Farrell has a yummy dad bod." He flicks his hand against his forehead as though he's brushing off sweat. "Second, what a poignant statement about the shackles of couplehood."

"Agreed on both counts. It's amazing how many people still idealise marriage when one in two weddings ends in divorce. I've read somewhere that it's an even higher divorce rate the second time around."

"I sure as hell don't buy into heteronormative relationship values," Wolfie says.

"Not even a white picket-fence house with a dungeon in the basement?"

"Not even."

"Your place or mine?" I ask, half hoping he'd suggest his pad in Oakland. I've been curious to see where he lives.

"I'd invite you over, but I don't think it's your scene." Wolfie explains that we wouldn't have much privacy. He shares an Edwardian house with a bunch of radical faeries, and apparently, there's a lot of partying and drugs.

Amos greets us with tail wags and a talking kind of howling that sounds almost human. *Where have you been motherfuckers?*

"Let's take him out," Wolfie says, as though we're a long-time couple.

We walk down Brannan Street to the Embarcadero and cross the draw-bridge behind AT&T Park. Near the pier, there's a small dog run overlooking a haunting view of the bay, its waters a dark inky colour, illuminated by a full moon.

"Tell me more about stereotype threat," Wolfie says, throwing Amos the ball.

"Okay, but it's getting late, and once I start talking research, it's hard for me to shut up."

"Sounds good to me." Wolfie picks the ball Amos has dropped at his feet like a well-trained human.

"How do you know what you're not good at?" I ask.

"Is that a trick question?"

"Alright, I'll answer my own question. When I was in elementary school, my teachers told me I was terrible at maths. The truth is, I didn't give a shit about it. It was a boring subject and I hated school, so I was more than happy to believe them."

"I hear you. I still have PTSD from long division."

"Anyway," I'm eager to continue, "maths aside, the problem was that someone put an identity label on me at such a tender age and I embraced it." There's fire in my belly. "And how did my teachers decide what I was good or so-called bad at, anyway? Objective truth? Stereotypes?" I hear my voice getting louder. "So, fast forward, I felt stressed out of my mind when I started caring about doing well in college, and at statistics no less. It was stereotype threat. This new and constant worry that if I didn't perform well, I'd be proving what my teachers, nay, what society has told me all along – that people like me didn't belong in intellectual spaces." Damn, I did what I promised myself not to, spiralled into a TED talk. "Sorry for going on and on."

"No worries, it resonates." Wolfie sits on a bench, Amos panting by his feet. "I was diagnosed with dyslexia as a kid, so my teachers didn't expect me to be a good writer. I believed them, but then I caught the journalism bug when I went to college."

"And what happened?"

"My professors told me I had a knack for writing about cutting-edge topics; I even got into Columbia's Graduate School of Journalism, but I didn't finish my master's."

"Did you miss exams or hand in assignments late?"

"Yeah, how did you know?"

"Self-sabotage can be a consequence of stereotype threat. What's more effective to avoid so-called inevitable failure and rejection than to shoot oneself in the foot pre-emptively?"

"That sounds about right." Wolfie rubs the back of his head. "I'm so embarrassed."

I sit beside him and put my hand on his thigh. "It wasn't your fault. It's high time we changed the system; not just put underrepresented folks on advertisements and brochures to signal virtuousness."

"I'm super curious to hear more, but—" Wolfie yawns.

"It's late. I know. Thanks for indulging me."

Home sweet home at last, Amos trots to his crate and collapses on his dog bed with a dramatic sigh.

"Race you to bed, my prince?" I ask.

"I need to take a shower first."

"Don't. I love your sweaty werewolf smell."

"It's just that I came straight to the movie theatre after seeing a gentleman caller." Wolfie makes his signature mock-coy expression, but I don't find it charming this time. And, no, I have no right to feel this stung. Wolfie and I met on a hookup site and have only been dating for a short time. Besides, I find polyamory appealing. So, why the hell do I feel like I've been kicked in the gut?

"Who was the guy?" I hate my tone, dripping green poison.

Wolfie smiles. "A hookup. Another day in the life of an ethical slut."

"We've never talked about having sex with other people."

"Yeah, I just assumed we were."

"I did too, but okay to ask what your sex life is like?" There, I asked it. Now there's no going back.

"I have regular fuckbuddies, but otherwise, I hook up two to three times a week."

"On the apps with random guys?"

"Yup. Is that a problem?"

"I dunno, maybe. I'm a kinky prude."

"What does that mean?"

I don't want to puke out my feelings and risk damaging what we have. He's too important for that. "Here," I point to my head, "I'm a prime member of the slut fan club. Give me a cheerleading outfit, and I'll use my pompoms to hurray sexual freedom, especially for those of us who've been told to be ashamed of our bodies and desires." I try to inject as much light-heartedness into my tone as I can. "But here and here," I point to my heart, then groin, "turn-on comes from connection."

"So, as long as we have intimate sex, does it matter what I do with other men?"

"In theory, no."

"Is there anything I can do to make you more at ease?"

"Keep doing what you're doing, but please don't share any sexual details."

"That's easy." He strokes my cheek. "Am I still staying the night?"

"You'd better." I usually like my bed to myself but falling asleep with Wolfie is like spooning a warm and fuzzy teddy bear. So, how about I drop my story of who I am – or at least some of the habits that so-call define me – and open to what unfolds in the here and now? Tomorrow will bring more clarity, right?

"Hi, Amos, love," I mumble, the bright morning light forcing me awake. The pup bumps his wet nose against my hand, tail wagging, ears back. I reach for Wolfie, but the bed's empty.

On the kitchen counter is a note and freshly made coffee, waffles and scrambled eggs. *Enjoy your breakfast. There's cut papaya in the fridge, the way you like it. Amos and I took a walk and he did his business, so you can take it easy before leaving for work. You mean the world to me, W.*

After two months of dating, Wolfie and I have developed a flowing and dare I say it, domestic routine. Night walks with Amos by the Bay Bridge, Indie horror films, experimental sex, breakfasts in bed and the highlight? Seeing Wolfie perform as his drag queen alter ego – a fierce, sharp-witted dancing queen with a full beard and glamourous makeup. Here I was, convinced that this self I supposedly knew so well needed more space. Ha!

"What does it feel like being on stage?" I ask, giving him a ride home after an especially wild performance where he spun like a rag doll to Kate Bush's "Running Up That Hill".

"It's like all my inhibitions lift and I'm ready to take over the world."

"Do you ever feel like a woman?"

"No, not at all. But tucking my junk and having an illusion of a Barbie crotch is liberating."

"In what way?"

"So much of gay male culture revolves around dicks, but my masculinity and the masculinity I'm attracted to, well, these have never been about dick size. So, yeah, it's freeing to tuck, dress in fabulous feminine clothing and still be a man."

"I wish I had the option to tuck."

"You can strap on a dildo and tape it to your butt."

I laugh. "What a jerk. How about I tuck it up your ass?"

Wolfie rolls his eyes. "Just as I was boasting about my intellectual boyfriend, he has to ruin the illusion."

"Boyfriend?" I repeat the word with a tinge of panic. I'm not sure I'm ready to shed my bachelorhood quite yet. Or maybe it's the elephant in the room – Wolfie and I haven't talked about his gentleman callers, and while I'm not clear on who they are and how many, I suspect the number is higher than I'd be comfortable hearing about.

"Oops. Too soon to call you that?" Wolfie asks.

"Hey, are you still up for our mini adventure tomorrow?"

"Totally." Wolfie looks at me, point blank. "I'm hearing loud and clear what you're not saying."

"You know I'm crazy about you, right?"

"Well, at least Amos is."

It's our first road trip – nothing fancy or far, just a drive down Highway 1, south of San Francisco towards Santa Cruz. The views of the Pacific Ocean are usually spectacular, but it's a foggy day.

Near Half Moon Bay, we stop for an English lunch at Cameron's Pub, Restaurant and Inn. It boasts a dubious history of murders and ill repute, a double-decker bus and the best fish and chips in town. It'd be cosier eating inside, but the music is blaring, so we head to the empty, dog-friendly patio.

"Delicious," Wolfie says, taking another bite of sizzling battered haddock wrapped in fake newspaper. His hands are shivering.

I inhale a couple of thickly sliced french fries doused with salt. "Heavenly," I say, hopping from foot to foot. Perhaps eating outside wasn't the best idea. The wind is biting and the fog hangs heavy and wet.

Weather be damned, we head to the beach. Unleashed at last, Amos does zoomies, wild and free. Who cares about stormy weather when there's a ball, a long stretch of sand and two humans wrapped around one's paw?

"Look," Wolfie points to a wind-carved cave. It's a risky proposition. The tide is low, but in a blink of an eye, shelter from the buffeting winds could turn into death by drowning. Still, it'll do as a quick refuge and its transience is a reminder not to take things for granted.

Toasty in our makeshift sanctuary, we spread out on a plaid blanket. Wolfie lays down with his head in my lap and Amos nestles against Wolfie's body, sandy and panting.

"Isn't your mother coming to visit soon?" I ask, unzipping my coat.

"Yup. I'm already regretting the whole thing; she drives me nuts."

"In what way?"

"Mommy dearest never asks me anything about my life. It's like she doesn't want to know who I am."

"I used to think of love as seeing and being seen." I reach under Amos's chin and give it a scratch. "But getting older, I realise that people love in different ways."

"What does it mean to love someone if they're a projection of what you want them to be?" Wolfie has that beguiling look, a crack in his well-honed drag queen shield.

"Moms know our histories. They intuit aspects of who we are, even if they can't articulate them. So, if we're holding them to an idealisation of love than they're capable of giving, aren't we as guilty of wanting them to be different from who they are?"

"No, you're wrong. There's no excuse for parents who make their kids' lives all about who they, the parents, are."

"I get that. For years, my mom never asked me what it was like to be queer or trans. My otherness embarrassed her. But ill and in her eighties, she's come out as a proud mother of a gay trans man." Imagining Mom's Parkinsonian face tugs at my heart. I've been missing her a lot lately. "Mothers. They can surprise us, you know."

Wolfie is quiet. Was I being too much? Am I ... too much?

"Avi, there's something I need to tell you." Shit, he's saying my name. That's never a good sign. Why can't he keep the illusion that everything's right with us, the world, for a bit longer?

"I'm listening," I say, but my inner kid is covering his ears.

"I've tested positive for gonorrhea."

He's being honourable, but our cave is no longer the shelter from the storm it had been only moments ago. "Thank you for telling me," I say.

"It's just a round of antibiotics, right? No biggie?"

I nod ambiguously. I don't know how to voice my discomfort without sounding shaming or losing gay male points. I'm sexually active, so an easily curable sexually transmitted infection shouldn't be a big deal, but ... it is, to me. I almost died from a rogue case of gonorrhea complications a couple of years ago. Sepsis. "Here you go, sailor," the doctor who ordered the intravenous antibiotics said, patting me on the shoulder.

Ultimately, this situation was my fault − I should've got tested every three months. The thing is, I had a monogamous agreement with my then-boyfriend, Pablo, so I didn't. Little did I know, Pablo cheated. Not once or twice, but tens of times, and without using protection.

The ocean waves smash against the giant, sharp-toothed boulders, drowning Wolfie's voice. Still, despite the relentless beatings, the boulders are teeming with life – tide pools with weird and wondrous creatures: anemones adorned by broken shells, hermit crabs, worms with feathery tentacles and warty sea cucumbers, to name a few. Beautifully hideous or hideously beautiful? And mortal, so damn mortal.

"Sorry, what did you say?" I ask.

"Are we on a boyfriend track?"

What Jon had been trying to tell me? I get it now. This familiar pit in my stomach, a desire to give Wolfie what I think he wants, a carefree persona that isn't me. Do I fish out the well-crafted, intricate nets from my so-called player repertoire to ensnare him? Then what? A few months of happiness? A messy ending?

"I have strong feelings for you," I say, placing my palm on his chest. "But I don't think we're compatible as long-term romantic partners."

"I'm not ambitious enough?"

"No, that's not it at all. You know that."

"Then what?"

"I'm a kinky prude, and you're—"

"A slut," he finishes my sentence.

"In the best of all ways." I smile, longing to show him how much I care.

"I understand and I so wish I could give you what you want."

"I want honesty and intimacy, and that's exactly what you're giving me." There's a heaviness in my chest – the mourning of what could have been – but there's also relief.

Wolfie opens his palm and wriggles his fingers. "Friends?" he asks.

"Chosen family forever," I say, putting my hand in his.

15

EVEN MOTHER SPIDERS DIE[9]

My phone barks a mundane, invasive ring. Who calls anyone on the spur of the moment anymore?

"She's gone," Gil whispers from the other side of the world. "Our mother is gone."

"Did she suffer?" I ask, afraid to know.

"No, and she wasn't alone. I held her hand till she took her last breath." Gil's voice is shaking. "Hurry, you have less than twenty-four hours to get here. They won't keep her body any longer than that."

By *they*, Gil means Chevra Kadisha – the ultra-orthodox Jews in charge of burials in our secular hometown. They believe that the body should be buried right away or else the spirit becomes trapped between worlds.

"Try to stall, okay?" I plead. A direct flight from San Francisco to Tel Aviv takes seventeen and a half hours. That's not factoring in the time it takes to pass through passport control and security and then take a cab from the airport to the cemetery.

"Rush to the airport," Gil says with urgency. "I'll

do my best, but you know how stubborn the Kadisha people get."

Just yesterday, Mom and I spoke on the phone.

"What's happening to me?" She asked, her voice paper-thin. "You're the only one that tells me the truth anymore."

I'd have told her whatever she wanted to know; of course I would have, but I didn't know shit. "Mom, what's going on?" I asked, and when she didn't answer, I begged, "speak to me. Please, say something."

"She fell asleep." It was Dad's senescent voice. At 89 and with Alzheimer's, he's still physically active, but his cognitive capacities have diminished considerably.

"Call for help," I yelled, too far away to be of use, a sham of a son.

"Avi, it's Fey. Don't worry! Your mother has dozed off." Fey is Mom's aide, not a doctor. So why didn't I make Fey get one or call an ambulane?

If I had only insisted, would Mom be alive?

Splashing cold water on my face snaps me into doing mode. Right! Buy airline tickets, call the dog sitter, beg someone to substitute-teach my classes, pack, turn the gas stove off, make sure it's off, make a pit stop at the pharmacy and what else? I'm forgetting something important. I know I am.

Don't forget to breathe, Mom whispers from the ether.

"I'll be there, Mom. I have to," I hear myself say. If I don't, no, I must, there's no other option.

It's like someone has taken over my body, crossing the items off my never-ending list, one by one, and finally, in a frenzied haze, I'm in an Uber to the airport.

The driver slaloms up and down San Francisco's steep

hilly streets, passing a trolley with waving tourists flashing toothy smiles. How dare the sky be blue, no fog in sight?

"See? We've made record speed." The driver comes to a full stop in front of Departures.

"I'll give you five stars," I say and sprint inside. Will I clear the scanner this time?

"Step aside," the TSA officer orders. It's the scanner. Must be; bodies like mine defy its settings.

A few questions into the interrogation, and my name is announced on the PA system — the final boarding call. *I repeat, proceed immediately to your gate,* the disembodied voice commands.

"Go," the man huffs, and I sprint faster than I thought I knew how.

The plane greets me with hissing air vents and hospital-beige fold-out trays. My seatbelt, grey and slick, clicks tightly into place, squeezing my thighs. The familiar is real but not; a facsimile of a world that once had Mom in it.

I didn't have time to write Mom a eulogy, but I brought a memento for inspiration — a studio photograph of us. I take out a pen and start to scribble. Whatever comes out, comes out.

When I was six, you took me to a photographer's studio. "I want a memento of just us girls," you said. Over the years, moving countries and cities, my collection of photos has dwindled to those that hold a special place in my heart. This photo of us isn't happy exactly, but it belongs.

Look, Mom, there's six-year-old me, staring at the camera, pigtailed and made to wear a dress, and look,

there's you, hiding behind me, shaking from fen phen -
anything to lose weight.

"What do you want to be when you grow up, little
girl?" the photographer asked.

"A bull," I said.

"A heifer? How come?" you asked, your brow deep-
ening its creases. You didn't expect me to become a
doctor or a lawyer, but trans-species? Definitely not.

"I love to play in the mud," I said, and we laughed,
ruining the photographer's meticulous staging.

I love, no, I loved your unarmed rolling laughter, how
you kept your promises, and, yes, it took you a while,
but you called me son.

Only seven hours after your death, memory is growing your wings, dulling the sharpness of your horns,
smoothing wrinkles, and covering liver spots - forcing a
monument to motherhood constructed from the glossy
marble of a tombstone.

No, I refuse the mind's propensity to lie outright.

Air pockets - a bumpy ride - and I'm holding on to
my bovine childhood wish for dear life.

Mom, I want, no, I need to keep you gloriously
messy.

The muck. I want the muck.

I was certain the cab ride from the Ben-Gurion airport to
Herzliya's cemetery would end in a fiery crash. Still, here I
am, frazzled but intact and in the nick of time. Or at least
I think I am. Gil said to meet outside the gates. Where is
everybody?

The Israeli sun's harsh rays bounce off the cemetery's
white walls. Blinking, I straighten my palm and touch
the tip of my index finger to my forehead like a military

272

salute. I forgot my sunglasses, so this makeshift visor will have to do.

Across the street, still standing in a glorious decay, is my elementary school. Is that Mrs Hamorah's ghost peering through the top window, batting her eyes at death in pornographic glee?

But wait, something isn't right. Did the funeral already start?

Dashing inside, the wheels of my carry-on screeching on gravel, I spot the procession mid graveyard, moving at a snail's pace, with Dad, Noam and Gil, at its head.

Thank goodness, it's not too late!

Damp and breathless, I weave in and out of the crowd, mumbling, "Sorry, sorry, sorry." Just a few more steps and I'll catch up with Dad and my brothers. I need to slow down, though. I don't want to startle Dad.

My father looks frail. His suit is at least two sizes too large for his body, a tilted skullcap threatening to slip and expose his once full head of hair. Noam and Gil are his crutches. Supporting Dad from each side, they trail behind a Rabbi and two strangers carrying a gurney. On it, bouncing up and down to the melancholic rhythm of the Rabbi's prayer, are Mom's remains, wrapped in a white shroud.

Gil's the first to notice I'm here. "You made it! I'm so relieved!" Turning to Dad, he says, "Look, it's our Avi."

"*Chabibi.*" Dad's eyes are puffy and red. "I should've gone first."

"Please, stop saying that," Noam kisses Dad's temple, then nods in my direction.

Forty degrees Celsius and humid, we persevere on the pebbly path that twists and turns. A primal life force pushes our feet, one in front of the other, the thin poplar trees trying but failing to provide relief from an unrelenting sun.

"We've arrived," the Rabbi announces, and we halt at Mom's open grave, her final resting spot.

"For you were made from dust, and to dust you will return," the Rabbi chants, and the strangers with the *yarmulkes* and *pe'ot* hover the gurney over a casket-less hole in the ground. A naked cavity. Then the men tilt the gurney, and, no, this piercing pain in my chest, I can't look.

A thudding of stiff meat and dry bones,
a smell of brambles, must and moss,
and now I do look, eyes stinging like bees,
a body disappearing under layers of shovelled earth,
and I finally get it, and I don't. You
will never return.

"Stop! Mom can't breathe," Noam yells, letting go of Dad and falling to his knees. Kneeling by my older brother on the arid ground, I place my hand on his shoulder, but he shrugs it off. I'm eight years old again, and Noam's back from war, and whatever I do, I can't console him.

"It's okay, Noam, let it out," Gil says, hugging Dad's skeletal frame close to his chest and all four of us weep, refusing to let you go.

Dina, Gil's Jewish-American girlfriend, has rented an Airbnb for the two of them and invited me to stay in the spare room. It's nice of her, I guess, but I need alone time, and she can get a bit overbearing.

But why am I being such an ingrate? Dina's gesture is generous, and, besides, having company might be a good thing.

"Wanna help with dinner?" Dina asks, emerging from the kitchen wearing an apron with the word "אחלה", *Achla*, printed in large font.

"I'm a horrible cook, but yeah, sign me up for food prep, washing dishes, that kind of stuff," I offer.

"How about making us some tea, then?"

It sounds like an easy task, but apparently, I'm doing it wrong. "Let me show you," Dina says, wrapping my teabag around a spoon and draining it to its last drop. The last thing I need is a lesson, but Dina's trying to be helpful, and to be fair, she's been in the kitchen for hours, cooking up a storm.

"I can set the table while we're waiting for the tea to cool off," I say.

"Great," Dina says and leaves me unsupervised. It's good to be useful, but a hot shower and a hug from Adva, who'll join us for dinner, can't come too soon.

Adva is one of my homes. No matter how long we don't see each other, we always pick up where we left off and with such precious ease.

Once upon a time, Henry was home. The last time we talked was the day before his wedding. Eight years ago or so? "Am I doing the right thing?" He asked out of the blue, as though Talia was there to answer. Then, radio silence.

Still, Henry emailed this morning. **My deepest condolences on the loss of your mother, Avi. I loved Rina very much.** Apparently, while Henry and his family had shunned me for decades, he had kept in regular touch with Mom and Gil. I don't know what to make of their secret liaisons, but I don't have the bandwidth to process any of this right now.

"Good job," Dina compliments my table settings, holding a cup of tea in each hand. "Listen, the three of you should take away your father's access to his bank accounts, or he'll spend it all on some *mishigas*." She might be right, but this is none of her fucking business.

"Look who's arrived to grace us with his presence," Gil announces as he enters the front door, Dad leaning on his arm gasping for air. Our dear father is in decent physical shape for his age but in no condition to climb up three flights of stairs on this hot and emotionally draining day.

While Dina keeps Dad company in the living room, I motion for Gil to join me in the hallway. "What's happened to Dad's face?"

"He was trying to look good for dinner," Gil says.

"By using black shoe polish on his eyebrows?"

"It's mascara, I think. Pretty grotesque, eh?"

"What's wrong with you two? If your father feels good about how he looks, that's all that matters," Adva barges into our private huddle.

"Dad used to be a dandy, and now, he looks like a demented clown. It's undignified. And anyway," I wag my finger, "you shouldn't sneak up on people like that."

"I adore you, but stop being selfish," Adva says. She's right. I need to get over myself, but am I giving up on Dad if I don't care about how he looks?

"Is Noam joining us?" Dad asks from his seat at the head of the table. The air conditioning is on its lowest setting, but he shivers as though he's weathering a blizzard.

"He'll be here for dessert, Daddy-O," Gil says, carrying a tray with bowls of chicken soup. He lays it on the dinner table, careful not to spill any of the piping-hot liquid, and kisses Dad's wrinkled forehead.

"Thank you, *chabibi*," Dad says with his famous ocean-wide smile. "I can't tell you what you all mean to me."

Poor Dad. I can't imagine how he'll go on without Mom, having shared the same bed for over sixty years. "Since we've moved to assisted living, your father has been leaving roses on my pillow," Mom had confided in me. How did they shift from tolerating each other, stuck in a loveless marriage, to such tenderness, romance even, in their twilight years?

"So, Gil tells me you're Avi's childhood friend." Dina gives Adva the once over.

"We were inseparable as kids and our mothers were besties, too," Adva says.

"I was lucky to have met Rina." Dina flashes perfect veneers. "She was such a beautiful soul."

"Beautiful? More like fierce," I say.

"Sorry, I get confused sometimes. My wife is dead, right?" Dad says.

"Yes, Mom passed away," Gil puts his palm over Dad's.

"My Rina. She was younger you know? It should've been me."

Dad's been saying that again and again, like a mantra, and I know I should let him grieve in his own way, and maybe the best thing to do is just listen, but I hear the words tumble out of my mouth, "You're the utmost gentleman for outliving Mom. It would have shattered her to have lost you."

"Thank you, *chabibi*." Tears roll down Dad's cheeks and into his soup.

"Eat Papa Bear," Dina says. I want to blame her for all that's wrong in the world, for sickness and loss, but she's trying her best; we all are.

"Can I sleep here tonight?" Adva asks. My bed is a small double – not the most comfortable arrangement for two people.

277

"Only if you cuddle with me."

"Deal. By the way, that Dina is such a princess."

"Right?" I yawn, forgetting to cover my mouth. "Sorry for being a bad friend. This whole time, I haven't asked how you've been doing. How's your heart?"

"Let's say divorce agrees with me. And you? Seeing anyone special?"

"I just broke up with a big-hearted, ultra-hairy bear."

"Good looking, I bet."

"Hyper-masculine until he opens his mouth, and the purse falls out, as gay men say."

"You like that, right?"

"Guilty." I fan myself, drag-queen style. "It was very romantic while it lasted. He even crocheted a pink skull for me."

"So what happened?"

The pain in my gut is scalpel sharp. For a split second, I forgot. "It's so fucking unfair," I bellow.

"I know," Adva whispers.

"I can't stand being in my body."

"I know, honey. A loss like this is impossible to comprehend." She offers to walk on my back, claiming intuitive Thai massage skills. I'm dubious, but the pain feels good.

Dad's flat at the assisted living facility is too small for sitting *shiva* – the traditional Jewish mourning period that lasts for seven days. We're lucky Management was kind enough to provide us with a vacant unit. It's spacious and has a garden – perfect for welcoming friends and family who'd be coming bearing loads of home-cooked food.

Adva and Dina stay with Dad while we brothers go shopping for provisions and recyclable dinnerware. Black seems too macabre for plates and silverware. "How about white and blue, Mom's favourite combo?" Gil asks. Surely, this trivial detail shouldn't matter, but it does.

We've only been away for what? An hour? But the *shiva* is going strong. Adva is by Dad's side, holding his hand, and Dina is busy setting dishes on the dining table. I count about thirty people and more are streaming in. "Oh, good, we have things to eat with," Dina says, grabbing the bags from Gil's hand.

"How about—?" I start saying when Mom's cousin, Chana, brushes against me, barrelling her way towards Dad.

"The woman's a nightmare," Noam whispers.

"I got this." I hurry after Chana who, in her eighties, is leaving me in the dust.

"Israel, what happened? I talked to Rina two days ago and she was fine," Chana yells, two metres from Dad's face.

"Mrs Peleg, Israel's hearing is normal," Adva mumbles. What's up with her meekness? Ah, yes, it's coming back – Chana was Adva's teacher in elementary school and had once slapped her hard across the face.

"I want the name of Rina's GP," Chana says with urgency. "Do you hear me, Israel? Rina was her normal self the day before she died." Oblivious to the panicked look on Dad's face, she adds, "I'd bet all my life's savings the blood thinner that murderer prescribed killed her."

"I know you loved Mom, but please stop." I give Chana a stern look. "Can't you see how badly you're upsetting Dad?"

"Listen here—" Mom's cousin is about to give me a piece of her mind, but Gil pulls her away. "Come with me, Auntie," he says.

"It's okay, Dad; I'll make sure Chana keeps her distance. Want me to walk you home? Rest for a bit?"

"No, I'm okay, *chabibi*," he says, sitting back on his chair. But he's not okay. Far from it. His mind keeps weaving in and out of lucidity. He gets paranoid that guests want to steal his meds but then musters what it takes to thank them for showing up.

Meanwhile, people keep coming and going, buzzing condolences. "Where's the daughter?" and "You are ...?" ask those who haven't stayed in touch with Mom recently enough to know that Talia is no longer with us.

On the sixth day of the *shiva*, a stranger stops by. She's in her late forties, early fifties tops. Fidgety, she straightens and re-straightens her perfectly ironed dress. "Is this the family-in-mourning of the esteemed librarian, Rina Ben-Zeev?"

"Yes, you're in the right place," I say. Despite barely finishing high school, Mom created a library from scratch in our town's modest community centre by knocking door to door and collecting book donations.

"God bless you, all of you," the woman says and takes both my hands. "I don't want to intrude, but is the husband still with us?"

"Follow me," I say and lead her to where Dad sits, flanked by Noam and Gil. "Dad, this is ..." I start saying, hoping the woman divulges her name.

"My deepest condolences, Mr Ben-Zeev," she says, dropping to her knees. "I am so sorry to disturb you at this time of great grief, but I had to come."

Noam gestures for her to take his seat, but she indicates *no*.

"Your wife saved me, *tehi nishmata tzrura bitzrur ha'chaim*; may her soul be bound in the bundle of life." Then, finally, the mystery woman tells us her story. She came from a home with very little food and no books, but even without a card, Mom welcomed her into the library and taught her how to read the newspaper. "I read it every day and was able to finish high school and get a job at the local municipality. My boss was impressed by how someone like me knew so much about current affairs."

"My Rina would have been very proud of you," Dad says in a moment of clarity.

"May I hug you?" I ask the woman, and enveloped in her embrace, Mom hugs me goodbye.

My brothers have tasked me with clearing Mom's closet. I'm leaving for San Francisco tomorrow, so it has to be now.

Not that I'm ready. Not that I'll ever be.

I knock on Dad's door and Fey flings it open, then throws herself into my arms. "I loved Rina as if she were my mother," she wails, leaving warm, wet spots on my shirt. She needs more room for her stuff now that she'll be taking care of Dad around the clock. "Do you want some tea?" she asks.

"Thanks, maybe later," I say and explain why I'm here.

"Let me know if you need my help," Fey says and shows me into the parents' bedroom.

Mom valued her privacy. It'd be sacrilege to go through her things, but it helps to think she'd prefer me to do it, even if it's my history as her daughter that would have made it more palatable.

On Mom's bedstand is a framed photograph of the five grandkids and her favourite book of short stories, tattered and dogeared — of all the authors in the world, it boiled down to O. Henry. "*The Gift of the Magi*, now that's a masterpiece," she'd say. She recounted this story to us kids a thousand times, each telling making it that much more off-putting.

"The husband and wife were destitute, but she loved him so much she was willing to cut off her luscious hair to buy him the thing he dreamt about most – a chain for his pocket watch."

"Noooo," I'd cover my ears. Who wants a chain for their pocket watch, or a pocket watch in the first place? The White Rabbit in *Alice in Wonderland*, that's who. And women with short hair looked better, anyway.

Mom would continue, undiscouraged, "And meanwhile, what does the husband do but buy his cherished wife her dream gift – a comb to adorn her lovely hair? But, unaware of her excruciating sacrifice, he sells the only treasured possession he has … his pocket watch."

"*Oye* and *vey*," I'd groan; What pathos! Kill me now.

But enough dawdling! I'm in the parents' bedroom on a mission and better get to it. Heart thumping, I open Mom's closet. The smell of her perfume fills the air. I used to be allergic to her scent as if it were a personal assault. Now, I stick my nose into her favourite woolly turquoise sweater, inhaling deeply for that citrusy smell of a bygone home.

Give to the granddaughters. Donate. Throw away.

Is this what a life gets reduced to – a body decomposing in an open grave, eaten by worms, its belongings in three piles? For the record, I'm not okay with any of it.

"What are you doing here?" Dad catches me mid-crying. I imagine he's exhausted and in need of rest before returning to welcome more guests to the *shiva*.

I blow my nose. "I'm taking care of Mom's things."

"Is that so?" Dad lies on the bed with his shoes on and props himself against the headboard. "Is *she* taking any of it?" His eyes narrow into slits.

"You mean Fey?" I whisper.

"Who else? She's a thief," he yells.

I try to distract Dad with the gold watch he had gifted

282

Mom on their 50th wedding anniversary. "Remember how the two of you read out loud from your courting letters? How, with time, *Dear Rina* became *Dearest Rina* became *My Rina*? It was so romantic."

"Put the watch back."

"Sure, *Aba'le*, I was only trying to—"

"I want my daughter," Dad says, his eyes a cloudy shade of grey. "My Talia. Where is she?"

"She's . . ." My voice trails. How can I even begin to explain?

"Leave, or I'll call security," this man, my father, says.

Death spared Mom from witnessing this scene, from untold suffering. This thought should comfort me, but it doesn't.

Settling into the long plane ride back to San Francisco, I try to meditate but I can't focus. It was hard to leave Dad to his paranoia and loneliness and to pray that he what? Wakes up to another day of confusion and pain?

Now, with Dad's dementia and Mom's passing, the bare thread that still attached me to my troubled homeland has been snipped. Untethered by her death, my heart is in free fall.

I take out a pen and start writing.

There were very few things I could count on in life, and at the top of the list were Mom's promises. She made them seldomly, and when she did, she kept each one.

When I was twelve, shortly after my Bat Mitzvah, I gathered my immediate family to deliver the devastating news. The lifeline on my right hand was broken - I would not live past my teens.

"Psychic expertise comes at a price. I know too much," I declared.

"Nonsense," Mom said, dismissing my powers and the powers that be. "You'll age like the rest of us!"

"You'll regret having said this when my young body is tossed into the grave," I said.

"I promise to celebrate your 20th together." Mom gave me her infamous blue steel glare. "I'll find you, no matter where in the world you'll be hiding."

"You promise?" My bad-ass voice turned into a quivering child's.

"I promise!" Mom exclaimed, her ginger mane burning on top of her head like a holy thornbush.

Sure enough, when I turned twenty, in Milan, Italy, Mom was there, holding a deeply cherished family heirloom - a pearl necklace that belonged to Grandma Rivka. "Take good care of it," Mom said with a commanding smile. "I'm going to ensure you wear it on your 30th!"

A decade later, Mom made a long and arduous trip from Israel to Providence, Rhode Island. "Happy 30th, my girl! Let's eat cake."

Since then, a birthday package arrived from the Middle East to America year after year, a few days short of or right on November 8th. "Happy Birthday to our beloved Talia!" became "Happy Birthday to our beloved Avi!"

Every year except this one.

"I didn't forget," Mom sighed. "I'm sorry to disappoint, but they put me in a wheelchair, so the present and card will have to be late."

"Hearing your voice is my gift," I said, aching to teleport through the ether and take Mom into my arms, letting her head hang heavy on my chest for as long as she'd let me.

Now that Mom's gone, I'm holding on to her citrusy smell, love for O. Henry, for pathos, how she grieved her daughter but opened her arms to her rebirthed son. I'm holding on, trusting that memory fades but the heart remembers.

Back in San Francisco, people walk about their business, as though the world had not just combusted.

It's Yom Kippur, and of all places, I find myself at Synagogue. I know, strange for a non-believer.

An ancestral calling? A homing instinct? All I know is that I'm wearing white on this Day of Atonement like Mom did after Grandpa Simcha died.

Far away from the home I've rejected, I look for glimpses of Mom in the Semitic faces of Diaspora Jews clad in ghostly attires. Greedy, I bargain with the god I don't believe in to bring her back for one stolen moment.

Stay strong, Mom whispers, but I could use some caretaking, a hug. I'd even hire one of those cuddling professionals – a no-nonsense lady, big-boned and buxom, who'd open her arms. "Come here," she'd say, squeezing me so hard I'd be forced to surrender.

This woman, well, she might look like Mom, but Mom rarely hugged me, and when she did, she arched her back, avoiding pressing her breasts against my unruly buds.

"You were an unhuggable kid," Mom said when I confronted her about the lack of physical affection, and I chose to believe her.

I chose to believe that some babies, like me, are born wrong.

*

I forgive you, Mom says.

"Thank you," I whisper, placing my hand on my heart. "I forgive you too."

You what? Her eyes bulge out of her head. *What's there to forgive me for?*

I could list a few things, but I don't. "You're right; there's nothing to forgive," I say.

16

JOSEPH'S KISS[9]

"So, why volunteer at a Buddhist AIDS hospice?" Jayden asks. On his desk, next to a nameplate bearing the title "Volunteer Coordinator", is a framed photograph – Jayden on a beach wearing black, yellow and green boardshorts, his arm draped around the broad shoulders of a blond, blue-eyed hunk.

"I'm a gay man who has lived through the AIDS epidemic as a 'hetero woman'." I gesture the quote marks around the last two words, hoping he gets my trans reference. "I wasn't involved in any activism or caretaking back then, and I'd love the chance to redeem that."

"Great, and just so you know, we're cool with trans guys here."

"There's another reason." I want to come clean. "Dying terrifies me."

"Oh?" He tilts his head.

"I have a spiritual practice, but this whole impermanence business – I want to learn to accept it more." Am I making sense? I'm not so sure volunteering will help demystify death, or accept Mom's loss, and, goddammit, the guy is distractingly handsome.

My weekly volunteer shift at the San Francisco Buddhist AIDS hospice starts with reading resident updates. There's a newcomer. Joseph. The photo stapled to his folder shows a dapper Black gentleman in his late 50s. His prognosis is three months or less.

Someone (the intake counsellor?) has left a handwritten note. "Joseph identifies as a heterosexual man and devout Christian who believes AIDS is a 'gay disease' and 'punishment from God.'" The commentator underlined the quotes in red pen and added two exclamation points.

Will Joseph and I get along? Wait, that's not the point, though, is it? I'm here to be of assistance.

I wave hello to Jayden and walk down the hallway and into the living room. Its dark chocolate walls feature paintings and photographs donated by local artists. My favourite is an aerial shot of the Golden Gate Bridge on a sunny day. Granted, it's a clichéd image, but the artist captured the structure's majestic quality, or perhaps this setting lends an edge – a reminder that even enduring American icons are sculpted from ice.

Two months, and I still need to take a deep breath before entering the residents' quarters. I'll start with Kevin and end with Joseph. Chin up!

"C'mon in," Kevin yells in a shrill voice.

Today's report sounded grim. Kevin's developed lesions on his legs that are, and I quote from his file, "weeping lymphatic fluid". Is weeping a medical term?

"Hey, fabulous man," I say, pushing the door into a bright yellow room.

"Avi, my favourite." Kevin's smile lightens up his sunken cheeks, his blue eyes as bright as a child's.

"I bet you say that to all the volunteers." I pray my face doesn't betray my horror at how much he's deteriorated. "Need anything?"

"Carrot juice, please and add a kick to it, okay? Ginger for this ginger?" That's an easy request. The kitchen has a juicer and lots of organic options.

"Where would you like me to set this?" I re-enter Kevin's room, holding a tumbler filled with nectar. The L-shaped side table by his bed makes the most sense, but Jayden has taught us to ask. "When people don't have much control over their lives, even a small choice feels humanising."

"This fuckin' sucks." Kevin gestures to his swollen, leaky legs.

"I bet." I used to believe in the healing power of words. I still do, but at this moment, words feel feeble at best.

"The docs are wrong about me, you know. I'm not planning on dying anytime soon." Kevin nods as if he needs me to agree.

I nod back, wishing him a better quality of life than his chart indicated, however long he has left.

"Hey, Magnolia's been beating the odds, so why shouldn't I?"

"That's right," I say. Fair point. Magnolia was given a few months to live and she's been at the hospice for almost a year.

"Her cruelty's been keeping her alive," Kevin says.

I snort, ashamed of becoming complicit in hospice gossip.

"Hey, I calls it as I sees it."

Hospice residents are encouraged to personalise their space with mementos, art, books and even small furniture pieces. What stuff do humans ache for when death is imminent? Kevin has chosen a portrait of Daisy, his golden retriever. "That's my sweet girl," he said when we first met. It seems like ages ago, but it's only been what? Three weeks?

"Looking at Daisy's mug makes me happy and sad." Kevin winces. "How come there's no one word for that?"

"But there is," I say.

"Love?" he asks.

Ajahn Chah, the Thai Buddhist meditation teacher, cherished drinking from his favourite cup because, in his mind, it had already been broken. Intellectually, I get that impermanence lends a preciousness to what's here and will vanish forever. Still, doesn't that mean love has built-in grief, and bittersweetness is the best one can hope for?

Next stop's Mary. She's propped up in bed with four fluffy pillows, drawing on a large sketch pad. How could this lovely lady have lost more weight when she was already skin and bones?

"Your hair looks amazing!" I say. It's not a platitude. Mary's platinum-coloured curls look straight out of a lady's glamour magazine.

Mary puts her pad down. "My son, Curtis, is a hairstylist. He wanted to feel useful, so I let him."

"That's sweet of—"

"I still can't believe it. AIDS," she cries, shaking her coiffed head. "I went to the hospital for pneumonia. AIDS, you have AIDS, they said, and now, I'm in hospice care."

Mary said the same thing last week, but I bob my head up and down to let her know I'm listening – that she can take up as much space as she needs.

"How does a woman in her seventies get AIDS? I mean, what did I do to deserve this? I'm not saying anyone does, mind you. I don't judge people's lifestyles. No siree! My son is gay. Did I tell you that? That Curtis is gay? I'd die if he had AIDS." Mary's talking so fast; her mouth is foaming. "I'm not ready to go. And why AIDS? I mean, I haven't had sex in years. I barely drink, sometimes wine with dinner, and that's it. I swear. I don't understand. I've been losing all this weight, and the doctors want me to eat, but I can't."

"Is there anything I can do?" Last week, we did a lap around the living room, hand in hand, but she doesn't look like she'd be up for that.

"Watch *The Golden Girls* with me?"

"Sure, I'm a fan."

"Yeah? What's your favourite line?"

"How Dorothy describes her mother. 'She really is a very sweet woman, she just doesn't like to show it'," I imitate Bea Arthur's husky voice.

Mary giggles. "Those two are something." It's my first time hearing her make happy sounds; now I'm greedy for more.

We sing along with the theme song, "Thank you for being a friend," and for short but precious moments, Blanche's sultriness, Rose's St. Olaf stories, Dorothy's eye rolls and Sofia's picture-this-reminiscences keep the Grim Reaper at bay.

"Thanks for the wonderful company, dear lady," I say, getting up.

"Hold on, this might be the last time I see you."

She's right. Even here, where existence isn't taken for granted, it's too easy to forget how precious time is.

"Would you like me to stay a little longer?"

"No, that's okay, but I want you to have one of my drawings. Pick your favourite."

I choose a sunset in golden red and yellows. "Thank you for this generosity," I say, trying to steady my voice.

"Remember me after I'm gone?"

"You'll be right here." I place my hand on my chest. It's where all my dead live. Mom. Dad, who fell and hit his head on the toilet a few months after Mom passed away. Grandma Rivka and Grandpa Simcha. The list is growing, but I trust that the heart space is vast, infinite, maybe.

My shift's coming to a close, but there's still one more person on my list. I knock on Joseph's door, anxious to get home and crawl under the covers. I'll make it a brief hello, and then, that's that; I'm done for the night.

"Come on in." He's fully dressed in a grey suit, black-and-gold tie, fedora and dark brown wingtip dress shoes. Is he expecting a visitor this late at night?

"Hi Joseph, I'm Avi."

"Avi – what kind of name is that?" His voice is raspy.

"It's a Hebrew name. I'm Jewish."

"I see." The lines on Joseph's forehead soften. "Man, I've dreamed of visiting the Holy Land."

"May I sit down?"

He motions to the leather armchair. "The people here seem nice, but I have a problem, you see. My nurse is a homosexual, and I'm not comfortable with him touching me." Joseph gives me a knowing look as though I, too, must harbour such sentiments.

I should feel upset, but Joseph's hands are trembling. Homophobic or not, it must be disorientating for him to be in a strange place with a death sentence hanging over his head.

"There's a female nurse working tonight. Would you like me to ask if she'd be willing to stop by?"

"That'd be very kind of you, Sir," he says in a brittle baritone.

The nurse, Rita, is in the breakroom, sipping tea. Her feet are dangling from the chair without reaching the ground. "He's going to have to get over himself," she says in a high-pitched voice, indifferent to Joseph's request. Maybe if I were working at the hospice every day, I, too, would become immune to pleas from the dying.

"But the man seems distressed."

"Gosh, you're a softie." Rita slaps me on the belly. "Suck in your gut, Avi; it's not becoming."

"What? I'm a bear, Nurse Ratched. I'm supposed to have a belly."

"Alright then, let's go see your Joseph."

Rita zooms down the hallway and storms into Joseph's room. "Yeah, yeah, I look like a twelve-year-old, but I'll have you know I'm one of the RNs here." She assumes the Wonder Woman pose, all four feet of her, arms placed on her waist.

Wide-eyed, Joseph tilts his hat. "Thank you for coming, Ma'am."

"I'm leaving you in good hands," I utter as I walk out the door.

"That one's gay, too," I hear Rita say. "No one wants to molest you here, okay? So just relax."

A new week, a fresh new volunteering shift, and as much as I've been hoping to avoid crossing Magnolia's path, it's inevitable. The woman is standing in the hallway, connected to a portable oxygen tank, shrieking at the top of her lungs, "Volunteer! volunteer!"

It's not just Kevin. Everyone here hates Magnolia, and

perhaps for a good reason. It's as though she's intent on preventing people from dying in peace.

"How can I help?" I ask.

"I want a jar of pigs' feet and pronto," Magnolia barks, her fuzzy pink pyjamas accentuating her scaly skin.

"You want what?" I have no clue what she's talking about. Israel wasn't exactly a pork-friendly country to grow up in.

"Are you deaf, stupid or what?" Magnolia sneers.

"You'll catch more flies with honey than vinegar," I say. Magnolia's been so over the top lately; it's hard to take her insults personally.

"Aw, honey bunny," Magnolia changes her tone into a sultry drawl. I bet she's used that voice on the street corners of the Tenderloin, where she sold her body and shot heroin between her toes. "Pickled pigs' feet are a delicacy in the South. Now be a dear and fetch 'em before the cows come home."

Sure enough, at the supermarket across the road, there's a jar of pickled pigs' feet on the top shelf of the aisle labelled "ethnic food". I'm not into woo, but I wouldn't be surprised if Magnolia used her witchy powers to manifest it into existence.

Back from my quest, I find Magnolia on the smoking patio with Brittney, tonight's other volunteer. At least by San Francisco standards, it's a large space, complete with a two-seater swing, blue Adirondack chairs and lush plants with a jungle vibe – ferns and birds-of-paradise in vibrant greens.

"Hey, Brittney, look at my feet," Magnolia says, kicking off her furry pink slippers, exposing grimy toes with overgrown nails curled into yellowed claws. "But my pussy, now that's the real problem. It itches like crazy. Take a peek, sweetie pie? Pick out some of the lice for me?"

"Gosh, well, I'm not sure I'm allowed to." I don't blame Brittney for being thrown off balance. It's hard to know how to respond to a bully, especially when said bully has a terminal diagnosis and one's in charge of helping her.

"Itching is for the nurses and doctors to resolve. We, volunteers, are here to serve pickled pig's feet," I say.

"Aw, honey bunny," Magnolia squeals, "you found some?"

I hand her the ghastly jar. "Here you are, milady." My mock-English accent might be embarrassing, but it does the trick. Magnolia's smile spreads from her toothless mouth into her honey-coloured eyes.

"Avi, my sweet, will you do me the great honour of taking me out for coffee?" Her voice is syrupy-sweet again. "And grab my leopard-print coat, will ya?"

It'd be a production. I'd need to get her a wheelchair and brave the unfriendly sidewalk. So, yeah, it's a pain, but I say yes. Magnolia has never asked for my company before, only my service. So, how could I resist?

At Orphan Andy's, the 24/7 diner down the road, my cruel mistress finds another unsuspecting victim – a newbie waitress eager to please. Magnolia's coffee is too cold, too bitter, too anything but right.

"This fourth cup will be perfect, right, Ms Magnolia?" Enough is enough; we're all dying here.

"Aw, honey bunny, you ruin all the fun." Magnolia stares out the window at the Castro neighbourhood's early-night revellers – a hodgepodge of local queers and out-of-town visitors flagging rainbow accessories.

"You okay?"

"Help me write a list."

"Sure." I take out a black notepad from my coat pocket. "What kind of list?" I'm readying myself for more gruesome requests.

"A list of things to do before I die."

The skies open as though on cue from a higher power – rain drumming a frenzied rhythm on the café's windowpanes.

"What's number one on your list?" I yell to make sure she hears me over the sudden storm.

"To die sober, with dignity," Magnolia mouths. I can't hear her, but it doesn't matter. I can read her lips.

I write it down and show her, "1. To die sober, with dignity."

"Thank you, honey bunny," Magnolia says, a tear rolling down her leathery cheek, joining an orchestra of raindrops. "Take me home?"

What does home at a hospice mean? What does home mean for any of us in this living-dying world? Maybe home is a prayer, a daily commitment to keeping the heart open no matter what. Or are we all homeless in the face of death?

No, it's love, right? It's got to be love.

"I need a bit of a break. Two weeks, maybe?" I hope I don't sound too defeated.

"Sure, no problem." Jayden looks concerned. "Is there anything you'd like to share?" There's a new photo on his desk – a puppy with a gem-studded collar.

"Okay if I get melodramatic for a second?"

"Go for it!"

"I'm angry we're born into open graves."

"Well, that's a gruesome image, but yeah, I get mad at death too."

"What helps, if anything?" I'm hoping for a crumb, anything.

"Well, for me, it's Thich Nhat Hanh's teachings."

"There's a gentleness there, for sure, but what does the wise Buddhist master offer those of us who don't believe in reincarnation or an afterlife?"

"The answer's staring you in the face." Jayden inclines his head to a poster above his desk. Printed in black lettering on a white background is Thich Nhat Hanh's saying: *No Mud, No Lotus*. "The lotus flower lives in swamps, nourished by mud. So, its essence, blossoming into a thing of beauty, depends on the muck at its roots," he explains.

"So, there's no happiness without suffering, no beauty without ugliness, no life without death? Is that what you're saying?"

"Yes, one can't exist without the other, and overall, life's a gift, don't you think?"

I didn't ask to be a fucking lotus, so I don't know what I think. How can I accept that after I die, I will never exist again – lost forever, forgotten, gone, gone, gone? And what about the ravages of AIDS and other sicknesses? War? The destruction of our mother planet? But, sure, life's a gift. I mean, what's the alternative?

"You look lost in thought," Jayden says, fiddling with his nameplate.

"Do you believe in god?"

"I believe in kindness." Jayden leans forward. "You're doing good work. I hope you know that."

"Thank you." I didn't realise I needed his affirmation, but I do. I so do.

"Joseph, for one, has been singing your praises."

"No way." Shit, now I'm full-blown tearing up.

*

Last week, Joseph and I shared an unexpected conversation while Googling a small Mississippi town on one of the hospice's computers.

"It's still Jim Crow in this country," Joseph frowned. "But you're white, so you can't understand."

"What makes you think I'm white?"

"What now? You, a person of colour?"

"No, I'm *other*."

"Other, what does that mean?" Joseph's dropped jaw reminded me of how he looked at Rita when she first blazed into his room. In hospice time, it was moons ago, but in the outside world, it's been only two months.

"My dad grew up in Peru, but that's beside the point. First and foremost, I'm Jewish, and the Nazis didn't put us in ovens because of our religion, but our race." There was no stopping me. "And my beloved Grandma Rivka, who was made to watch her father hung from a tree by Russian villagers? That wasn't a faith-based lynching either."

"Strange Fruit," Joseph said.

"I was twelve when I heard Billie Holliday bellow this song on a vinyl record all the way in the Middle East." Maybe I should have stopped there, but an inner voice whispered to continue. "I don't know what it's like to be Black in this country, and I don't pretend I ever will, but the "Strange Fruit lyrics—the trees with blood on their leaves—man, did that hit home"

"I hear you, brother." Joseph hovered his palm over my arm, then pointed at the screen. "See here, this Ole Towne Church is where I got married." He shook his head. "I've been doing a lot of reckoning. But you know what? God is good." Had he received uplifting news, or was that my wishful thinking?

*

298

It's good to take a two-week break, and now that I'm back at the hospice, I can't wait to start my shift. I've missed Joseph and even, dare I say it, Magnolia, and I'm beyond relieved to hear they're alive.

According to the psychiatric social worker's latest notes, Magnolia's still the bane of residents' existence, but Joseph's come a long way. "He's no longer resisting medical treatments from gay male attendants. I wonder why that it. Does reckoning with mortality ease bias?

So far, it's been a (knock-on-wood) mellow shift — I've greeted new residents who seemed in good spirits, all things considered, then helped serve dinner. I even got to catch up briefly with Rita, who shared that she met a special someone online. "Gallant," she called him.

Now, it's time for my favourite activity. Movie night. I poll residents on what film they'd like us to watch in the living room together, and the winner is *Shutter Island* with Leonardo DiCaprio. An oldie, but goodie.

Seven people promised to come, but only three turn up — Joseph, Magnolia and Oli. Oli is our newest resident, a thirty-year-old with a mop of dirty blond hair and thick-rimmed glasses. Having 20/200 vision, he's legally blind and would benefit from sitting closer to the screen, but Magnolia has claimed what would have been his ideal seat.

The movie starts and Magnolia offers Oli to switch armchairs with unprecedented magnanimity. "It's yours if you want it, four-eyes."

"*Nah*, I'm good. I'm having fun just hanging with you guys."

"But sweetie pie, you're blind as a bat." Magnolia waves her hand in dismissal like Grandpa Simcha used to do, deflecting affection. Emotion was a weakness for a Jewish boy-turned-man who, against all odds, escaped pogroms, constructed his family's house with his bare hands and fixed his own false teeth.

But enough reminiscing. Show time means pop-corn time.

Stretching out in our seats, we munch on the sweet-and-salty puffed kernels. The crunching is satisfying, but the movie's plot twists make us bolt up. The Leo character, Teddy, isn't who we thought he was! "Noooooo," we cry, attached to our hero. We've been rooting for him this whole time, and we're not stopping now. Hope springs eternal, even when the odds are grim.

"They're taking Teddy away and the doctor looks upset," Joseph narrates, then describes the climactic scene's silent parts blow-by-blow.

"Amazing. It's like I'm inside the movie," Oli whispers.

I'm not ready for an ending, but just like that, the screen fills up with the closing credits. Two hours and change flew by in an eye blink.

"Thank you, honey bunny." Magnolia rubs her eyes. "It's time to hit the hay." I've heard from Jayden that Magnolia's sister visited this morning. Is that why she's been in such a good mood? Whatever it is, I'll take it.

"Rest well and till soon, fabulous people," I say, stretch-ing my arms. Nights like these keep me going. Still, I'm exhausted, and tomorrow's workday starts too early. It's high time to go home.

"So sorry. You have your coat on and all," Joseph lowers his head and raises his eyes, "but could you kindly spare a few moments?"

"Sure." I follow him to the smoking balcony. His gait is unsteady, so I walk close behind him like a mother hen.

"I want to show you something." Joseph reaches into his jacket and takes out a letter. It's worn and creased as

300

though it has been folded and unfolded. "It's a note from my daughter."

Strange. He's never mentioned a daughter.

"I'll read you what she says." He takes a deep drag on his cigarette and coughs. "Dear Joseph, or should I write Dad? Your letter arrived on the day of my baby shower. It's a sign from god this baby is blessed."

"Wow, that's—"

"There's more," Joseph says, wiping his eyes with his sleeve. "I'm so sorry to hear about your cancer. I'm praying for your full recovery with all my heart. And, yes, I was mad when you left us, but with hard work and time, I've learned to forgive you. Mom told me about your depression, womanising, the drugs, so in the end, I choose to believe you tried to protect me by walking away."

The letter is shaking in his hand. "My daughter's grown up to be a fine woman."

"It sure sounds like it, buddy," I say.

Shoulder-to-shoulder, we overlook the Castro's late-night hustle and bustle – two men from different walks. Straight. Gay. Cis. Trans. Christian. Jewish. Black. Other. And mortal, so damn mortal.

Joseph pats my shoulder. "You're alright," he says. I ache to put my arm around him, but touch is tricky, so I don't.

"My daughter says she'll visit after the baby is born." Joseph places the letter back in the safety of his inner pocket and lights up another cigarette. "Want one?" he asks. It's been decades since I quit, but I can still feel that sweet relaxation on the inhale. What if I had one? Would it really be that bad?

"I pray I get to see her before I die." Smoke from Joseph's throat and nostrils mixes with the cold night's mist.

"Amen," I plead.

The city is loud, but its rumbling pales compared to the life force right here on this tiny balcony, on this grain of sand.

After a resident dies, Jayden organises an in-house memorial. Today, residents, staff and volunteers have gathered once again around a makeshift altar in the living room. Its centrepiece is a photograph of a smiley eighteen-year-old woman, Michelle, surrounded by candles, a pink statue of the Buddha and white chrysanthemums. Jayden invites us to share. "No pressure, whatever your heart tells you to."

"Rest in peace, courageous young lady," Rita says.

I'm full of feelings and out of words. Memorials have been bleeding into each other – Mary's and Kevin's, to name a few. I've witnessed irreplaceable individuals arrive and pass away without comprehending death any better.

Michelle's loss is an especially tough pill to swallow. She came in with a rare complication, a type of meningitis caused by a fungus that assaults the lungs and spreads to the brain. At least, that's what I understood from her chart.

Her prognosis was forty-eight hours or less.

I stopped by Michelle's room to say hello and see if she needed anything. "Where am I?" she murmured, looking lost, but before I could explain, she clutched her stomach and projectile vomited bile and blood.

"Rita," I howled, and Rita appeared like she always does, a fierce angel ready for action. "Step outside. We'll take it from here," she said.

I wish I hadn't read Michelle's full report. Sometimes it's better not to know. But read it, I did. Michelle was raped when she was twelve. Untreated HIV turned into ravaging AIDS.

"You can go in now." Rita emerged into the hallway, looking pale.

"I don't know if I can," I mumbled.

"It's okay, hon. We'll take good care of Michelle. I promise."

It was hard to accept Rita's kindness while I brimmed with self-hatred. What was up with my sudden, self-centered paralysis?

And yes, I'd bet my life that Rita did her best, and Michelle felt cared for, but fuck this peaceful altar! Weep and accept Michelle's brutal young death? Hell, no — throw the Buddha statue against the wall, burn down the house.

The floodgates are pushing against my eyelids, but by the grace of something, I manage to wait until the ceremony's over to stumble into the bathroom, lock myself in a stall and bawl my eyes out. These are tears of rage, you hear me? You, the cruel god who doesn't exist.

Puffy-eyed, I run into Magnolia. I can't deal with her tantrums right now, no matter how ill she is, so she'd better behave.

"Hey honey bunny, have you been cryin'?"

"Yes," I say, wanting her out of my way.

"I know what will make you feel better."

"Yeah? What?" I smile, despite myself.

"You can get me a—"

"No," I say.

"No?" Magnolia's eyes widen. "You don't even know what I want."

"How about doing something for me for a change?"

"Like what?" she scoffs.

"Tell Rita she's doing a good job, okay?"

"You're a sensitive one." Magnolia winks. "But for you, honey bunny, I'll do anything. Anything at all."

*

The phone call shouldn't catch me by surprise, but it does. "Joseph's on his deathbed. He's asking for you," Jayden says.

"Did you notify his daughter?"

"What daughter?"

"There's a letter in his pocket."

"I'll see what I can find out, but Avi, you'd better hurry."

Pedal to the metal, I slalom up and down San Francisco's hilly streets, passing the iconic rainbow flag on Market and 16th. Arriving at Joseph's door, at last, my hand reaches for the handle. But, no. Stop. I'm no good to him like this – sweaty and anxious.

Breathe. One, two, three, four, five, six on the inhale; One, two, three, four, five, six on the exhale. Ready or not, it's time to say goodbye.

"You've made it," Joseph manages to whisper, his hands collapsed on his chest, one palm on top of the other.

"Of course I did, buddy."

Rita is by Joseph's side, wetting his lips with ice. She looks at me with what I understand as an encouragement to get as close as I can to this frail, ghostly-looking man who is still here, fully human.

I rest my hand on Joseph's clasped palms. His skin is cold, or maybe my fingers are burning. With immense effort, his breaths getting shorter and shallower, Joseph lifts his head and grazes his lips against my flesh.

Joseph's kiss, this precious gift, is a rebirthing mirror. This time, what looks back is formless, a pure human-to-human love.

I vow to honour your bequest, dear Joseph, to carry it in my pocket like a forgiveness note from those I've abandoned but crave to hold. In the moments I forget to live from love, may this letter await – stained with tears, tattered with hope – to be folded and unfolded countless times until I, too, drift into that final void, that endless night.

17

FUCKING MYSELF GOODBYE[10]

Jon's new office is in the top suite of a spanking-new hotel, where the Castro borders the Tenderloin, San Francisco's grittiest neighbourhood. Is this location why the security guard followed me all the way to the thirteenth floor? Should I be flattered I look like a tough guy?

"So, how's the memoir project coming along?" Jon asks.

"Still daunting, but I'm making progress." I've been alternating between writing and recording myself. Kipling wrote about the daemon in his pen (yes, I know, but I like this image), and Talia is mine.

"Any insights?"

"I want to ask for Talia's forgiveness."

"What does that look like?" Jon strokes a beard with new specks of grey.

"I'm still figuring it out.

Last night, I woke up at 4 a.m. and, like a man possessed, wrote a rough short story draft. Avi meets Talia in modern-day San Francisco, tempts her into his loft, and fucks her goodbye.

Fiction is a deviation from my usual real-life writing, but there was something about venturing into make-believe that uncovered a truth. I want my Avi character to eroticise Talia's body – to make love to parts that had once caused shame, or at least try.

As luck would have it, I'm meeting up with my new writer friend, Claudette, tonight. If I feel brave, I'll pitch this story for her new anthology. We'll see.

Dinner at this Chinese hot pot restaurant in the Outer Sunset was Claudette's idea. The walls are a dirty shade of pink and the tablecloth is a flowery vinyl in canary yellow and mint green. So, yeah, not a hipster foodie spot for the local literati yet, but I can't wait to taste our dishes. The woman's a harbinger of cool.

"The *Screwing Claudette* anthology is almost done," she says, tossing raw, headless shrimp into a pot with boiling broth that covers half our table. Submissions for her book weren't confined to writers who had sex with her or were hoping to. Nope! As Claudette, the editor, explained, Claudette, the character, could symbolise anything and everything erotic.

"Two seconds and go!" she yells, and we both fish out the freshly cooked critters and dip them in garlic sesame sauce.

"Congrats on the book," I sputter. A sip of green tea dislodges the barnacle stuck in my throat but burns my tongue. "Too late to pitch a short story? Granted, it's very, very rough."

"And here I was, oblivious of your interest in shagging me." Claudette raises a manicured eyebrow.

"If I ever switched teams, you'd be the first woman I'd lure into my den."

Claudette chuckles. "What a charming liar." Her full lips are a shiny metallic purple. "So, what's your story about?"

"Talia materialises into modern-day San Francisco. Avi is shocked when he runs into her at Paxton Gate, you know, the curiosities store in the Mission, and—"

"I love Paxton Gate." Claudette points to her human tooth ring. "And placing Talia in a shop filled with taxidermy mice in Victorian dresses adds a nice, macabre touch. Anyway, go on."

"So, Talia doesn't recognise Avi, but she trusts him right away. I mean, how couldn't she? He makes her feel seen more than anyone she's ever met. Long story short, Avi lures Talia into his bachelor pad and fucks her goodbye."

"You'd give her *la petite mort*?" Claudette snorts.

"It's more about making love to the parts that caused her pain and self-loathing," I overexplain, feeling somewhat cheapened. "I killed Talia prematurely. I want a chance to redeem that."

"I like the concept, but timing's tight. You have two weeks to submit a polished piece," Claudette says.

A week passes, and all I've managed to finesse are two scenes – Avi's surprise encounter with Talia at a store filled with esoteric trinkets and his clunky but hopefully endearing attempt at seducing her over coffee.

Now that my protagonists' sex scene is imminent, I'm stuck, and the deadline feels impossible.

Scene 5: Sex

[To fill out later – Avi and Talia have been hanging out at Avi's loft for a couple of hours.]

"It's getting late. Should I head back to my hotel?"

Talia was right to be impatient. Avi had been sending her mixed messages the whole night.

"I have to tell you something, but I don't know how to do it without freaking you out."

"You're gay?"

"Yes, but that's not the issue."

"So, you weren't trying to seduce me?"

"I was, I mean, I am," Avi said, feeling and looking the fool.

Talia laughed. "What a comedy of errors."

How could Avi have even begun to explain? So, he kissed her, and instead of fending him off like he feared she would, Talia reciprocated.

Emboldened, Avi reached for Talia's breasts and flicked his fingers on her nipples. He had sacrificed erotic sensation for gender alignment. Could he regain it by touching his past?

"Suck on my titties," Talia whispered.

Suck on my titties? Really? That sounds so cartoonish. So not what I'm going for.

Talia unbuttoned her shirt and waited for Avi to do something, but he stared at her chest, frozen.

"Are you okay?" she asked.

"You remind me of someone I've been trying to forget," he said, holding back tears.

Wait, what did Talia's breasts feel like? Touching my chest, I try to imagine what had been there, but my hard pecs have erased its heaviness and texture.

Googling breasts brings up medical and hetero, X-rated sites. The former's too sterile and the latter isn't exactly my cup of tea – it's all about the guy's pleasure. Still, memory beggars can't be choosers. After the tenth clip, I'm ready to give up. Maybe I'm looking in all the wrong places. Besides, the visual and auditory aren't enough. What about touch, texture and smell? A fuller embodiment?

My Avi character desires to worship the feminine instead of associating it with disgust simply because it didn't belong on his body – to fuck Talia goodbye lovingly and, in doing so, integrate what used to be his compartmentalised selves. And if I'm going to write that semi-convincingly, there's only one way forward. It sounds insane, I know, but I need to find a woman who looks like Talia and make love to her. After all, Intellectualisation and imagination can only go so far.

A tall order? An impossibility? Probably. But if there's a San Francisco institution that might just produce a Talia stand-in, it's Craigslist.

Gay Trans Man in search of
His Past's Doppelganger

Are you a high femme on the outside but a tomboy on the inside? Have sensitive nipples, fashion sense, imagination and are kinky? Then you might just fit what I'm looking for.

I'm a bearish, gay trans guy who once upon a time "passed" as a straight, femme woman.

Early in transition, I rushed to erase my fabulous drag-queen past. But, now, I'm craving a proper ritualistic goodbye – to make love to her as she once was, sucking on nipples that'd harden despite themselves, fisting her forbidden front hole and making her come so hard she'd cry out in abandon and pleasure.

I'd want her to feel cherished, hold her like she'd yearned

for but never let anyone do, let alone me.

Does role-playing this scene with me as the dominant, calling the shots, and you as the submissive, following directives, sound like a turn-on? If so, tell me why.

Pic for pic.

P.S. I'm not sexually attracted to women.

What woman would be mad enough to reply to my ad? And if there were such a woman, she'd likely be someone I wouldn't be interested in, right? This thought is freeing, and besides, writing the ad was all I needed to get the creative juices flowing. Lighter and with a fire in my belly, I type away when the ping of an incoming email stops me dead in my tracks.

Hi mystery man,

I'm a graduate student visiting San Francisco for a sex work conference. I leave the day after next.

I'm responding to your ad because I'm attracted to impossibilities. I realise that sounds heady, and I don't know what it's like to be trans, but I know what it's like to be unkind to my past.

My appearance is feminine, but I'm a tomboy at heart. Photo attached.

Do I fit the bill? Set up an audition for tomorrow afternoon?

Kisses,
Maya

My back-and-forth with Maya is flirty and informative. We even exchange some background stuff. I have major issues with Israeli politics, Maya writes. Don't worry; I'm a traitor to my people, I respond.

She's versed with kink, having worked as a pro-dominatrix

to help pay for university, and excited about the prospect of switching roles for a change. Not sure you'd be able to handle me, though, she teases the way Talia would have.

We decide to meet up for tea. If there's chemistry, Maya will come over to my place. I'd direct the scene, and she'd role-play Talia, the object of desire.

So, I should be pleased, excited even, but instead I'm a bundle of nerves. I've never been with a woman before. Well, there was the Talia and Teddy affair, but Teddy never did let Talia reciprocate. And even though I'd like to think of myself as a fast learner, what if I won't know what to do? An eye roll about my lacking sexual skills isn't what I'm going for.

Enough with the neurotic chatter. It's the opposite of sexy, and besides, I can do this. I'll just keep repeating this mantra to myself, and who knows? I might even have fun.

The Samovar Tea Lounge is bustling. I claim an outdoor table and order an iced chai. It's not the warmest of days, but San Francisco doesn't get warm, especially in summer.

Where's Maya? Re-checking my phone for the thousandth time doesn't help soothe my jitters. It only slows time down.

It's one thing to fantasise about reconnecting with my past self, but expecting a flesh-and-blood woman to materialise from an online existence and embody her? What was I thinking?

Still, there's hope my plan won't come to fruition. Talia was as punctual as the angel of death, maybe timelier, but Maya is ten minutes late. A sign from the god I don't believe in that Maya and I weren't the right match after all? Five more minutes, and I'm out of here.

Getting up, I spot Maya across the street, looking

like a modern-day, tattooed Betty Page or one of the *SuicideGirls* – glamorous soft-porn models with an alternative, pinup aesthetic.

I wave. Maya waves back, turning heads as she jaywalks towards the lounge in a black-and-white, low-cut swing dress stamped with red vampire kisses. Drawing this kind of attention in the Castro is no small feat. It's a queer, anything-goes neighbourhood, where spotting a Sister of Perpetual Indulgence – a bearded man in a nun's attire with grotesquely beautiful makeup – strutting his stuff, or a group of naked people biking around is just another day in the life.

"Sorry I'm late." Maya collapses into the wicker chair. "This city's public transport sucks." Up close, she's drop-dead gorgeous – dark brown eyes with thick, long eyelashes, round lips and supple skin.

"What are you studying in grad school?" I ask, professor-like. I can't help myself sometimes, even if that means ruining the mood.

"Clinical psychology. I want to help people."

Ah, the beauty of youth – smooth skin, agile body, bright eyes and a beguiling lack of cynicism – endearing? Yes. Annoying? Sometimes. Sexy? No. At least not to me. I'm attracted to bears around my age, give or take a decade – men who've earned the wrinkles around their eyes.

"Please order whatever you'd like. My treat."

"'The Iron Goddess of Mercy' sounds fabulous."

"I like the words goddess and mercy, but caramel and shiitake mushrooms? Interesting."

"Interesting is an interesting word, but before we get ahead of ourselves, I have a confession." Her expression sours. "It might be a deal-breaker."

"Really?" I try not to sound too hopeful. "An STI?"

"No, worse. I'm blood-related to a notorious

313

Israeli ex-prime minister. Think more right-wing than right-wing."

"That fascist? I'll have to bend you over my lap and spank you."

"But I'm such a good girl, Daddy," Maya purrs and pouts her lips. Damn it; I should have watched more hetero porn. What would a straight guy have said about now? My gaze travels to Maya's cleavage. Yup, I'm in over my head.

"So, what was Talia like?" Maya asks, raising a glass with amber liquid to her red lips.

"An outsider." Of all the words I could have chosen, why had this one blurted itself out of my mouth?

"An outsider in what way?"

"You had to be there."

Maya laughs. "Now, that's what I call a cop-out. If I'm going to role-play Talia, I'd like to get a sense of her."

"I respect that. I've been trying to be more empathetic than critical towards my past lately, so I'll try to be kind." Fuck, how do I even begin to summarise her? "Talia was sassy, outspoken, a survivalist. She was full of feelings but didn't know how to express her needs or wants." I need to slow down; this isn't a therapy session. "Sexually, she was disconnected from her body."

"I'm not trans, but I hate my body, so I get that part."

"Hate?"

"Look," Maya says, circling her hand in front of her torso and face. "I have a long nose, my boobs are huge and my legs are way too short for my body. And if I gain even two pounds, I become too fat for my clothes."

"You're gorgeous."

Maya looks pleased. "I wasn't fishing but thank you."

"Listen, I'm gay, so what if I can't get aroused? After what you just said, I'd hate for that to feel rejecting."

"I can take care of myself. And I might not get aroused either, so there."

"So why are we doing this again?" My tone is playful, but asking this question out loud feels right.

"Impossibilities are hot," Maya says.

"Yes, you wrote that, but I'm not sure I follow."

"We're an unlikely pair, but we can help each other heal, don't you think?" Maya leans forward, puts her elbows on the table and interlaces her fingers to create a cradle for her face. "Besides, we're two pervs who can't help ourselves," she says, gazing up.

"Have you been with a trans guy before?"

"My ex-boyfriend was trans."

"Your safe word?" I hear myself ask.

"Zionism."

"Alright then. Eight o'clock tonight, my place. I'll send you an email with my address and instructions. Make sure to respond within half an hour of getting it."

"Yes, Daddy."

"Sir," I correct her.

Maya grins. "Yes, Sir."

It hasn't even been ten minutes since I sent the email and Maya's already written back. She copied my instructions, italicised them and inserted short responses under each one.

Play will start from the moment I buzz you into the building. Walk into the courtyard, eyes gazing at the ground. Do NOT look up to greet me when I approach you.

– Yes, Sir.

Once inside my apartment – don't speak unless spoken to. I want you to make sounds like moaning but keep your voice low because of the neighbours.

– Will do, Sir.

As we've already negotiated, if whatever I'm doing feels good but too intense and you want me to slow down, say yellow. If you want to stop role-play altogether, say Zionism.

– Thank you. That's super clear.

If, during play, you need clarification or want to voice something, ask permission to speak. I will, of course, grant it. Trusting you to use your safe words and share needs as they arise will allow me to go deeper.

– Your Talia understands.

Finally, as we've discussed at Samovar, ours is a one-off. Happy to unwind after play and be our natural selves for a while, but we're spending the night separately.

– Totally on board, Sir.

Maya will be here in less than an hour and I have no one to blame for this folly but myself. It's been a whirlwind, but she'll be leaving town tomorrow, so it's now or never.

Armed with a vacuum cleaner, I inspect the apartment. Dust bunnies are peering from under the couch. Why do they make themselves visible only when I have a guest coming over?

Do I want to have sex with Maya, or does my desire stem from a more analytic, research-like place – the alluring trappings of the mind? What does my heart tell me? My gut?

I still have a couple of hours to cancel. Should I?

We can help each other heal, Maya said earlier today. It felt right then and it feels right now.

Breathe, just breathe.

The intercom rings. Ready or not, it's showtime.

I usher Maya into my bedroom with dogged determination. At the end of the day, what could go wrong?

Everything.

I'm the anti-dom, a schoolboy in top's clothing, prodding Maya's soft skin, inhaling her talcum scent and lingering at first base.

"I'm not breakable," she scoffs, standing with her back to the bed.

I laugh, utterly humiliated. I've never been accused of being too tentative before. And, sure, I'm only an adolescent in trans years, but c'mon! I can do this!

I give Maya a gentle push and she goes flying into the mattress. Goddammit, I'm not used to playing with someone so petite.

"Don't move!" I say in what I hope sounds like an authoritative voice, trying to suppress a chuckle. Laughter can be sexy and connecting during play, but not this early on.

Straddling Maya's body, I unbutton the front of her dress. Her erect nipples stick through her bra like swollen transmale dicks. I suck on them through the soft, silky fabric, alternating from one to the other.

"This feels so good, Daddy, Sir," Maya moans.

Is she lactating, or has my saliva left large, milky spots on the red sateen? Gasping, I pull off her bra and squeeze her breasts. Her nipples taste sour, or perhaps it's the acid reflux shooting up my oesophagus and into my mouth.

"Do you like my boobies, Sir?"

"They're perfect."

I sink my head into Maya's cleavage and press her breasts against my cheeks. A phantom pleasure surges through my nipples. Chest surgery was a welcome relief, but the cost of gender alignment was a loss of erotic sensation in my nipples.

"Spank me," Maya pleads.

It's hard to stay present when she's taking over the scene. How do men and women negotiate power in kinky play,

317

anyway? I'd slap a guy's butt in a heartbeat, but it feels wrong, sexist even, to dominate a woman. Or is it sexist not to?

"Be quiet but keep your mouth open," I say.

Maya shuts her eyes and parts her lips.

What if I expanded the script and allowed the past to make love to the present? My hand reaches to unzip my pants. It'd be vulnerable to take them off, but the show must go on, or I'd be an asshole, coward, or both.

"I want your spit, Sir. Please, may I swallow your spit?"

As a Jew, I've learned to spit for good luck. It's like knocking on wood. Not this time. The viscous substance that shoots out of my mouth and into Maya's is the stuff of what? Sex-positive play? Shame? Both? Is it even what I want?

Maya takes a big gulp. "Thank you," she whispers and reaches her tongue to lick the rest of the sticky liquid off her lips. "I'm your slutty girl, Daddy, Sir."

She's violating our agreement, topping from the bottom, as folks say in kink community and I should be the one to call out "Zionism" and kick her out. I need to see this through, though, whatever this is.

"Tell me what you are again," I say, my tone filled with judgment.

"Your slut," Maya murmurs.

"Louder!"

"A dirty whore," Talia howls.

Finally, *she*'s here. Not the way I've wished for, but still. And, yes, I've developed expertise in humiliating her; I could orgasm from demeaning her, but it will not bring relief.

I motion for Talia to sit in my lap. She wraps her arms around my neck and rests her heavy head against my hairy chest. "My sweet, wounded girl," I say. Rocking her from side to side, I reach my hand inside her lacey underwear. She's wet.

"This feels so good," Talia murmurs.

"I want you to look at yourself." I carry her to the rebirthing mirror and dismount her two feet from her reflection. "What do you see?"

"A strong daddy."

"What else?"

"An ugly impostor." Talia lowers her head. "I can't stand looking at myself."

"You're powerful and beautiful, inside and out." I wrap myself around her from behind like a weighted blanket.

Our breathing synchronised, I cup Talia's cheeks and watch my mirror hands slide down her mirror neck, then pause on the soft spot *he* molested with nicotine teeth and alcohol breath. I kiss that spot, sucking residual poison into my throat, bitter and lava hot.

Breathe in the suffocating and breathe out the lightness, my internalised Pema Chödrön whispers. It's counter-intuitive to inhale poison – abuse and self-condemnation – and purify it on the exhale. But leaping on faith, we breathe in hardship and breath out hope; me and my Talia, a clear light emitting from our pores.

"Tell yourself you're a fierce goddess," I say.

"I can't."

"You don't have to believe it yet."

"I'm a fierce goddess," Talia whispers.

Turning her around, I kiss her for the first time. She returns the kiss, hungry for something I can't name. It matters; she matters, and she matters, even if, at this moment, I'm not sure I can give us what we need.

"I'm yours to do with whatever you please," she says.

"Spread your legs for me." Kneeling, I flick my tongue

on her swollen clit-dick, then venture two fingers inside her. Curling my fingers, I rub them against her G-spot, her clit-dick erect against my tongue.

Two fingers become four; four turn into a fist. I push and pull my hand back and forth in rapid movements, going harder and faster. "I'm coming," Talia yells, splashing in an ecstasy I never dreamt we'd share.

I hold her, or maybe she and she are holding me – Talia, Maya, Talia, Talia, Maya, naked, shivering and wet.

"Thank you," I whisper.

"I got you," Maya says.

I sink my head between her soft breasts. Like a child, I cry out for my mother, for who I once was, for our lineage of big-breasted Jewish women with stretch marks like road maps that lead anywhere but home.

Maya and I have been cuddling for half an hour or so. I'm different. I can't articulate how exactly – words sometimes take a while – but I sense it, this new spaciousness.

"Was it what you'd hoped it'd be?" Maya asks.

"Different from what I had expected and exactly what I needed. You?"

"It was powerful, Sir."

"Even though you behaved like a brat?" I sound light-hearted, or so I hope.

"I know I went off script. I couldn't help myself."

"I almost ended play."

"Really, you—"

"Yes, I was close to calling it."

"Why didn't you?"

"This was different from any scene I'd ever role-played. And, somehow, you breaking the rules was fitting with who Talia was in her twenties, so I rolled with it."

320

"I wanted to make you come. Why didn't you let me touch you?"

"I didn't need to orgasm. I'm content, truly."

"Content? How about on Cloud Nine?" Maya slaps me on the arm. "Hey, what side of the bed do you sleep on?"

"Wait, you're not expecting to—"

"So, I'm not staying the night?"

There's a new tightness in my chest. "We discussed this, remember?"

"But that was before. What we shared was romantic, right? I mean, you felt things for me?"

"Aw, my lovely, this was a one-time thing, and we were both very clear about that and spending the night separately."

"I know, but it hurts that you want me to leave."

I'd love to have my space back, but I also want to do right by her. "I guess I've become used to how gay men have sex. It usually ends with calling an Uber, then a quick hug and thank you if things went well."

"I get that," Maya mutters.

"I'm sorry. I should have been more thoughtful about our," I stammer, "our differences." In the hetero universe I once roamed in, it would have been rude, callous even to ask Maya to leave.

"You were honest with me; it's just—" Maya buries her head in the pillow. Oh no, is she sobbing?

"Please, let me hold you," I say.

"Okay," she mumbles and snuggles against me.

I hug Maya until her body relaxes into mine. "You're my first woman and I'll always cherish that." Does she hear my sincerity?

"So why don't you want me to spend the night?"

"I need alone time, but instead of calling an Uber, how

about I take you to your hotel? And if you want me to, I'll give you a ride to the airport tomorrow."

"All of the above." Maya's eyes are still wet, but she's smiling. Thank goodness. I'd hate for this night to end on a sour note. Still, I'm plagued by a nagging thought. Is Maya expecting me to be more empathetic and emotionally available because I'm a trans man? Then again, if she does, so what?

Early this morning, Maya and I said our warm goodbyes at the San Francisco International Airport, but now I'm stressed again. Claudette's deadline is tick, tick, ticking. I swear I'm striving to finish my submission on time, but I want to get the story right and I'm drawing a blank.

Scene 5: Bedroom

[Note: Insert sex scene here. Don't make it pornographic but don't shy away from being explicit, either. Somehow convey without getting too didactic that those of us who have been shamed by having so-called wrong bodies could use a heavier dose of eroticism, especially from our future selves.]

I email Claudette the final draft moments before the deadline. I've sacrificed sleep and work commitments, so this version will have to do.

She emails back an hour later. I like this piece, especially the sex scene, but your writing's still too rough. There won't be enough time for revisions, so it's a no-go for the anthology. Still, she offers encouragement: Keep going; your story will find a good home one day.

Home. It's a word that breaks my heart.

*

Jon's new office is shockingly bland. I get it; the black leather armchair and sofa were showing signs of wear and tear, but replacing them with a beige Scandinavian set? It doesn't compute. I accept change; of course I do, but when it comes to this man, my heart demands he stay quirky and fiery, live forever.

"Are you disappointed?" he asks.

"About my story not being publication-ready yet?" I shake my head. "Not at all. I kind of expected that. Besides, I wouldn't have had the Maya experience if I hadn't tried for that crazy deadline."

"Did sex with Maya teach you something new?"

"It did."

"Well, don't keep me in suspense." Jon mock rolls his eyes.

"I was trying to get the wording right, but fine. I heard myself sight. "I used to think of Talia as the wounded, but when Maya, no, when Talia held me during play, it finally dawned on me here," I place my hand on my chest, "and not just here," I point to my head, "that I had it wrong all along."

"In what way?"

"It wasn't Henry who saved us, was it?"

Jon's ocean-wide smile reminds me of Dad's. "How does it feel to be this generous with your past" he asks.

My smile must be Dad-like too. "Weird, but dare I say it, good."

"You've done a lot of work, and it shows. I'm proud of you."

"Wait, you're not suggesting terminating therapy, are you?" I'm seized by a wave of panic. "I still have a way to go."

"I'll leave termination up to you, my dear Avi, but it's been a while, and you've internalised my voice."

323

It's a now-or-never moment, so I go for it. "Can I ask you for something you'll likely say no to?"

"What's that?"

"A Jon hug."

"You know it's not something I do," Jon says, but then he opens his arms. "Alright, come here, you."

After over a decade of verbal exchange, I dissolve into his embrace. It's warm here and quiet, like on the most hallowed of retreats. Then a meditation bell rings. And again. And again.

Home, a female voice intones. *Can you feel it?*

Grandma Rivka? Mom? Talia?

It's all three harmonising as one.

Acknowledgements

Writing this book took a village. I'm deeply grateful to everyone who contributed critique, wisdom, and encouragement, helping me embrace self-doubt and transform vulnerability into storytelling. A heartfelt thank you to each of you (in semi-alphabetical order):

Matt Bates, for invaluable ideas and edits and for pitching the book to Muswell Press. Your generosity and support mean more than I can say.

Sarah and Kate Beal of Muswell Press for believing in my work and showing outstanding professionalism and caring. Thank you for involving me in each step of the way and for being such enthusiastic and outspoken allies for queer literary voices. Working together has been a great honour.

Julia Bell, my Birkbeck, University of London Creative Writing tutor, for transformative critique and insights, pushing me to dig deeper, and for coming up with the book title after my many failed attempts. I'm deeply grateful for and moved by your guidance, advocacy, and friendship.

Toby Litt, my Creative Writing MFA director and tutor, for taking a chance on this academic turned creative writer. I've learned tremendously from your teachings and my fabulous MFA cohort: Anna, Daisy, Dee, Farha, Karen, Marcella, Norman, Philly, Serena, and Sonia.

Writers Anonymous – Karen Constantine, Marcella Marx, Farha Quadri, and Philly Stock – my talented, inspiring, and committed group members for sharing our writing process, however tender and raw, and showing up for each other weekly. You guys are my rock.

London-based queer mindfulness meditation friends: Spencer Clark, Dominic Janes, and Fiorenzo Palermo, for maintaining a semblance of sanity during the COVID pandemic, your warm communal welcome for this Jewbu nomad, and our enduring, heartful connection.

Adam Zimbardo for being the best therapist ever. I wouldn't be here without you.

Last but not least, my brothers, Gil and Noam Ben-Zeev, and my beloved San Francisco Bay Area friends and chosen family: Monica DuClaud, StormMiguel Florez, Mark Geisler, Zev Lowe, Ezequiel Morsella, Ben Stefonik, and Sue B. for your love, feedback, and support throughout my life's transitions and writing journey. Despite the physical distance, you're always in my heart.